"VALUABLE INSIGHTS... AMONG THE MOST IMPORTANT BOOKS PUBLISHED ABOUT THE WATERGATE SCANDAL"
—*The New York Times Book Review*

"Coherent, penetrating assessment of the characters of those involved and the practices of government"
—*Los Angeles Times*

"If you are only going to read one volume about Watergate, this is the one... Sussman has done the best job of putting Watergate into the perspective of this country"
—*The Houston Post*

"This book is a necessity"
—*Bestsellers*

About the author: BARRY SUSSMAN received his B.A. from Brooklyn College. He was Managing Editor of the Briston, Va.-Tenn., *Herald Courier* from 1962 to 1965, when he left for the *Washington Post*, where he became city editor, a job he held at the time of the Watergate break-in arrests. Sussman was then named Special Watergate Editor, one of the team directing the *Post*'s Watergate investigation. In 1972, he won the Drew Pearson Award for Investigative Reporting, and in 1973 he received a Washington Newspaper Guild First Place Award for National Reporting, and was named "Editor of the Year" by the Guild. His book *The Great Coverup: Nixon and the Scandal of Watergate* was named one of the best books of the year in 1974 by both *The New York Times* and the *Washington Post*. Sussman has lectured widely on Watergate and has appeared on major network television programs. Currently he is known for his work as a public-opinion analyst and serves as the *Washington Post*'s Director of the Washington Post-ABC News poll.

MENTOR and SIGNET Titles of Interest

☐ **NIXON AGONISTES by Garry Wills.** In this rich study of Richard Nixon, Garry Wills presents an exciting new combination of on-the-spot reporting and political analysis for anyone who hopes to understand one of the most complex American Presidents. "One is tempted to quote constantly from *Nixon Agonistes* because Mr. Wills writes with a scalpel ... an astonishing book."—*New York Times*
(#ME1750—$2.50)

☐ **THE PUBLIC PHILOSOPHY by Walter Lippman.** A study of the challenges facing democratic societies by America's leading political analyst. Urges free men everywhere to take a responsible interest in government in order to preserve their liberties and defend themselves against totalitarianism. (#MW1866—$1.50)

☐ **THE UNITED STATES POLITICAL SYSTEM AND HOW IT WORKS (revised and updated) by David Cushman Doyle.** A brilliant account of how the world's greatest democratic government has developed and how it functions. (#MJ1980—$1.25)

☐ **THE MAKING OF THE PRESIDENT 1960 by Theodore H. White.** The masterful Pulitzer Prize winning account of the 1960 campaign and election of John F. Kennedy. (#ME1874—$2.50)

☐ **HENRY KISSINGER: The Private and Public Story by Ralph Blumenfeld with the staff and editors of *The New York Post*.** The book that says it all ... Kissinger's rise step by step to the summit of power ... his dazzling triumphs and the troubling questions about them. ... The most candid and revealing portrait ever of Henry Kissinger. With 16 pages of photographs.
(#E6343—$1.75)

Buy them at your local bookstore or use this convenient coupon for ordering.

THE NEW AMERICAN LIBRARY, INC.,
P.O. Box 999, Bergenfield, New Jersey 07621

Please send me the books I have checked above. I am enclosing $_____ (please add $1.00 to this order to cover postage and handling). Send check or money order—no cash or C.O.D.'s. Prices and numbers are subject to change without notice.

Name_____

Address_____

City _____ State _____ Zip Code _____
Allow 4-6 weeks for delivery.
This offer is subject to withdrawal without notice.

784 DAYS
THAT CHANGED AMERICA

From Watergate to Resignation

by Barry Sussman

REVISED AND UPDATED EDITION OF
The Great Coverup

A MENTOR BOOK
NEW AMERICAN LIBRARY
TIMES MIRROR
NEW YORK AND SCARBOROUGH, ONTARIO

*For my wife, Peggy, and our daughters,
Seena and Shari.*

NAL BOOKS ARE AVAILABLE AT QUANTITY DISCOUNTS
WHEN USED TO PROMOTE PRODUCTS OR SERVICES. FOR
INFORMATION PLEASE WRITE TO PREMIUM MARKETING
DIVISION, THE NEW AMERICAN LIBRARY, INC., 1633
BROADWAY, NEW YORK, NEW YORK 10019.

Cover photos: UPI

Copyright © 1974, 1982 by Barry Sussman

All rights reserved

Originally appeared in a Signet edition

Library of Congress Catalog Card Number: 82-81661

MENTOR TRADEMARK REG. U.S. PAT. OFF. AND FOREIGN COUNTRIES
REGISTERED TRADEMARK—MARCA REGISTRADA
HECHO EN CHICAGO, U.S.A.

SIGNET, SIGNET CLASSICS, MENTOR, PLUME, MERIDIAN AND NAL
BOOKS are published *in the United States* by
The New American Library, Inc.,
1633 Broadway, New York, New York 10019,
in Canada by The New American Library of Canada Limited,
81 Mack Avenue, Scarborough, Ontario M1L 1M8

First Printing, June, 1982

1 2 3 4 5 6 7 8 9

PRINTED IN THE UNITED STATES OF AMERICA

CONTENTS

INTRODUCTION ix

PART I
The Break-In 1

PART II
The Great Coverup Begins 31

PART III
The Washington Post 57

PART IV
Sirica, Gray, and McCord:
The Turning Point 109

PART V
Collapse of the Coverup 153

PART VI
The Senate Watergate Hearings 181

PART VII
"Saturday Night Massacre":
The Road to Impeachment 209

EPILOGUE 261

INDEX 265

A NOTE FROM
TELEVISION CORPORATION OF AMERICA

WHILE THIS BOOK and our television program share the same title, they are vastly different. At Television Corporation of America we recognize Barry Sussman as an acknowledged authority on Watergate, a distinguished writer whose views are highly respected, but in our opinion those views as presented here represent only part of the overall picture. We do not altogether agree with him and while his viewpoint is reflected in our television program, it is only one among many different views we present. In fact, we deliberately show viewpoints that are contradictory to his.

When we began work on our television program last year, we sought contributions from dozens of experts, including Barry Sussman, and at that time we encouraged him to revise his earlier book, widely acclaimed as must reading for the student of Watergate. The result is this volume. However, to clarify matters for the reader and to prevent confusion, we point out that this book is not a guide for or a blueprint to our television program, which at this writing is still deep in the creative stages of production.

Our objective in producing *784 Days That Changed America* is to put Watergate in historical perspective in a documentary that shows how American democracy worked, struggled and finally survived the dreadful scandal that for a period of time crippled our government.

> Nancy Dickerson, Executive Producer
> Television Corporation of America
> Washington, D.C.
>
> *March 19, 1982*

Introduction

I BEGAN WORKING on the Watergate story on June 17, 1972, only hours after the break-in arrests at the Democratic National Committee headquarters. I was city editor of the *Washington Post* and had seen my share of crime stories. But from the start, I had never seen one as tantalizing as this. The five men captured wore business suits and surgical gloves, had thirteen brand-new hundred-dollar bills in their pockets, and carried sophisticated camera and electronic bugging equipment and a single walkie-talkie. Though they made no telephone calls after their capture, two lawyers appeared at police headquarters to represent them.

The following day it was revealed that one of the five worked for Richard Nixon's re-election committee. The day after that the mystery deepened when we at the *Post* learned and reported that the name and telephone number of a White House operative, E. Howard Hunt, Jr., formerly of the CIA, was listed in two address books belonging to the arrested men, and that a check for $6.36 from Hunt to a local country club had been left behind in one of their hotel rooms at the Watergate.

From those early moments on, I was part of a team that viewed from close in the uncovering of what many have called the worst scandal in the nation's history. Week by week, the Watergate disclosures led nearer to Nixon, engulfing his closest associates. On the first day in July, John N. Mitchell, who as attorney general had been the chief symbol of law and order in Nixon's Administration, resigned as chairman of the re-election committee because of the scandal. A month before the presidential election, the *Post* reported that the Watergate bugging was only one incident in a massive campaign of political spying and sabotage waged against the Democrats by the Nixon forces.

Even before those charges were aired, one Congressman, Wright Patman of Texas, had called for an inquiry into Watergate because of obvious violations in the financing of the Watergate burglars by the Nixon re-election committee. Patman sought as witnesses many of the conspirators, and successful hearings had the potential to expose the coverup at the outset. But with the White House intervening, a majority of Patman's House Banking and Currency Committee, including all the Republicans and a sufficient number of Democrats, blocked the inquiry. Nixon was thereafter able to keep Watergate a minor side issue in the election campaign. In November, 1972, he defeated George McGovern, the unpopular Democratic candidate, in one of the greatest landslide victories ever.

By spring of the following year, the Watergate coverup had collapsed, largely through pressure exerted by an aggressive jurist, John Sirica, and stunning, inexplicable disclosures made by the temporary head of the FBI, L. Patrick Gray III, who destroyed his own career and reputation in the process. In April, Nixon dismissed his chief aides, H. R. Haldeman, and John Ehrlichman, his counsel, John Dean, and Mitchell's replacement as attorney general, Richard Kleindienst. By going through the motions of cleaning house, the President tried to make it appear that he had no personal involvement in the scandal and that he was attempting to get to the bottom of it. But by late May, people who studied the public record could see that Nixon was guilty of criminal conduct in the Watergate coverup and in more serious earlier crimes or perversions of the presidency. The Oval Office tapes were still secret then, but no tapes were needed. There was more than enough evidence, as this book shows, to persuade a jury that the President of the United States had engaged in criminal activity.

It was then that I began writing the earlier version of this book, *The Great Coverup: Nixon and the Scandal of Watergate*. I did so with the conviction that Nixon's guilt had been established but the concern that Congress would not move against him.

Nixon's most obvious complicity was in the obstruction of the FBI's Watergate investigation. In his own words, in a statement issued on May 22, 1973, Nixon said he used the leaders of the CIA to have L. Patrick Gray curtail the Watergate inquiry and keep it from touching on "national security" matters. It was clear to me and others who studied it that Nixon was not talking about national security at all, but about his own security.

By then, other of Nixon's illegal or repugnant activities were coming out in a gush. It was revealed, for example, that burglars for the White House had broken into the offices of a West Coast psychiatrist in 1971, looking for material to discredit Daniel Ellsberg, whose gift of the *Pentagon Papers* to *The New York Times* had done so much to impugn the U.S. government's conduct of the war in Vietnam.

It was disclosed that as early as 1969, Nixon had ordered illegal wiretaps of government officials and newspaper reporters and columnists in an attempt to prevent "leaks" about Nixon's handling of the war. Astoundingly, the chief leak was the fact that the United States had bombed Cambodia, a neutral nation—an act of war that Nixon had managed to keep hidden from the public. By law, congressional consent was required for such an action, but only a handful of Congressmen knew of the bombing.

It was revealed that Nixon had set up a domestic spying operation, to be run from the White House, that would have used the CIA and the FBI to conduct illegal burglaries, read the mail and tap the telephones of antiwar dissidents. In addition, evidence was produced showing that some of the men involved in Watergate had for years been spying on Senator Edward M. Kennedy, the most-feared likely presidential opponent, and had forged State Department cables from early in the Vietnam war to defame the late President Kennedy.

The mentality that created Watergate had its beginnings in a White House that viewed any action as proper if it could help thwart antiwar protest among the citizenry or serve Nixon politically. As a result of these unchecked activities, an air of arrogance took hold. And with the spying apparatus in place, it was only a natural and small next step to use it, when the time came, for the election in 1972. The Watergate bugging was simply a continuation of past White House activities, with a slightly different goal.

I watched with incredulity from the spring of 1973 on as Nixon, with characteristic boldness, appeared able to withstand every new disclosure and all the pressures on him. In private, he ordered his aides to pay out hush money and to "stonewall" inquiries and he feared for his survival. But in public he depicted Watergate as a partisan witchhunt, charging that his enemies were using it not to get at the facts but to weaken him and further their own political ends.

In response to such posturing, with evidence of Nixon's come before them, the Congress, which could have controlled Nixon, began reacting in strange, contradictory ways. On the one hand, members called for the appointment of a special prosecutor to investigate Watergate independently. Then, led by Sam Ervin, Congress undertook the most dramatic inquiry in the history of the nation, the televised Senate Watergate hearings. By July, only die-hard supporters remained loyal to Nixon; the country had been repulsed by his activities as revealed by the U.S. Senate.

At the same time, however, even as Congress seemed to be moving toward Nixon, it was moving away from him. Before the end of April, 1973, Nixon and Ehrlichman were privately discussing the possibility of impeachment. "I think it's entirely conceivable that if Dean is totally out of control and if matters are not handled adroitly that you could get a resolution of impeachment in the Senate," Ehrlichman warned, and Nixon agreed, saying, "That's right."

Less than a month after that conversation, Congress knew, through abundant testimony, almost all the details of the matters that Ehrlichman and Nixon feared could lead to impeachment. And within six weeks, Dean had gone "totally out of control," filling in what few blanks were left. Despite that, there was no move toward impeachment. A few members of Congress spoke out, but they were widely ignored. The subject was not really discussed.

Furthermore, despite the sensational Watergate hearings, as summer turned to fall in 1973, leaders of both political parties began saying that the nation had "had enough" of Watergate. Despite the national disgust caused by the hearings, no move to impeach the President was begun or seriously considered. The reason was simple: rather than being his enemies, most in Congress were either Nixon's friends or people more concerned with keeping their own power than in further arousing large numbers of voters by venturing into a politically risky assault on a president.

What we were watching then was no longer a scandal limited to Richard Nixon and his Administration, but one that threatened to encompass almost the entire government. The question was whether the Congress would move to oust a criminal president, and for a long time the indication was that it would not. Only a handful of elected leaders spoke out against Nixon; the rest kept quiet or rallied to his side at crucial times.

Two immense counterpressures were at work, however, and they ultimately prevailed. The first was Nixon's own conduct, especially his defiance of the courts and the horrendous Saturday Night Massacre in October, 1973, when he took steps so violent that it seemed a madman was at the helm of government. The second pressure was that of the citizenry. A majority of the public had decided early on that Nixon was guilty and that he was lying. That was shown in opinion polls and in millions of letters and telegrams—literally tons of mail—descending on Capitol Hill.

And in November and December, another issue, Nixon's personal finances, came to a head. The President had a colossal tax problem. In 1970, it was revealed, he had paid $789 in federal income taxes, and in 1971 he had paid $878, having taken a $570,000 deduction for donating his vice-presidential papers to the government. It was also reported that hundreds of thousands of dollars of government money had been spent to improve Nixon's private residences in Key Biscayne and San Clemente. Government funds had been used to improve the private property of other presidents, but not to the same extent.

The financial scandal presented a new dimension in the battle of Nixon v. the people. Parts of Watergate may have been confusing, but there was no intricacy to the financial improprieties. The public outrage grew so enormous that Congress finally was forced to begin a serious impeachment inquiry.

In this revision and updating of my earlier book, I have discarded some of the details of the case against Nixon that were included in the 1973-1974 version. Proof of his involvement in the coverup has long since been established. I have tried instead to focus on the spectacle and drama from the break-in arrests until Nixon's resignation. It is a story of how a great nation watched its President go about trying to subvert the political and justice system, while powerful leaders did little to block him.

Washington, D.C.
March, 1982

BARRY SUSSMAN

PART I

The Break-In

1

It was Friday, June 16, 1972. Richard Nixon had been back from his trip to Russia for two weeks. During his journey, he had also visited Austria, Iran, and Poland, and he capped the 16,000 miles of air travel by dramatically convening a special joint session of Congress upon his return. The President had been gone thirteen tiring days, but the moment Air Force One landed at Andrews Air Force Base on June 1, he flew by helicopter to Capitol Hill—the first time a president had ever so descended on Congress. He delivered a speech that was carried live on radio and prime-time television, and was interrupted ten times by bursts of enthusiastic applause.

Now he was looking forward to leaving Washington for a weekend at a private Bahamas island owned by Robert Abplanalp, his friend for ten years. The White House entourage, aides and press, would stay at Key Biscayne. It was to be a relaxing weekend, not one for news. The re-election campaign had been mapped out and put in action, and it was a period of waiting: three and a half weeks for the Democratic Convention, nine and a half weeks for Nixon's nomination.

The campaign plan was for Nixon to appear above the fray, running as the President and not as a partisan candidate. The Moscow summit trip had been important for detente between the two super powers; but, as with Nixon's visit to Peking four months earlier, it was also the kind of statesmanlike action that seemed to place the President above party politics, and as such, it was politically helpful as well.

The visit to Russia, Nixon told Congress, portended "an historic opportunity" to achieve "man's oldest dream—a world in which all nations can enjoy the blessings of peace." Opinion polls indicated that a more immediate result of the trip was an increase of two to twelve percentage points in the

President's lead over his prospective Democratic opponents in the November election.

Even the name of the Nixon campaign committee, the Committee for the Re-election of the President, seemed to suggest that a nonpartisan leader, not a man known as an attack-style politician, was running for office. The committee, known as CRP, or CREP, and later as Creep, furthered the theme by arranging for several dozen "surrogates"—Cabinet members, U.S. senators, and others—to do much of the campaigning that would normally occupy the time of the candidate.

As the President flew south on that June 16, his wife went to the West Coast, where she was to be the guest of honor at a weekend "Celebrities for Nixon" party in Beverly Hills. John N. Mitchell, the former attorney general and now director of the Nixon campaign, also went to California on Friday, to attend the party and other campaign events. Mitchell had made it known that he was to approve all important campaign decisions, and that in line with the desire to avoid low politicking, there were to be no slashing attacks on the press or the rest of the media by the CRP surrogates. So it was not surprising that only the day before, a CRP press aide, DeVan Shumway, and another official—one who always wanted to please the boss—had come to Mitchell's office to ask approval for a proposed letter to the editor of the *Washington Post* taking issue with statements made in an article on campaign financing.

The man with Shumway was present in his capacity as counsel to the Finance Committee to Re-elect the President, the money end of the campaign committee, but he had other campaign duties as well. His name was George Gordon Liddy. Mitchell read the letter, approved it, and waved the two out.

Perhaps because it was such an easy stage of the campaign, Mitchell took his wife, Martha, and his daughter, Marty, to California with him. His closest aides also took their wives, to attend the parties if not the political meetings.

Among those aides were Frederick C. LaRue, a wealthy Mississippian who held no fixed position in the campaign but who had been as close as any man was to Mitchell for six years; Robert C. Mardian, who had been assistant attorney general under Mitchell but who left the Justice Department when Mitchell asked him to help in the campaign; and Jeb

Stuart Magruder, formerly a White House aide and now listed as Mitchell's number-two man at CRP. Magruder, only thirty-seven years old, had left his position as an aide to White House chief of staff H. R. Haldeman in May, 1971, to organize the re-election committee and run its day-to-day activities until Mitchell was ready to take over in March, 1972.

Gordon Liddy stayed in Washington, and on Friday evening, he headed over to the Watergate Hotel on business.

The Watergate complex was the most valuable piece of privately held real estate in the nation's capital. Built in the mid-1960's, it consisted of six buildings—the hotel, two office buildings, and three apartment cooperatives in which units sold for from $40,000 to $250,000 in 1972. Overlooking the Potomac and the new Kennedy Center, and with majestic views sweeping from the Lincoln Memorial eastward across the mall to the Washington Monument, the White House, and the Capitol, the Watergate attracted some of the better known figures of the Nixon Administration as residents, including John and Martha Mitchell, and Nixon's private secretary, Rose Mary Woods.

Across the street from the Watergate, in room 723 of the Howard Johnson's Motor Lodge, two men who worked for Liddy spent the evening of June 16 tinkering with electronic equipment. From their room they could peer across at the sixth-floor offices of the Democratic National Committee.

One of them, Alfred C. Baldwin III, followed the other's instructions, soldering batteries together, connecting antennae onto listening devices, testing them first on a television set and then on a telephone. By 11:30 the tests were completed, and Baldwin went downstairs for an ice cream sundae. When he came back, his partner, James W. McCord, Jr., was on the telephone, saying he "didn't know whether or not somebody was still working across the street, and possibly we'll have to call it off."

McCord was a man who exuded confidence. A colonel in the Air Force Reserve, he had the appearance of a pilot—sober, strong, intelligent-looking, certain of himself. In a world of guardians, those who are guarded, and intruders, he had always been a guardian. He had been an FBI man and had spent the bulk of his career as a security official in the Central Intelligence Agency. Only recently had McCord switched roles and became an intruder.

Baldwin saw a man get up from a seat at Democratic headquarters and turn off the lights. He told McCord, and McCord said into the telephone, "It looks all right."

McCord, Baldwin was to recount later, then "furnished me a walkie-talkie unit and told me to observe anything that was going on, if I saw anything unusual to take the walkie-talkie and call immediately. He went over to the bed, emptied his pockets, took his wallet out, his change and other papers, and placed them on the bed and left the room. . . . It was after midnight, I don't know the exact time, but approximately 12:30 or 1 o'clock."

Baldwin turned on the television. He could watch it and still keep an eye out across the street. The building containing Democratic headquarters was patrolled by twenty-four-year-old guard Frank Wills during the midnight to 7:00 A.M. shift. Sometime between 12:15 and 1:30 A.M.—accounts are conflicting—Wills noticed something peculiar. He was on the second basement level, a garage, and he found a piece of tape drawn tautly over a door lock. "I took the tape off, but I didn't think anything of it. I thought maybe the building's engineer had done it," Wills was to tell reporters. He checked the door again at about 1:50 A.M., found a new piece of tape, and called the police.

Upstairs, McCord and four men from Miami removed the hinges from a rear door of the Democrats' offices. They had been there before, on Memorial Day weekend, when they had photographed documents and planted two eavesdropping devices: one in a telephone in the office of Democratic Party chairman Lawrence F. O'Brien, the other in a telephone used by Spencer Oliver, a liaison officer between the national committee and the various state Democratic Party leaders.

In the intervening weeks, the bug on O'Brien's phone proved faulty, but Baldwin monitored two hundred calls on Oliver's phone. Oliver was not paid by the Democratic Committee, but because of his function as liaison to state chairmen, the committee wanted him close at hand and gave him the use of a large office that had been a conference room and was equipped with a refrigerator. Secretaries at the committee sometimes kept food in the refrigerator, ate their lunch in the office, and, when it was empty, made personal calls on Oliver's phone.

It was private conversations like these as well as business calls by Oliver that Baldwin had an opportunity to overhear.

He would transcribe them almost verbatim, type them, and give them to McCord, who gave them to Liddy. A secretary at CRP would retype them on special stationery with the letterhead GEMSTONE in large type, and Liddy would give those to Jeb Magruder. But Lawrence O'Brien, with his political experience, savvy, and clout, was a much bigger fish than Oliver, and Liddy wanted the bug on O'Brien repaired, or a new one installed.

As they entered the Democrats' offices, the Gemstone team immediately went to work. They began removing the ceiling panels above O'Brien's office and setting up camera equipment to photograph more documents. One of the men, Bernard L. Barker, an American born in Cuba, carried a walkie-talkie, but he didn't have it on.

Elsewhere in the Watergate complex, also carrying a walkie-talkie and supervising the operation from a safe distance, were Liddy and E. Howard Hunt, Jr., whose special talents had brought them together as secret agents for the White House in 1971.

Hunt had been employed by the Central Intelligence Agency from 1949 to 1970. He had been a cold-war spy, Bay of Pigs planner, author of almost two dozen dime-store novels; and at fifty-three, he was still practicing intrigue and bragging about it. He was listed in the 1972–73 *Who's Who* as a correspondent for *Life* Magazine during World War II, a Guggenheim fellow, a movie scriptwriter. He gave his business address as: Office, The White House, Washington, D.C.

Liddy was forty-one years old. He had failed as an FBI man, drummed out in 1962 after five years. He had been an attorney and a flamboyant prosecutor in Dutchess County, New York, where he fired a revolver in a court, waved a knife under the noses of a jury, hid in the bushes at a raid on the commune of Dr. Timothy Leary, the LSD experimenter. He ran unsuccessfully in a Republican congressional primary election in 1968 and decided to enter the general election as an independent, prompting local Republicans in Poughkeepsie to seek help in Washington for fear that Liddy's candidacy would elect a Democrat. Gerald Ford, who was then House Minority Leader, visited Poughkeepsie and helped Liddy get a job at the Treasury Department in Washington. There he repeatedly got into trouble until he was picked up by the White House.

After getting the call from Frank Wills, a metropolitan Washington police dispatcher radioed officer Dennis P. Stephenson and asked him to head to the Watergate. Stephenson had just pulled into Second District police headquarters, a few minutes from the Watergate. He begged off the assignment, saying he was low on gas and had paper work to catch up on. Had he answered the call, wearing his police uniform and driving a marked police car, there probably would have been no Watergate scandal. He would have been spotted by Baldwin from across the street, and Baldwin would have put out an alarm on his walkie-talkie. Even with Barker's walkie-talkie turned off, Hunt and Liddy would have heard the alert and had time to rescue their cohorts.

The nearest other police car was an unmarked sedan with three plainclothes members of the tactical squad in it. Dressed in plain clothes, their hair long, trained at being unobtrusive, these officers had completed their shift and spent some time at an after-hours spot in Georgetown, according to a ranking police official. They were back in their cruiser when the call came from the Watergate. They told the watch commander they would respond. In about three minutes, just before 2 A.M., they met Wills.

Baldwin saw the three policemen arrive but thought nothing of it. "A car parked in front of the Watergate and three men got out and went inside. I wondered if that meant anything, but I didn't use the walkie-talkie at that time."*

Wills showed the policemen the taped door in the basement. The officers sent him to the lobby to watch for anyone trying to escape. They then went up the stairwell.

The officers, informed of previous break-ins at the sixth and eighth floors, went to the eighth floor first and found the door taped there. They checked the office doors on the eighth floor but found nothing out of order.

One policeman, John Barrett, went to the ninth floor. The other two, Sergeant Paul Leeper and Carl Shoffler, started to work their way down.

The door on the sixth-floor landing was taped open. Leeper went up half a flight, summoned Barrett down, and the three began their search of Democratic headquarters. They started

---

*The account of events of the Watergate arrests is taken from a composite of later testimony by those involved. This quote from Baldwin comes from a lengthy interview with two reporters from the *Los Angeles Times*, made public in early October, 1972.

with the offices facing the Howard Johnson's, turning the lights on and off as they proceeded.

Leeper and Shoffler walked out on the terrace facing the Howard Johnson's. Baldwin was on the balcony outside his room, holding his walkie-talkie and peering at the two men. Shoffler, wearing old clothes and carrying a flashlight and a gun, feared that the man across the way might mistake him for a burglar. "Do you think he'll call the police?" he asked his partner.

Baldwin became frantic when the lights started going on and off. "I noticed the figures of three men. At least two of them came out on the balcony. They were casually dressed and were carrying flashlights and guns. I could see one man in the office holding a gun in front of him and looking behind desks. Watching from the balcony outside my room, I grabbed the walkie-talkie and said, 'Base to any unit.' A voice came back: 'What have you got?' "

The voice was that of Howard Hunt.

"Are our people dressed casually or are they in suits?" Baldwin asked.

"What?"

Baldwin repeated the question.

"Our people are in suits."

"Well," Baldwin replied, "we've got a problem. We've got some people dressed casually and they've got guns. They're looking around the balcony and everywhere, but they haven't come across our people."

Hunt seemed to panic. "Are you reading this! Are you reading this!" he pleaded. There was no answer. "They don't have the unit on or it's not turned up. Are you still in the room?" he asked Baldwin. "Stay there, I'll be right over."

The policemen searched methodically, working from the front of the building to the rear. Officer Barrett approached a corner office and stood motionless, staring into the darkness. He discerned a slight motion, just off the floor, and was able to make out the outlines of a man's arm. "Hold it and come out," the policeman shouted.

"Be careful, you got us," one of the men said.

Barker turned on his walkie-talkie momentarily and whispered, "They've got us." He left it on long enough for Baldwin to hear McCord ask, "What are you people? Are you metropolitan police or what?" Then it went silent.

The men came out of hiding, "arms all over the place," as

Sergeant Leeper recalled it, their raised hands sheathed in blue surgical gloves. They were lined against a wall, advised of their rights, and searched.

"By now," according to Baldwin, "there was all kinds of police activity—motorcycles and paddywagons driving up and guys jumping out of patrol cars and running up to the Watergate. Then I saw two men carrying suitcases casually walking out of the hotel section. I recognized one as Hunt, he glanced up at the balcony where I stood, and then with the other man walked over and entered a car parked in front of the Watergate Apartment complex, that is almost directly in front of Mrs. Mitchell's apartment. . . . The two of them drove away."

Arrested with McCord and Barker were Frank Sturgis, also known as Frank Fiorini; Eugenio Martinez, and Virgilio Gonzalez. All except McCord were from Miami. The latter two were Cuban emigres; Barker and Sturgis were American but had lived in Cuba. Sturgis was carrying $215, including two hundred-dollar bills; Martinez had $814, including seven hundred-dollar bills; Gonzalez and Barker had $230 each, including two hundred-dollar bills each. McCord had only an identification card borrowed from Hunt, with the alias "Edward Warren" on it. He had left his wallet, change, and car keys on the bed in Baldwin's motel room.

Later, in Rooms 214 and 314 of the Watergate Hotel, police found four packets of hundred-dollar bills, eight in a packet, all new and consecutively numbered. They also found two address books with the name "Howard Hunt" in them and notations suggesting that Hunt worked in the White House. There was a check from Hunt for $6.36 in an unmailed envelope, addressed to the Lakewood Country Club—one month's dues.

The five men were taken to Second District police headquarters, McCord in a scout car, Barker in the unmarked car that had responded to the break-in, and the others in a patrol wagon. At headquarters they gave false names.

The police at the stationhouse called the local FBI field office, an official of the Democratic Party, and the acting police chief that day, Charles Wright. Wright, who has since retired, remembered that no one knew the significance of the arrests early that morning. He said that the Democratic official who came to police headquarters, deputy chairman Stanley Greigg, speculated that "it will be a good thing if we can blame it on the Republicans. But we had nothing here, and we don't talk important things over on the telephone, we take a walk."

At about 9 or 9:30 A.M., two Washington attorneys, Douglas Caddy and Joseph Rafferty, Jr., mysteriously appeared at police headquarters to represent the arrested men, who had made no telephone calls.

2

THE OFFICES OF the Committee for the Re-election of the President were across the street from the White House complex, at 1701 Pennsylvania Avenue, N.W. Among those at work Saturday morning, June 17, 1972, were Hugh W. Sloan, Jr., the treasurer of the Finance Committee to Re-elect the President, and Robert Odle, the campaign committee's office manager. Sloan was stopped briefly in a hallway by Gordon Liddy, who was in an agitated condition.

"My boys got caught last night," Sloan recalled Liddy saying. "I made a mistake by using someone from here, which I told them I would never do. I'm afraid I'll lose my job."

Liddy found Odle and asked him where a big paper shredder was kept. He began shredding papers with his name on them, hotel soap wrappers that showed his travels, and, reportedly, even hundred-dollar bills.

Liddy telephoned Magruder in Los Angeles, interrupting a large, group breakfast. Liddy told him what had happened; Magruder told LaRue, and LaRue told Mitchell. Mitchell asked that Mardian be instructed to handle any immediate legal problems. Later, Liddy went to see Attorney General Richard G. Kleindienst at the Burning Tree Country Club and asked that McCord be released from jail, saying John Mitchell had requested it. The Attorney General refused.

Liddy told Kleindienst he believed that some of the men arrested at the Watergate might be employed by either the White House or CRP. Kleindienst still refused. The information Liddy had given him put Kleindienst in a compromising situation. The chief law enforcement officer in the land, he was among the first to be told that the White House might be involved in the Watergate break-in. Kleindienst knew Liddy and regarded him as a disreputable character, and from what

Kleindienst has revealed publicly of their conversation, there is little doubt that the Attorney General immediately recognized that Liddy knew details of, and was quite possibly involved in, the break-in.

Yet it was twelve days later before FBI agents stumbled onto the existence of Gordon Liddy, by accident and not through anything Kleindienst had said. To harbor information about a crime is a criminal act, termed "misprision of felony." By not seeing to it that Liddy was immediately investigated, Kleindienst left himself open for such charges to be placed against him had legal authorities decided simply to pursue what was a matter of public record. None did.

Kleindienst spoke three times that morning to Henry Petersen, the Assistant Attorney General in charge of the Justice Department's criminal division, and told him to handle the break-in in a normal manner. Kleindienst also spoke to D.C. police chief Jerry Wilson. Wilson reportedly told Wright, the officer in charge, to handle the arrests as he would an ordinary burglary.

Throughout the day, people and agencies that respond to momentous crimes such as hijackings or riots or assassination attempts began responding to this one. The police, the Secret Service, the Justice Department, FBI agents—all proud networks of investigators—started their ripples of inquiry, touching base with the White House, the re-election committee, the Democrats, unaware that other counter-ripples were also starting, that some of the guardians, like McCord, had become intruders.

The assistant chief of the Secret Service, Patrick Boggs, called John Ehrlichman, the President's domestic adviser and the ranking White House official in Washington, and told him that McCord, one of those arrested, was the security coordinator for the Nixon campaign committee. Boggs also called John J. Caulfield, who had been another White House secret agent. Caulfield, a friend of McCord's, had helped him acquire the job at the re-election committee. Caulfield too called Ehrlichman. They discussed McCord and the trail that Howard Hunt had almost certainly left behind. Ehrlichman reportedly said, "I guess I had better call John Mitchell."

Ehrlichman called Charles Colson, Hunt's longtime friend, the presidential aide who had pushed for Hunt to be hired in the White House and who directed most of Hunt's work there. "In candor," Ehrlichman told investigators ten months later, "I and perhaps others thought Colson was involved and we had to know." Ehrlichman also called Ronald Ziegler, the President's press secretary, in Key Biscayne.

Alfred Wong, the head of the Secret Service technical division in the White House, telephoned deputy assistant to the President Alexander P. Butterfield and told him that the name of a White House consultant, Hunt, had been found in an address book left behind. Butterfield, keeper of one of only three lists of the White House payroll, told Wong there was no consultant by that name. Wong said he believed Hunt worked for Colson.

Butterfield checked with his staff secretary, Bruce Kehrli, asking if there was a consultant for Colson whose name was not listed on the payroll. Kehrli said, yes, "Haldeman told me not to list him." Kehrli indicated that Hunt's work was of a clandestine nature. Butterfield was fond of Colson, but, like Ehrlichman, he immediately suspected that Colson might have been involved in the break-in.

About 5 P.M. June 17, an FBI agent telephoned Butterfield and asked how to find Hunt. By then Butterfield was able to tell him.

About two hours later, after calling to verify that he was home, two FBI agents visited Howard Hunt. Their meeting was brief. "Hunt admitted that the check for $6.36 was his, but refused to discuss the matter or the individuals involved without consulting his attorney," reads the first FBI report prepared on the break-in.

John Mitchell had a press release prepared Saturday deploring the incident at Democratic headquarters and attempting to disassociate CRP from McCord, its security chief. But the press didn't know who McCord was on Saturday, and no one asked Mitchell for any statement.

In California, Jeb Magruder called re-election aides at 1701 Pennsylvania Avenue—"We had numerous conversations that day," he said—and asked that certain files be removed from his office, including a folder with the marking "Gemstone" on it. "We never considered that there wouldn't be a coverup," Magruder would later say.

On Sunday, in response to an inquiry from the Associated Press, Mitchell released the following statement:

> We have just learned from news reports that a man identified as employed by our campaign committee was one of five persons arrested at the Democratic National

Committee headquarters in Washington, D.C., early Saturday morning.

The person involved is the proprietor of a private security agency who was employed by our committee months ago to assist with the installation of our security system.

He has, as we understand it, a number of business clients and interests, and we have no knowledge of those relationships.

We want to emphasize that this man and the other people involved were not operating either on our behalf or with our consent.

I am surprised and dismayed at these reports.

At this time, we are experiencing our own security problems at the Committee for the Re-election of the President. Our problems are not as dramatic as the events of Saturday morning—but nonetheless of a serious nature to us. We do not know as of this moment whether our security problems are related to the events of Saturday morning at the Democratic headquarters or not.

There is no place in our campaign or in the electoral process for this type of activity, and we will not permit or condone it.

The model for all future Administration statements about the break-in was contained in this first response. It consisted of three parts:

1. Deplore the incident.
2. Disassociate responsible Nixon aides from any part in it.
3. Point out that both political parties may be victims of such events—that spying is "just politics."

The Newporter Inn, a resort motel in Newport Beach, California, was probably the favorite stopping place in Orange County for ranking members of Richard Nixon's Administration. L. Patrick Gray III stopped there between a speaking engagement on Saturday at Pepperdine College and another one on Monday, June 19, at Palm Springs to the National Sheriffs Association. He and Mrs. Gray went to a motel swimming pool Sunday afternoon to relax, and ended up chatting for a while with John Mitchell's good friend, Fred

LaRue. They talked about the strange bugging incident in Washington as well as about other things.

On Sunday, John and Martha Mitchell also checked into the Newporter Inn, taking a villa. On Monday, Mitchell left and his wife stayed behind. How much she knew about the events of June 17, or the events leading up to and immediately following them, is not clear. It was from the Newporter Inn that she made her now famous telephone call to Helen Thomas of United Press International, saying that she was "sick and tired of politics," that she had given her husband an ultimatum that she would "leave him unless he gets out of the campaign," and that "politics is a dirty business." As she spoke, the telephone was yanked away from her and jerked out of the wall.

Days later, Mitchell resigned from the Nixon campaign on the grounds that he needed more time to spend with his family. Yet his own calendar shows that he spent more time on the campaign after he vacated his title than he had before.

3

RICHARD NIXON WAS not given to small talk. In his book, *An American Life*, Jeb Magruder described how in his second week at the White House, when he was introduced to Nixon, he was "struck by how ill at ease the President seemed in greeting me. This was in contrast to how good he was with groups and receiving lines."

Sometimes Nixon's discomfort became a real problem, even with people close to him. In March 1969, a few high-level staff members held a party in the recently renovated west wing of the White House for Paul Keyes, a comedy writer who had worked for Nixon in the 1968 campaign. As the President walked in there was a sudden hush, as there sometimes is at office gatherings when the boss enters. This time the hush wouldn't go away.

Keyes, who felt himself a pretty good man with a one-liner, tried to break it: "Gee, Mr. President," he said, "you're losing your touch. When I came in everybody cheered." The silence continued. Nixon looked at the new red rug and a woman aide's pretty green dress, and tried his own brand of humor. "Red rug, green dress. Christmas colors. Ha, ha." No one laughed or said anything. The President turned and went back to his Oval Office. In a moment he buzzed for his chief of staff, H. R. Haldeman, to join him. A moment after that, Nixon could be heard screaming at Haldeman: "I never want to see whiskey in the west wing of the White House again."

It was everyone's job to see that Nixon was saved from uncomfortable situations, but it was Haldeman's job more than anyone else's. Only Haldeman entered the Oval Office without knocking; it was Haldeman, acting on behalf of Nixon, who saw to it that Cabinet members were kept away, forced to deal with low-level White House aides when they wanted to discuss matters involving billions of dollars and important national policy with the Chief Executive.

The President found time to personally meet twice with a veterinarian when his dog, King Timahoe, had mange. But he never met more than once a year privately with Elliot Richardson, who held three Cabinet positions under him. It was not that Nixon was too busy to meet; it was a matter of personality and style. The President was deeply involved with endless details of the most meaningless sort—he would, for example, pore over guest lists for social functions at the White House, noting the names of the few people with whom he wished to mingle, issuing orders that all others be kept away from him.

Long before Watergate, then, Nixon had established for himself a policy of insulation. He made decisions on minutiae, but he kept most people he didn't trust at a great distance. His policies usually reached the Executive departments through Haldeman or *his* underlings. All orders from Haldeman were assumed to be orders from Nixon. Still, there existed a small coterie slightly removed from Haldeman who had access to the President and who had gained his trust: men like Ehrlichman, Colson, John Mitchell.

Monday morning, June 19, 1972, at the White House: Ehrlichman, preparing to report to Haldeman or Nixon on their return from Key Biscayne, began a succession of meetings with men who knew something about what had happened at the Watergate and about how federal investigators were pursuing the incident. At noon he called on a young man who had already been doing some fact-finding on his own.

John Wesley Dean III rarely met directly with President Nixon, but he served him the way the most efficient administrative aides served congressmen or senators. By virtue of his personality, intelligence, and background, he was an ideal second-rank official.

A lawyer, Dean served for a year in 1966 to 1967 as minority counsel to the House Judiciary Committee, where he became involved in preparation of legislation dealing with crime. In college at Staunton, Virginia, his roommate was Barry Goldwater, Jr., and when Dean married for the first time in 1962, it was to the daughter of the late Missouri Senator Thomas Hennings. Dean understood Capitol Hill, then, from the vantage point of one intimately acquainted with how elected officials and their staffs combined to mold the legislative process.

In 1967, he became associate director of the National Commission on the Reform of Criminal Laws, and his work contributed eventually to a section of the Omnibus Crime Control Act of 1970. That section established the principle of "limited immunity" from prosecution, or "use immunity," a means of providing members of a conspiracy incentive to implicate their leaders. Such immunity was aimed at fighting organized crime; it was later used frequently by prosecutors in the Watergate scandal. Dean himself, though pleading guilty to certain charges, received use immunity to testify freely on other matters.

Dean's work on crime laws brought him in contact with the Justice Department. In Feburary, 1969, he became associate deputy attorney general under John Mitchell, serving as liaison for the Department with members of Congress. During the great antiwar rallies of the late 1960's, the Justice Department often negotiated with the leaders of protests over demonstration permits and the like, and Dean became involved in that work.

By 1970, when Ehrlichman gave up his title of counsel to the President to become Nixon's chief adviser on domestic policies, Dean had shown that his thinking on important issues appeared in line with that of the White House, and that he was someone who was able to get things done as well. He moved to the Executive mansion and was given Ehrlichman's vacant title of counsel, but not his full range of responsibilities.

Wearing expensive, conservative suits and driving to work in a sports car, Dean was one of a number of young men of similar appearance who reported to Haldeman. His knowledge of Capitol Hill was helpful in certain White House lobbying efforts; his experience with antiwar demonstrators led him to play an active role in the Administration's handling of difficult May Day protests of 1971, and his legal ability was put to use on many of the President's private affairs. Associates in the White House considered him very bright, very loyal, and very ambitious.

As time passed, Dean assumed more and more responsibilities, especially on personal projects for Nixon—the handling of his estate, his private papers, legal matters in connection with the re-election drive.

Dean was at a college commencement in the Philippines

when the Watergate arrests took place. He arrived back in the United States on the evening of June 18 and called an aide, Fred Fielding, from San Francisco. Fielding told him about the break-in, the arrest of McCord, and the tell-tale check left behind by Hunt. Dean, like so many others, later said that he thought immediately that Colson might have been involved.

On the morning of June 19, Dean arrived at work at about 9:15 and began receiving calls about the break-in.

Jack Caulfield, McCord's friend, phoned. Magruder called and blamed Gordon Liddy for the trouble. Haldeman's principal political aide, Gordon Strachan, called; Hugh Sloan of the re-election committee called and was frightened. Dean meanwhile placed calls to Colson, to Liddy, and to Attorney General Kleindienst.

When Dean and Ehrlichman met for the first time that Monday, Dean already knew far more about the bugging incident than did the federal investigators. He had taken a stroll with Liddy, and he told Ehrlichman what Liddy had to say.

At 1:45 P.M., Ehrlichman met with Attorney General Kleindienst. Later, Ehrlichman was the ranking White House official present at a group meeting in which decisions were made to empty the contents of Howard Hunt's White House safe and to tell Hunt to leave the country.

Patrick Gray, acting director of the FBI for only six weeks, had not yet returned to his office from California on Monday. "Two-day Gray" they called him, because of the speeches and visits to FBI field offices that so frequently took him from Washington two days at a time. He had taken over on the death of J. Edgar Hoover, who had made the FBI the proud, independent agency that it was. Hoover himself had been put in charge of the old Bureau of Investigation in 1924, at the height of the Teapot Dome scandals, when the reputation of the investigative agency was so low that it was known as the Bureau of Easy Virtue.

Gray had been kept informed all weekend of the first FBI moves in the bugging investigation. Now, in Palm Springs, California, he was told of the FBI's first summary report, which identified the arrested men and mentioned the possible link to White House consultant Howard Hunt.

Two extra copies of the report had been prepared, one to be sent to Attorney General Kleindienst, Gray's boss, the other addressed to H. R. Haldeman at the White House.

Gray stated later that he refused to forward the summary to either man. "I stopped both of them," he said, because of the need to keep investigative findings closely held.

That day FBI agents had their first interview with an official at the Committee for the Re-election of the President, to be followed by six more in the next few days and by two interviews with White House personnel. FBI field offices across the country were notified of the urgency of this new investigation, first by telephone, then by written messages.

At the beginning, Gray and his assistants were doing everything right.

In the evening on Monday, June 19, 1972, as dusk turned to dark, Nixon and Haldeman sat together in the presidential plane, *The Spirit of '76*, high over the east coast, returning to Washington from Key Biscayne. Haldeman had been in touch with Jeb Magruder, with John Ehrlichman, and with others who had either plotted the bugging of the Democrats or were suddenly forced to turn their efforts to finding out exactly what had happened, who was involved, what had gone wrong, and how, as the President was to say a few days later, they could "cut the loss."

Nixon himself had spoken three times Sunday and Monday to Charles Colson, the man others in the White House suspected of being responsible for the bugging. Their last conversation, according to information supplied by the White House to Watergate investigators later on, had been Monday morning and was fifty-nine minutes long, and Watergate was discussed, Colson later testified. Nixon had initiated each call. To this day, one wonders what Nixon and Haldeman were saying and thinking as they headed back to the nation's capital.

4

JOSEPH CALIFANO, WHO had been counsel for President Johnson in the White House, was an attorney for the Democratic Party in 1972. He had a house guest from New York the weekend of June 17–18, and on Sunday, when they learned that one of the Watergate burglars had worked for the re-election committee, they were perplexed. Were other campaign people involved? What did they want in Democratic Party headquarters? There was hardly anything there.

"You're a lawyer," the house guest said. "Why don't you sue and find out?"

On Tuesday morning, June 20, 1972, the Democratic National Committee filed a one-million-dollar civil suit against the Committee for the Re-election of the President and the Republican National Committee. Lawrence F. O'Brien, the Democratic Party chairman, called a press conference to say that there is "a developing clear line to the White House" and to explain the suit as an attempt to force examination of the bugging by the courts.

"I believe we are about to witness the ultimate test of this Administration that so piously committed itself to a new era of law and order just four years ago," O'Brien said.

O'Brien homed in on John Mitchell's attempt to disassociate the Nixon campaign from McCord:

> We know that as of the moment of his arrest at gunpoint just ten feet from where I now stand, Mr. McCord was in the pay of the Committee for the Re-election of the President.
>
> If John Mitchell's reflex attempt to conceal that fact is any signal of what is to come from the Republican Party and the Administration, I fear we shall be long in get-

ting at the truth. . . . We learned of this bugging attempt only because it was bungled. How many other attempts have there been? And just who was involved?

When O'Brien filed his law suit, John Mitchell had a response prepared.

> This committee did not authorize and does not condone the alleged actions of the five men apprehended Saturday morning. We abhor such activity.
> The Committee for the Re-election of the President is not legally, morally, or ethically accountable for actions taken without its knowledge and beyond the scope of its control.

He called the suit "a political stunt," "another example of sheer demagoguery on the part of Mr. O'Brien."

The Democrats' charges and the Republicans' denials and countercharges immediately became a regular backdrop to the play of election-year politics. It was the end of June and the Democrats had not yet chosen a candidate for President, although it seemed fairly certain that the nomination would go to George McGovern, who had been running since almost four years earlier, when he made a bid for the 1968 Democratic nomination after the assassination of Robert F. Kennedy.

In the following years McGovern made his appeal as an antiwar, populist candidate. The South Dakota Senator traveled widely to promote reform measures in the selection of delegates to party nominating conventions—campaigning as he did so, long before anyone else entered the 1972 race. He formally announced his candidacy in 1971 and began holding meetings with small groups across the country. He promised to end the war in Vietnam immediately if elected, attacked the party's "establishment center," called for amnesty for those who had refused to fight in Vietnam, pledged huge cuts in defense spending and a program of income redistribution. It was early, and the press did not take his campaign seriously.

Instead, the press and the rest of the media focused on Senator Edmund Muskie of Maine as the most likely Democratic candidate. Muskie had sent out good vibrations to voters as the vice-presidential running mate of Hubert Humphrey in 1968, and in a series of Louis Harris polls from

February, 1971, through July of that year, Muskie repeatedly ran ahead of Richard Nixon in head-to-head contests. These polls indicated that Muskie would beat Nixon in 1972 whether or not Alabama Governor George Wallace ran as a third-party candidate, as he had in 1968.

The Nixon camp, threatened by Muskie, decided that it too would begin election work early. The Committee for the Re-election of the President was formed in May, 1971, and a campaign of so-called "black politics"—dirty tricks—was instituted to block Muskie and aid the candidacy of McGovern, who seemed to be the easiest opponent for Nixon to defeat. At the same time, Nixon and his aides had great fear of one other Democrat, Senator Edward M. Kennedy, whom they considered more than just an opponent. He was an enemy. From 1969 on, the White House was compiling information on Kennedy. In July, 1971, one of Howard Hunt's first White House projects was to find whatever dirt he could on the Senator and other members of the Kennedy clan.

The Democrats campaigned oblivious to the black politics being conducted by the Nixon forces, their party thrown into confusion anyway by the entry of George Wallace in key primaries. No one expected the Alabama governor to win the Democratic nomination, but it was feared that his appeal would so skew the primary results that no Democrat would emerge with a clear mandate.

Without a standout candidate, others put their names in the running: Senator Henry Jackson of Washington, projecting an image similar to Nixon's on issues such as the war and amnesty; Mayor John Lindsay of New York, who had just switched parties; and Hubert Humphrey, as he saw the field growing. Shirley Chisholm, the first black congresswoman, entered the race. So did Sam Yorty, the mayor of Los Angeles, for reasons not exactly discernible.

Muskie as frontrunner couldn't stand up under all the scrutiny. He won the first primary, in New Hampshire, but several bizarre incidents there apparently cut into his margin. The press was tough on him, and sources of campaign contributions began to dry up.

One of the incidents that appeared befuddling at the time was a series of phone calls made to Democratic voters in New Hampshire. Awakened in the middle of the night, citizens were told that the caller represented Harlem youth for Muskie, that the Senator was good to blacks, and that a vote for him would be appreciated. It was simple, obvious campaign sabotage.

But what helped ruin Muskie's presidential campaign was a more subtle piece of sabotage. On Thursday, February 24, 1972, the Manchester, New Hampshire, *Union Leader* ran a picture of a scribbled letter to its publisher, William Loeb, in the space usually reserved for an editorial page cartoon. The letter charged Muskie with condoning a slur on Americans of French-Canadian descent.

On the front page of his newspaper that day, Loeb ran a signed editorial calling attention to the letter, criticizing Muskie for finding the remarks amusing, and charging that the Senator was a hypocrite.

The following day Loeb ran a reprint of a *Newsweek* magazine item about Jane Muskie, the Senator's wife, in which she was quoted as telling reporters on a campaign bus, "Let's tell dirty jokes" and "Pass me my purse—I haven't had my morning cigarette yet." The item, a condensation of an article from *Women's Wear Daily*, said Jane Muskie owned up "to a preference for two drinks before dinner and a crème de menthe afterwards."

On Saturday morning, February 26, Muskie, with sixty to seventy newsmen and supporters huddled before him in a snowstorm, stood on a flatbed truck in front of Loeb's building, attacked the publisher as a "gutless coward" for involving Mrs. Muskie in the campaign, and denied condoning any slur on Americans of French-Canadian descent.

David S. Broder, who was there for the *Washington Post*, reported that "in defending his wife, Muskie broke down three times in as many minutes—uttering a few words and then standing silent in the near blizzard, rubbing at his face, his shoulders heaving, while he attempted to regain his composure sufficiently to speak."

Broder quoted Loeb as saying later in the day, "I think Senator Muskie's excited and near-hysterical performance this morning again indicates he's not the man that many of us want to have his finger on the nuclear button."

As routine politics in the 1972 primaries faded, this moment stood out as one of the few memorable ones. There is no question that it was terribly damaging to Muskie.

Seven months after it occurred, White House aide Kenneth Clawson reportedly looked back on it boastfully and told a *Washington Post* staff writer, his former colleague, that he had written the Canuck letter. It had been an act of sabotage, apparently conceived and executed by aides to the President, that helped do in Muskie.

Failing to live up to press expectations in New Hampshire on March 7, but at least winning with 48 percent of the vote, Muskie was overcome by disaster in Florida the following week, where he was the victim of more overt campaign sabotage, some of it practiced by a political saboteur named Donald Segretti.* Several days before the primary election in Florida, a flyer was distributed by saboteurs for Nixon using Muskie letterhead, charging Senators Jackson and Humphrey with improper sexual escapades.

"Senator Jackson of Everett, Washington, was involved with a 17-year-old girl . . . when he was a senior at Everett High School. The result was an illegitimate daughter . . . born February 7, 1929," the flyer said.

"Senator Hubert Humphrey has similar skeletons in his closet. He was driving in Washington, D.C., on December 3, 1967, after hitting two parked cars and a mail box. In his car at that time was a known call girl . . ."

The charges, which were false, were intended to tar Jackson, Humphrey, and Muskie with the same brush. Muskie placed fourth in the primary with only 8.8 percent, behind Humphrey and Jackson and far, far behind the winner, George Wallace. McGovern didn't even do that well—he came in sixth. But McGovern wasn't the candidate the nation was watching.

Muskie was now effectively out of the race. In popular vote, the primaries became a three-way battle among McGovern, Humphrey, and Wallace, with Wallace ahead. But McGovern, the champion of reform in the process of selection of delegates to the national convention, was picking up far more than his share of delegates in state after state.

On May 15, Wallace was shot and crippled in a shopping center in Laurel, Maryland. Whatever the Alabama Governor's intentions had been, whether he meant to run as a Democrat or as an independent, he was now out of the race altogether. Following three tragic assassinations in the previous eight and a half years, the shooting of Wallace by Milwaukee busboy Arthur Bremer was another sharp jolt to the nation's psyche.

---

*It was when Segretti's existence was uncovered, in October, 1972, that it became clear that the Watergate bugging was only one incident in a widespread campaign of political spying and sabotage for Nixon.

By this time, according to later testimony, a spy for Nixon was transferred from Muskie's headquarters to McGovern's, and the Nixon forces must have begun to realize that everything they were striving for was falling into place. Operation Gemstone had been approved at the end of March, when the Democratic race was still wide open. It seemed possible then that Edward Kennedy, the most feared Democrat, might emerge to challenge Nixon, and such a fear may explain the decision to monitor Lawrence O'Brien's telephone. O'Brien was close to the Kennedys and was recognized as the most skillful of all Democratic politicians.

At the end of May, when the bugs were first installed at the Watergate, McGovern was his party's frontrunner. Only one key primary election hurdle remained, that in California, and McGovern was a heavy favorite over the sole remaining announced opponent, Hubert Humphrey. Looked at in this light, the bugging of the Democrats was not only illegal, it could offer little or no gain. The risk was great and the likely rewards minimal.

There are indications, however, that the Nixon forces continued to fear the possible entry of Senator Kennedy into the campaign, and Watergate conspirator Bernard Barker later testified that he was instructed to look for any documents that had Kennedy's name on them during the break-ins at Democratic headquarters.

As it happened, the bugging began at McGovern's most glorious moment, while he was at the peak of his popularity. But that moment was short-lived. Taking a striking lead in the polls over Humphrey in California, he met twice with his opponent in nationally televised debates, losing ground each time. McGovern was unable to explain how he would fund his program for income redistribution. He said he would cut $33 million in defense spending, but "I would not close a single air base in California." In these and other specifics, his promises were put under scrutiny for the first time and were found to be either contradictory or not well thought out.

McGovern took California, but like Muskie in New Hampshire, not by the margin that had been predicted for him.

The stakes had changed for George McGovern, now virtually assured the nomination. Perceived as the candidate of antiwar groups, the gay alliances, and the women's liberation movement, he was faced with the challenge of extending his appeal to a broader base of the electorate. Benjamin Spock, the presidential candidate of the People's Party and considered by many to be a radical because of his outspoken dissent and activities in antiwar demonstrations, announced that *he* would vote for McGovern. With friends like this . . . McGovern began to move to the center.

Party regulars across the nation had warned that a McGovern candidacy would be devastating. In the South, Democratic leaders predicted the wholesale loss of House and Senate seats. "I like George McGovern, he's a nice fellow," said Robert Vance, the Democratic chairman of Alabama. "We'll just lose Alabama by a tremendous majority if he's the nominee." Georgia Governor Jimmy Carter said that McGovern's candidacy, with its call for cuts in defense spending, "would be a tremendous blow to Georgia."

McGovern was nominated on the first ballot, and he selected Senator Thomas Eagleton of Missouri as his running mate. When Eagleton's history of mental problems was made public, George McGovern found himself in a damned-if-you-do, damned-if-you-don't situation. He was roundly criticized for not doing the homework that would have either prevented him from selecting Eagleton in the first place or allowed him to announce to the nation upon his selection that Eagleton had in the past been mentally ill but had overcome it and was fit to run.

McGovern began vacillating, telling reporters he was "1,000 percent" behind Eagleton publicly but making it clear privately that he wanted Eagleton to drop out. Finally, when Eagleton succumbed to pressure on July 31, McGovern the reformer had shown, at least to many members of the press, that he could be as cynical and dishonest as any hack candidate.

Trying to recuperate from the Eagleton debacle, McGovern actively sought help from Chicago Mayor Richard Daley and labor union leader George Meany, both of whom were symbols of bossism. He went to Texas to meet with former President Lyndon Johnson, whose Vietnam War policies he had so often condemned. These moves were seen by many, including some in the McGovern camp, as a betrayal by the candidate of all that he had stood for before his nomination. McGovern, who had appeared to be vilifying the establishment center, now seemed to be chasing after it. He gave every indication of becoming exactly what he had not been during the primaries: a politician who winks at principle as he sees his goal near at hand but beginning to elude him.

In September and October, 1972, when McGovern began to refer to the Nixon Administration as the most corrupt in the nation's history, his charges were not accepted by many voters. McGovern was seen by great numbers of Americans as just another deceitful politician, and a feckless one, to boot. What he said about Watergate was what any opponent of Nixon might be expected to say.

PART II

The Great Coverup Begins

1

JOHN EHRLICHMAN AND Bob Haldeman hed known each other for many years. While classmates at the University of California after World War II when Nixon was first elected to Congress, Haldeman helped direct the campaign of Ehrlichman's fiancée for a student government office. At one point he released a poll showing her with a commanding lead. But Jeanne Fisher, later Ehrlichman's first wife, lost decisively. When people singled out Haldeman for blame in the Watergate scandal, there were those old UCLA grads who recalled that campus election and viewed the poll for Jeanne Fisher as Haldeman's first venture into attempting to manipulate public opinion and thereby win votes in an election.

Haldeman went into advertising after college, rising to the position of vice president at J. Walter Thompson, the largest advertising agency in the nation, according to the trade publication *Advertising Age*. He was in charge of the Los Angeles office, and starting in 1956 he took leave to work for Nixon in each of his election campaigns.

Ehrlichman went to law school at the University of Southern California and then into private practice in Seattle, specializing in zoning, a field that had opened up with the rapid suburban expansion after World War II. Haldeman called on him for help in the presidential campaign of 1960. At one point during the primaries, Ehrlichman, on something of an intelligence-gathering mission, was placed in the camp of Nelson Rockefeller and drove a car for Rockefeller as he toured North Dakota.

In 1969, Nixon asked Ehrlichman to join the White House staff, with the title of Counsel to the President. In Washington he and Haldeman were very close, both working extremely long hours, getting some relaxation by playing tennis together.

Haldeman and Ehrlichman came to be called the "Berlin Wall," as though they always shared the same White House relationship to the President. They didn't. Their roles were quite different. Haldeman played no part in establishing government policy. He was an implementer, not a policymaker. He was the President's personal public relations firm, guarding Nixon's every move, controlling access to him, seeing that the entire White House staff realized immediately in 1969 that the foremost goal of the first Nixon Administration was to win re-election in 1972. Haldeman did his best to make a Boy Scout camp of the White House, with himself scoutmaster and all second-rank aides subservient to him, selflessly and absolutely devoted to the re-election of Nixon.

Ehrlichman, on the other hand, dealt with substantive policy issues in the field of domestic affairs. Efficient, calm, Ehrlichman inspired confidence in aides below him and among Cabinet members and their assistants who could never get to Nixon. But from the beginning, he did other work as well. In May, 1969, according to later testimony, he met at a New York airport with a retired New York City detective, Anthony Ulasewicz, who had been recommended as a prospective snooper for Nixon, a White House private eye. Ehrlichman approved his hiring and occasionally filtered orders down to him to satisfy Nixon's demands. Still, Ehrlichman never stood as close to Nixon as Haldeman did; the public could infer this when it was revealed that Haldeman but not Ehrlichman knew of the President's practice of taping his conversations.

The public seldom heard of either man at all in the first Nixon years. In a capital that lionized power, Haldeman and Ehrlichman could walk into a department store without being recognized.

At 8 A.M. Tuesday, June 20, 1972, Ehrlichman entered Haldeman's office for their first White House meeting since the bugging arrests the previous Saturday. Fifteen minutes later they were joined by John Mitchell. Mitchell was to say later that it was at meetings that began on this morning that the potential damage of an unfettered Watergate investigation was discussed and decisions were made to protect the President at any cost.

The problem was not so much Watergate, Mitchell said,

but rather the earlier activities of Howard Hunt and others in the White House. Mitchell called these activities "White House horror stories." If revealed, they could conceivably have destroyed Nixon's political career.

The horror stories included incidents of past wiretapping, a break-in at the office of Daniel Ellsberg's psychiatrist, snooping on Senator Kennedy, fabricating State Department cables to make it appear that the late President Kennedy had conspired in the assassination of South Vietnamese President Ngo Dinh Diem in 1963, and Hunt's mysterious call on International Telephone and Telegraph lobbyist Dita Beard in a Denver hospital that further implicated the White House in shady dealings with the huge corporation.

Mitchell said that he, Haldeman, and Ehrlichman "had an innate fear" from the first that these stories might be uncovered in the investigation of Watergate.

At 9:45 A.M., June 20, 1972, according to John Ehrlichman's logs, the meeting between Haldeman, Ehrlichman, and Mitchell was joined by John Dean and, ten minutes later, by Attorney General Kleindienst.

In that morning's *Washington Post* was the first story publicly linking Howard Hunt to the five men arrested on Saturday. At about 10:30 A.M., Ehrlichman met privately with President Nixon for an hour. Even as they were talking, Democratic Chairman Lawrence O'Brien was announcing the filing of his one-million-dollar civil suit and charging that there was "a clear, developing line" from the bugging incident to the White House.

In this first meeting between Ehrlichman and Nixon since the arrests, Ehrlichman may have known more about what had occurred and how it was being investigated than any other man who had Nixon's trust. He had talked to Colson, to Dean, to Mitchell, to Kleindienst, and to others as well.

About 11:30 A.M., Ehrlichman left Nixon, and Haldeman entered the Oval Office. A tape of this conversation was produced in court in November, 1973. The voices were largely inaudible, and there was a gap of 18½ minutes near the beginning of their conversation. The White House confirmed that Nixon and Haldeman discussed Watergate. Some talk that is discernible, as well as Haldeman's notes of the conversation, indicate that they talked about adopting a "PR offensive to top this."

(At 1 P.M., at the end of the conversation, the President can be heard saying he wanted to take a little rest. One mark of the peculiar approach to public relations by Nixon is the fact that the American people were never informed of his habit of frequently taking an afternoon nap for at least twenty minutes. Other presidents took naps, and many Americans were thought to regard a little afternoon rest as an endearing practice.)

At 1:27, Nixon met with General Alexander Haig, who was then assistant to chief foreign affairs adviser Henry Kissinger. At 1:45 Nixon placed a telephone call to Clark MacGregor, who was then on the White House congressional relations staff. Haig left the President's office at 2:10, according to summaries of Nixon's meetings that were later sent by the White House to Watergate investigators.

At 2:16 P.M., Nixon placed a phone call to Charles Colson, and at 2:20 Colson came to the President's office in the Executive Office Building next to the White House for their first face-to-face meeting since the bugging arrests. Colson, everybody's suspect, met with the President for an hour and ten minutes.

Throughout the day, on even past midnight, Nixon continued to meet or speak on the telephone with men who had already begun to make Watergate their number-one priority. At 4:35 he met again with Haldeman, for fifty minutes. At 6:08, he put through a telephone call to John Mitchell, reportedly their first talk since the bugging arrests. A tape of this conversation was among the first to be subpoenaed by the Watergate Special Prosecutor's office in July, 1973. After months of wrangling in court over that subpoena, the President released seven of the nine tapes that had been sought, including the Haldeman conversation with the 18½-minute gap. Nixon said his talk with Mitchell and one other conversation had never been taped in the first place.

At 7:52 P.M. on June 20, 1972, Nixon called Haldeman, speaking until 7:59. At 8:04 he called Colson, speaking until 8:21. At 8:42 Haldeman called Nixon, the only telephone conversation among seven that day between Nixon and people concerned with Watergate that was not initiated by the President. At 11:33 Nixon telephoned Colson again, speaking with him until 12:05 A.M.

So on the President's first day back from Key Biscayne, according to White House summaries provided to investigators, he had ten meetings or telephone calls lasting more than five and a half hours with Haldeman, Ehrlichman, Colson, and John Mitchell, men who could collectively tell him virtually anything he might have wanted to know about the bugging and how this bungled venture at political intelligence-gathering could jeopardize his career.

The next day, June 21, the coverup strategy meetings continued. Ehrlichman was in Haldeman's office at 8 A.M., joined by John Mitchell at 8:15. After the meeting, Mitchell entered on a succession of other meetings with his CRP assistants, Magruder, Mardian, and LaRue, seeing one or more of them six different times during the day. By then Mardian and LaRue had spoken to Liddy. All were aware of or were taking part in the destruction of documents at 1701 Pennsylvania Avenue, according either to their own admission or to criminal charges later lodged against them.

At 9:30 A.M. Haldeman called on Nixon. At the same time, Ehrlichman telephoned acting FBI director Patrick Gray and told him that John Dean, who had worked with Gray years earlier at the Justice Department, "was going to handle" Watergate for the White House. At Ehrlichman's request, Gray called Dean to set up a meeting, and at 11:30 A.M., Dean visited Gray at his office.

Despite his plans to keep FBI findings closely held, Gray, an impulsive man, became somewhat expansive with the President's young counsel. He told Dean he was starting out with three theories of the bugging attempt:

- Since so many of the arrested men had past affiliations with the CIA, the bugging might have been perpetrated by that agency. Gray had already made contact with the CIA and was awaiting word back from its director, Richard Helms.
- Because the break-in had been so badly bungled, there was the possibility that someone wanted the men to be caught. It was an election year, and the Democrats stood to gain by publicity that reflected unfavorably on Nixon. This was called the double-agent theory.
- And, of course, there was the possibility that the break-in had, indeed, been committed by the re-election committee. As Orson Welles once said in a movie, just because a man looks guilty doesn't mean he's innocent.

Dean and Gray talked about the status of the investigation. Gray mentioned that FBI agents had traced the hundred-dollar bills found at the scene to one of suspect Bernard Barker's bank accounts in Miami. He mentioned that the account showed some extraordinary transactions, with $114,000 being deposited and withdrawn in a matter of weeks.

That afternoon Dean told Haldeman and Ehrlichman of Gray's progress. They asked him to go back the next day and find out how the FBI was pursuing the bank transactions, if at all.

The meetings between Nixon and his close aides continued much as they had the previous day. He met with Haldeman at least twice; he met with Colson or spoke with him on the telephone at least five times.

On June 22, the FBI was continuing to press its investigation aggressively but was beginning to meet interference. Lawyers at CRP were sitting in on FBI interviews with workers there. Two agents requested an interview in the White House with Charles Colson and a procedure was established through which the President's counsel, Dean, sat in on this interrogation and others like it.

The FBI sent out new messages to selected field offices, repeating to special agents in charge the urgency of the investigation: "It is again reiterated that all leads in this matter must be given the highest priority with sufficient personnel assigned to insure maximum effort in covering all leads."

In Miami, according to an FBI report dated June 22, Michael Richardson of Rich Photos "advised that about noon, Saturday, June 10, 1972, one white male who he tentatively identified from a photograph as Bernard Barker, came to this store" with a rush order for the development and printing of thirty-eight negatives.

On most negatives were documents headed "Chairman Democratic National Committee," the report said, and "all documents were photographed with a shag carpet background and hands covered with clear-type gloves held down each corner of each document. . . . Investigation at the Howard Johnson Motel, 2601 Virginia Avenue, N.W., Washington, D.C., determined the carpet utilized by the motel is similar to that noticed in the photographs by Richardson."

At 6:30 P.M. on June 22, Dean met with Gray and asked how the FBI was intending to pursue the strange transactions discovered in Barker's bank account. Gray gave the obvious answer: agents were attempting to interview the two people involved. Their names were Manuel Ogarrio D'Aguerre, a Mexican, and Kenneth H. Dahlberg, an American.

For Dean, that was the worst possible news. A successful

investigation of the money would lead to Liddy, and would link Maurice Stans, the re-election finance chairman, and John Mitchell to the Watergate burglars. The $114,000 had been given to Liddy by re-election treasurer Hugh Sloan to be "laundered"—made untraceable—so that the names of campaign contributors and the circumstances surrounding their donations could be kept secret. Liddy used Barker to launder the money, a sum so large that Stans and Mitchell would have had to give authorization for it to be moved around.

Dahlberg was a key fund raiser for Nixon, and a check for $25,000 with his name on it was one of those deposited in Barker's bank account. The check represented a contribution from Dwayne Andreas, a Minneapolis businessman who had previously been a major contributor to Hubert Humphrey. Andreas wanted his donation to Nixon kept secret.

The other $89,000 consisted of four Mexican checks that had gone through the hands of the attorney Ogarrio but did not originate with him. Ogarrio was a middle man, representing a number of American corporations in Mexico, including Gulf Resources and Chemical Co., a conglomerate based in Texas.

After a fund-raising tour by Stans earlier in the year, Gulf Resources transferred $100,000 from its treasury to Ogarrio's account in Banco Internacional, the start of a transaction that FBI agents were to liken to methods used by organized crime in the laundering of money. Ogarrio converted $89,000 of the funds into cashier's checks and the balance to cash. The entire $100,000 was returned to Texas, where it was put on a private plane with other campaign cash, perhaps $600,000, and flown to Stans in Washington.

The Ogarrio money arrived at CRP on April 6, 1972, the day before a new campaign financial disclosure law took effect. The Dahlberg money arrived April 10. CRP reasoned it could keep the later contribution secret on the shaky grounds that it had been committed earlier, and possibly because of the conviction that if it was turned into cash, the transaction would never be discovered anyway.

At the time of the change in the campaign disclosure law, Sloan was trying to hide from view hundreds of thousands of dollars in additional secret campaign funds. In this period, Sloan also made advance payments to firms that would do work later on in the campaign. By keeping income and expenditures secret, CRP could give the appearance of having less money than it actually did, which was helpful in encouraging further large campaign contributions.

Sloan had so much cash on hand that he was afraid to go downstairs from his office to the bank to deposit it alone. On one occasion he asked Liddy to accompany him. Liddy said, "Wait a minute," went for his pistol, and then escorted Sloan.

Now less than a week after the Watergate arrests, with the FBI on the trail of Ogarrio and Dahlberg, the money end of the campaign, rife with illegalities, stood to be fully exposed. It was illegal for corporations to contribute to candidates in federal elections. The Ogarrio contribution had every appearance of being a corporate contribution, and it represented less than one percent of the funds that had been raised secretly at the time Barker's bank records were being scrutinized.*

So on June 22, when Patrick Gray told John Dean that the FBI was pursuing Ogarrio and Dahlberg, Dean tried to stop him, warning falsely that such an investigation might jeopardize activities of the Central Intelligence Agency. Gray said that if such were the case, the CIA should tell him.

---

*At the time, the Nixon treasury was thought to have between ten and fifteen million dollars in secret contributions. In 1973, after a successful court suit by Common Cause, it was revealed that Nixon received $22 million in secret contributions in all. Much of the money represented illegal corporate gifts. Some, like that which originated with Gulf Resources, was returned. In other instances some of the nation's leading corporations were fined after executives pleaded guilty to using company money to comply with demands from Maurice Stans and others for huge contributions.

2

PRESIDENT NIXON HELD a news conference on June 22, his first since the arrests. He was asked whether he was conducting "any sort of an investigation" to determine whether, as Lawrence O'Brien had charged, there was a link between the bugging and the White House. Nixon answered:

> Mr. Ziegler and also Mr. Mitchell, speaking for the campaign committee, have responded to questions on this in great detail. They have stated my position and have also stated the facts accurately.
>
> This kind of activity, as Mr. Ziegler has indicated, has no place whatever in our electoral process, or in our governmental process. And, as Mr. Ziegler has stated, the White House has had no involvement whatever in this particular incident.
>
> As far as the matter now is concerned, it is under investigation, as it should be, by the proper legal authorities, by the District of Columbia police, and by the FBI. I will not comment on those matters, particularly since possible criminal charges are involved.

By then, Nixon had been fully briefed on Watergate. The news conference presaged his future public behavior: he repudiated the break-in, disassociated himself from it, and lied. And on the following day, June 23, the private Nixon sprang into action, ordering the CIA into the Watergate coverup.

That morning, Dean reported back to Haldeman and Ehrlichman on his latest conversation with Patrick Gray. Haldeman then met with Nixon for thirty-five minutes, beginning about 10 A.M. (More than two years later, in August, 1974, the transcript of this meeting was released to the public after a Supreme Court order. It was one of three transcripts that immediately became known as "the smoking gun," the evidence that once and for all tied Nixon to the coverup in its first stages and forced him to resign.)

After Nixon and Haldeman met, Richard Helms, the director of the CIA, and General Vernon (Dick) Walters, the deputy director, were summoned to the White House at the request of the President. They were told at first to be there at 1 P.M. for a meeting with Haldeman and Ehrlichman. Then the time was pushed back slightly. At 1:04, Haldeman and Nixon met for a second time, for nine minutes, according to the White House summaries of logs. Shortly after that, Helms and Walters arrived.

"Mr. Haldeman said there was a lot of flak about the Watergate burglary, that the opposition was capitalizing on it, that it was going to—it was apparently causing some sort of unified trouble, and he wanted to know whether the Agency had anything to do with it," Helms said later.

"I assured him that the Agency had nothing to do with it. He then said that the five men who had been found in the Democratic National Committee headquarters had been arrested and that that seemed to be adequate under the circumstances, that the FBI was investigating what this was all about, and that they, unified, were concerned about some FBI investigations in Mexico.

"He also at that time made some, what to me was an incoherent reference to an investigation in Mexico, or an FBI investigation, running into the Bay of Pigs. I do not know what the reference was alleged to be, but in any event, I assured him I had no interest in the Bay of Pigs that many years later, that everything in connection with that had been dealt with and liquidated as far as I was aware and I did not care what they ran into in connection with that.

"At some juncture in this conversation, Mr. Haldeman then said something to the effect that it has been decided that General Walters will go and talk to Acting Director Gray of the FBI and indicate to him that these operations—these investigations of the FBI might run into CIA operations in Mexico and that it was desirable that this not happen and that the investigation, therefore, should be either tapered off or reduced or something, but there was no language saying stop, as far as I recall."

At the end of the meeting, Helms said later, Ehrlichman "made his sole contribution to the conversation, which was that he [Walters] should get down and see Gray just as fast as he could." Ehrlichman later testified that the President's concern was aimed specifically at blocking FBI interviews wth Ogarrio that could have been damaging to Nixon personally.

When their conversation ended, the White House officials had their assistant, John Dean, telephone Patrick Gray and notify him that Vernon Walters would be calling on him shortly.

Like Gray, Walters had been in his position only six weeks before the arrests at the Watergate. At 2:30 P.M., Friday, June 23, 1972, Walters called on Gray. They have been in dispute over some of what was said in this and later conversations, but they both agreed that Walters warned Gray that an FBI investigation in Mexico could uncover CIA activities and be damaging to the Agency.

When Walters returned to CIA headquarters that afternoon, he made inquiries and determined to his own satisfaction, he said later, that an FBI investigation in Mexico would not be damaging to the CIA. But he neglected to so inform Patrick Gray.

Gray immediately ordered a halt to FBI efforts to interrogate Manuel Ogarrio. In addition, he began getting frequent telephone calls from John Dean advising him that interviews with Kenneth Dahlberg could also jeopardize the CIA.

On the morning of June 23, 1972, the most pressing problem for those in charge of the Watergate coverup was the prospective FBI interviews with Ogarrio and Dahlberg. That afternoon, the problem was taken care of, at least for the time being.

3

PATRICK GRAY WAS to describe himself as a man who was not suspicious by nature, a former submarine commander who was used to saying "Aye, aye, sir." John Dean, in a taped conversation with President Nixon, described Gray as someone who would "do what we want," who would "want to play ball," but who was being watched closely and pressured by high-ranking associates at the FBI. Nixon, in another of those conversations, said once, "Well, let's talk about Gray—the problem with him is, I think, he is a little bit stupid."

Gray was acting director of the FBI from May, 1972, to April, 1973. He was forced to resign in shame for having destroyed documents from Howard Hunt's safe that had been handed him by Ehrlichman and Dean. He was the head of the nation's proudest investigative agency, forced to beg Ehrlichman and Dean to cover up for him, and Dean wouldn't.

It may be that Gray was a man of good intentions who was used by stronger men. It may be that his intentions were not so good, that he knowingly took improper actions in his lust for J. Edgar Hoover's job. It may be that the Nixon view of Gray is the correct one; a lack of intelligence helps explain actions that are otherwise unintelligible.

In June and July of 1972, when the FBI was working as hard as it could to get to the bottom of Watergate, Gray continually gave John Dean information and data that allowed the White House to stay a step ahead of investigators. In 1973, when Gray seemed to have gone over to the White House side and was nominated as permanent FBI director, his revelations at Senate confirmation hearings did more damage to Richard Nixon than all the investigations, trials, and newspaper accounts until that time.

I once asked Samuel Dash, the chief counsel of the Senate Watergate Committee, to tell me how he felt about Patrick Gray, the man, about what motivated his actions. It was just before Christmas, 1973, a year after Gray had destroyed the Hunt files, and Dash had spent the previous nine months scrutinizing almost every person involved in Watergate. He threw up his hands and said, "I don't know. He is an enigma."

On June 23, 1972, when Vernon Walters asked Gray to "taper" his investigation in Mexico, Gray succumbed—but not entirely. Pressured by his chief assistants, W. Mark Felt, the number-two man in the FBI, and Charles W. Bates, an assistant director, Gray kept coming back to the need to interview Ogarrio and Dahlberg.

On June 27, as the three FBI officials were meeting, Dean telephoned Gray and Gray warned him, according to his later testimony, that Dahlberg might be brought before a grand jury because he was evading the FBI.

Gray, Felt, and Bates were coming to a point where they wanted the CIA to state in writing why Ogarrio and Dahlberg should not be interviewed. After Dean's phone call, Gray spoke to Richard Helms to ask directly whether the CIA "had any interest in Ogarrio." Helms said no. Having now received conflicting information from Dean, Walters, and Helms, Gray scheduled a meeting for 2:30 P.M. the next day with the two CIA leaders. Minutes later, Dean called once more and, to Gray's best recollection, told him that Ogarrio and Dahlberg had nothing to do with Watergate and implored him to keep FBI agents away from them.

On the morning of June 28, Gray returned a call that Ehrlichman had placed to him. Ehrlichman's "first words, issued abruptly," Gray later testified, were, " 'Cancel your meeting with Helms and Walters today; it is not necessary.' "

Gray said he asked Ehrlichman "point-blank" who made decisions on FBI interviews, and Ehrlichman responded, "You do." But Gray called Helms and canceled the meeting. It was later that day that Gray, summoned to the White House by Ehrlichman, was given the documents from Howard Hunt's safe by Ehrlichman and Dean. He took them home, put them in a drawer underneath his shirts, and thought nothing about them for months. He was told they were politically explosive but on matters quite apart from Watergate. He said he didn't even examine them.

In the days that Dean kept pressuring Gray to stay away from Ogarrio and Dahlberg, the young counsel was trying to cope with another problem as well. At 10 A.M. Monday, June 26, he called Vernon Walters, who had been so useful to Haldeman and Ehrlichman the previous Friday. Dean asked to meet with Walters and told him, "You can call Mr. Ehrlichman to see whether it is all right with him."

Walters checked with Ehrlichman, and at 11:45 A.M. he called on Dean. Dean went over some of the ground that had been covered by Haldeman earlier; then, according to later testimony of both men, he told Walters that some of the arrested men were getting frightened and were wobbling. Dean asked whether the CIA could arrange to pay bail for them, and if the Agency could covertly pay their salaries.

In a memorandum Walters wrote several days after the meeting, he said he told Dean that he had no authority to approve such a scheme and that "if the Agency were to provide bail and pay salaries, this would become known sooner or later in the current 'leaking' atmosphere of Washington and at that point the scandal would be ten times greater."

The following day, according to Walters, he returned to Dean's office. He said he had discussed the matter with Helms and that both agreed that "involving the Agency would transform what was now a medium-sized conventional explosive into a multi-megaton explosive and simply was not worth the risk to all concerned."

A day later, on June 28, Dean called Walters and they met again in Dean's office. According to Walter's memorandum of that meeting, Dean said that "the problem was how to stop the FBI investigation beyond the five suspects." Dean asked Walters for advice.

"I said that this affair already had a strong Cuban flavor and everyone knew the Cubans were conspiratorial and anxious to know what the policies of both parties would be towards Castro. They, therefore, had a plausible motive for attempting this amateurish job which any skilled technician would deplore. This might be costly but it would be plausible."

In later testimony, Walters said he told Dean that he was "quite prepared to resign before I do anything that will implicate the Agency in this matter." Walters discussed the matter with his boss, Helms, and they agreed not to have the CIA make illicit payments to the arrested men. But neither Helms nor Walters brought his knowledge of the conspiracy to federal investigators, and Walters failed to notify Patrick Gray that it was all right for the FBI to investigate in Mexico.

Helms also was less than open with Gray. On June 28, when Gray called to cancel their appointment, Helms asked Gray to postpone scheduled FBI interviews with two other CIA employees who knew about assistance the CIA had given Howard Hunt in 1971, after Hunt joined the White House staff. Helms was well aware of this assistance, especially in connection with the clandestine White House research on Daniel Ellsberg. By keeping the FBI away from this agent, Helms helped prevent exposure of the so-called White House horror stories that later proved so damaging to Nixon.

It was now only eleven days after the Watergate arrests. But already a seemingly never-ending web was beginning to ensnare government leaders who were far removed from the inane bugging at Democratic headquarters.

That afternoon, after Vernon Walters told John Dean for the last time that the CIA would not make payments to the arrested men, Dean called Nixon's attorney, Herbert Kalmbach, and asked that he come to Washington immediately.

"He told me that it was a matter of extreme importance that I return to or come back to Washington, preferably by the first available flight, to undertake a very important assignment," Kalmbach said later.

The next day Kalmbach was in the nation's capital, assigned to make secret payments to the arrested men to buy their silence. He was to be directed by Fred LaRue, Mitchell's right-hand man, and Nixon's private detective, Anthony Ulasewicz, would distribute the funds. Kalmbach knew them both. Ulasewicz in fact had been on Kalmbach's payroll for private political snooping he conducted on Nixon's behalf.

On Saturday, July 1, John Mitchell resigned as Nixon's campaign director, saying, "I have found that I can no longer (carry out the job) and still meet the one obligation which must come first: the happiness and welfare of my wife and daughter." To many the statement rang true because of Martha Mitchell's violent behavior in the previous two weeks. It was not until almost two years later that the real reason for Mitchell's resignation was spelled out.

Mitchell had gone to the White House to meet with Nixon and Haldeman on June 30, 1972. Before the meeting, he gave no appearance that he was about to resign, according to his closest aide, Fred LaRue. On May 17, 1974, the tape of a five-minute portion of the conversation between Mitchell, Nixon, and Haldeman on June 30, 1972, was made public. In it, Haldeman said, "The longer you wait, the more risk each hour brings. You run the risk of more stuff, valid or invalid, surfacing on the Watergate-caper type of thing. . . . As of now there is no problem there. As, as of any moment in the future there is at least a potential problem."

"Well, I'd cut the loss fast," Nixon said. "I'd cut it fast. If we're going to do it I'd cut it fast. That's my view, generally speaking. . . . I think the story is, you're positive rather than negative. . . . A hell of a lot of people will like that answer. They would. And it'd make anybody else who asked any other question on it look like a selfish son of a bitch, which I thoroughly intended them to look like."

4

> *Once the FBI was given the green light in its investigation of the Hiss case, it did a magnificent job. The blame for failing to act before that time rests not on the FBI but squarely on those officials of the Executive branch who had full access to FBI reports and who failed or refused to order a full investigation.*
>
> —RICHARD NIXON, *Six Crises*

ON JULY 28, 1972, the Washington prosecution team in the Watergate case issued a subpoena demanding that Maurice Stans appear before a grand jury. Then five weeks into their investigation, Earl Silbert, Seymour Glanzer, and Donald Campbell were moving along two lines of inquiry: the commission of burglary at Democratic headquarters and the interception of oral communications, or wiretapping, there.

Silbert, thirty-six, the principal assistant U.S. attorney, had been in charge of the investigation since immediately after the break-in arrests. He was considered a bright and capable prosecutor.

Before Watergate, Glanzer dealt almost exclusively in fraud cases. His work was so thorough that he seldom had to take defendants to trial; they almost invariably pleaded guilty when confronted with his findings. Campbell was the junior of the three. He told me much later on that he was so shaken by Watergate that in May or June, 1973, he considered leaving the practice of law entirely.

The U.S. Attorney's office is at the center of the pursuit of criminal justice in federal cases in the United States. There are 94 U.S. attorneys across the country, each appointed by the President. While they function independently, they are responsible to their superiors in the Justice Department. Prosecutors direct investigations through grand juries which decide by a majority vote whether there is sufficient cause to return an indictment and thereby send a suspect or suspects to trial, where guilt or innocence is decided.

Prosecutors hold great sway with their grand juries. Grand jurors may request that certain witnesses be called before them and are free to ask any questions. But prosecutors have come more and more to lead almost all grand juries and not be led by them.

In cases of great magnitude, such as the investigation of a congressman, prosecutors report to their superiors in the Justice Department and look to them for guidance. It would be almost unthinkable for a prosecutor to run a grand jury investigation of a congressman without the approval of the Attorney General, the head of the Justice Department.

The Watergate investigation, of course, was of such magnitude. The prosecutors worked closely with D.C. police on the burglary aspects and with the FBI on the interception of oral communications. Silbert and the FBI kept Assistant Attorney General Henry Petersen informed of their findings step by step.

Petersen stayed in touch with Attorney General Kleindienst or with officials in the White House, agreeing within days of the arrests on June 17, 1972, that he would not allow any investigation to become a "fishing expedition" into the Republican Party.

Watergate was a patently political crime. But Petersen was to testify later that "I decided at a very early stage that the investigation ought to be as isolated from the political element as it possibly could be." Judges and politicians were to make the same high-sounding assertions.

At the very first, FBI agents, working from Howard Hunt's long-distance telephone-call records, discovered a number of conversations between Hunt and a young California attorney, Donald H. Segretti. They interviewed Segretti on June 26, 1972, and learned that he seemed to have been deeply involved with Hunt—but not in the Watergate break-in. Silbert made a decision to question Segretti on his relationship to Hunt only as it might be helpful in the Watergate break-in and bugging case. Though he got indications of Segretti's dirty tricks practices, he discussed the problem with Petersen and decided not to investigate them.

Silbert told me later that he was no expert on the political Corrupt Practices Act, that he was investigating burglary and wiretapping. He took full responsibility for the decision not to probe Segretti. Glanzer was known to feel that Segretti's actions were reprehensible but very likely not criminal. He had no trouble with Silbert's decision.

The prosecutors persisted in this view even after FBI agents interviewed the President's personal attorney, Herbert Kalmbach, and were told that Kalmbach had paid Segretti between $30,000 and $40,000 between August or September, 1971, and March 15, 1972, at the request of Dwight L. Chapin, the President's appointments secretary in the White House. The FBI interview with Kalmbach was held at Silbert's request, an indication that he did not shy from pursuing leads to high places. But Silbert maintained that he saw no connection to Watergate, and he did not expand his investigation.

Unbeknownst to Silbert, John Dean applied pressure to Henry Petersen to have the prosecutors keep hands off Segretti. He told Petersen that Segretti's activities might be politically embarrassing to Nixon in the waning weeks of the campaign, but that they had nothing to do with Watergate.

Such a communication might be expected to make a veteran investigator more rather than less aggressive. Instead, Petersen encouraged Silbert to shy away from Segretti, Kalmbach, and Chapin.

FBI agents, however, wanted to pursue the Segretti leads. Patrick Gray testified that he discussed the matter with Petersen and was told to forget it, so important findings that could conceivably have made a significant difference in the 1972 presidential election were put away in Justice Department files, left unexplored, held irrelevant to the investigation at hand.

After consulting with Petersen, Silbert also decided to forego investigating a second element in the Watergate affair that was at least as crucial as Segretti: the question of illegal campaign financing.

Silbert knew of the mysterious transactions in Bernard Barker's bank account by June 21, 1972. When the FBI finally interviewed Ogarrio and Dahlberg, Silbert was on the wide-open assault on illegal campaign contributions and ties between Nixon chieftains and the Watergate bugging that trail of what those in charge of the coverup feared most, a would lead to an examination of past White House activities.

But Silbert decided that campaign financing was not part of his investigation and referred it to the Justice Department for examination, where it was ignored.

Once again, FBI agents felt differently and asked for a decision on whether they should make their own inquiries. Gray and others in the FBI consulted with Petersen, and, according to Gray, Petersen recommended against it.

Silbert pursued the $114,000 and scores of thousands of additional dollars that CRP officials had given Gordon Liddy. He got no cooperation at all from Howard Hunt or Liddy or any of the five arrested men, but Jeb Magruder and other CRP officials testified that the money given Liddy was to be spent on an elaborate but legal "Intelligence-gathering" plan. CRP, Magruder said, feared young radicals as a threat to surrogate candidates and to the Republican convention in August. Liddy was said to have been given $100,000 to infiltrate ten young people on college campuses for ten months. He was to be given another $150,000 for other legal intelligence-gathering, but received only $99,000 when, Magruder said, Liddy caught CRP officials in total surprise by his illegal venture at the Watergate.

Silbert, Glanzer, Campbell, and Petersen were suspicious of the story. It was far too much money for such projects. But other members of CRP, including Herbert Porter, who was in charge of scheduling for the surrogates, supported Magruder. So in an area where Silbert pushed his investigation, he was thwarted by false testimony.

By July 20, 1972, the FBI had compiled provocative information from its many interviews, and Silbert attempted to make use of it. Ogarrio told agents he had learned that the $100,000 he had handled was given over to Maurice Stans. Stans had told FBI men that he had received the $25,000 Dahlberg check and given it to campaign treasurer Hugh Sloan, but he could not explain how it had gone to Barker.

An FBI summary report dated July 21, 1972, stated that several persons at CRP

> contacted the FBI Washington Field Office and requested to be further interviewed away from committee headquarters and without the knowledge of committee officials. These persons advised that the presence of the [CRP] attorney during the interview prevented them from being completely candid. These sources further advised that all committee people subpoenaed before the

Federal Grand Jury were subsequently debriefed by committee attorneys as to what occurred at the federal grand jury hearing.

One of the foregoing persons confidentially advised that Hugh Walter Sloan, Jr., who supervises committee finances, reportedly maintains a brief case full of money in his office safe. During the period of February through April, 1972, according to this source, Sloan allegedly disbursed large sums to various committee officials for unknown reasons, such as $50,000 to Jeb Magruder, $100,000 to Herbert L. Porter, and $89,000 to George Gordon Liddy.

Another cooperative source at the committee advised confidentially that committee officials during interviews were sending FBI agents on fishing expeditions to keep them from getting to the truth.

Given this information, Silbert and his colleagues began calling leading officials before the grand jury. After much discussion, on July 28, 1972, they issued a subpoena ordering Maurice Stans to appear the following week. CRP attorneys asked for a delay, saying an appearance by Stans would interfere with planned campaign fund-raising activities. Silbert agreed to a delay but said Stans would have to appear later.

On the weekend of July 29–30, Silbert later wrote, "I was informed by Henry Petersen that he had received a very strong complaint from John Ehrlichman of the White House about the potentially unfair and prejudicial publicity generated by appearances of White House staff members and former Cabinet officers before the grand jury at the United States courthouse."

Ehrlichman was at Camp David, the President's mountain retreat, that weekend. In July, 1974, John Doar, chief counsel to the House Judiciary Committee, charged that it was Nixon who ordered that Stans be kept from appearing before the grand jury.

Early Monday, July 31, 1972, about 8:30 A.M., Silbert met with Petersen and Kleindienst. It was the prosecutor's only face-to-face encounter with the Attorney General to that point. They discussed the Stans grand jury appearance and other aspects of the investigation. The meeting lasted an hour.

As a result, Silbert said, "It was subsequently agreed that well-known persons such as Mr. Stans and White House staff members whose testimony was sought by the grand jury would be examined by an assistant U.S. attorney in the offices of Mr. Petersen at the Department of Justice."

The procedure for Stans was adopted for White House Staff members Charles Colson; Colson's secretary, Joan Hall; and the leaders of the White House plumbers, Egil Krogh and David Young, who had worked so closely with Liddy and Hunt.

Of these people, only Stans, Colson, and possibly Krogh (who held the position of White House–D.C. liaison officer) might have attracted any attention at all at the courthouse. Even they probably could have slipped in and out without being noticed. There was very little attention being paid to the courthouse by reporters in August, 1972; the building had many entrances and exits, including a basement entrance that cars could drive into, a tactic frequently used to successfully elude reporters and photographers at times when they were anticipating an appearance by a figure in a criminal trial.

Silbert agreed to the general principle that high aides should not be subject to embarrassing publicity. He told me later, however, that he informed Petersen that "it was ridiculous not to have Joan Hall" before the grand jury on those grounds and that Petersen seemed to agree with him. "My own feeling was that Henry didn't want to make a fight," Silbert said.

By agreeing to the procedure, Silbert gave away what every prosecutor regards as a valuable weapon. An appearance before a grand jury is a threatening moment for any person. Faced with twenty-three informed and suspicious people in surroundings familiar to them but not to the witness, even an ordinarily confident person may lose his or her composure and unintentionally make very revealing remarks. While grand jurors don't always ask difficult questions, sometimes they do.*

Each of these witnesses was privy to sensational information that was to remain secret for a great many months. Of course, there was no guarantee that any of them would have said more to a grand jury than to an assistant U.S. attorney. But it certainly must have been less foreboding to be interviewed in the office of Henry Petersen, where the assistant

---

*Exactly that reportedly occurred when Segretti appeared before the grand jury and was asked little of consequence by Silbert. A juror demanded to know who had financed Segretti and also asked other harsh questions.

U.S. attorney himself was not quite at home, than it would have been before the grand jury.

By the end of July, then, the pattern for the Watergate criminal investigation was set as though in concrete. Silbert pursued burglary and the interception of oral communications, and with some aggressiveness. But he ignored leads to other campaign violations, asking advice from Henry Petersen at a time when Petersen was promising White House aides that he would narrowly restrict the investigation.

At moments when it appeared that Silbert was getting close to matters that could prove dangerous to the White House, John Dean and John Ehrlichman worked through either Kleindienst or Petersen to cut Silbert off.

With the limits Silbert either accepted from his bosses or drew for himself, and because of perjured testimony, he was unable to take the original Watergate prosecution beyond Gordon Liddy. He, Glanzer, and Campbell were skeptical that the conspiracy stopped there, but they had insufficient evidence to present a case against anyone else.

One investigative agency that had the imagination and desire to cope with Watergate was the FBI, but its findings were often locked up in Justice Department files. The words Nixon used in describing the Hiss case applied in Watergate: the FBI became the victim of officials in the Executive branch who "failed or refused to order a full investigation."

Later on, in 1973, Petersen and Kleindienst quite dramatically pressured Nixon to release information that helped reveal the full scope of the Watergate scandal. But the role played by the two Justice Department officials in the first Watergate investigation will forever be an embarrassment to themselves, their families, and members of the proud agency they worked for. Kleindienst stood further removed from the handling of the initial investigation than did Petersen, but he intervened at crucial times.

On July 31, 1972, after his meeting with Silbert that resulted in keeping Stans and others away from the grand jury, Kleindienst spent a long period of time with Ehrlichman and John Dean at the Justice Department, discussing, among other problems, one Jeb Magruder.

According to Ehrlichman, Dean had informed him on June 19 "that Magruder may have had some involvement" in Watergate, and "Magruder was specifically discussed" with Kleindienst on July 31—just after Kleindienst had debriefed Silbert for an hour. Ehrlichman has testified that Kleindienst presented suggestions to "smoke out" leaks from the FBI. The Attorney General may have been more interested in keeping damaging information secret than he was in trying to "smoke out" criminal activities.

All during the 1972 campaign Kleindienst served as one of Nixon's chief surrogates, vigorously praising the Administration for its law enforcement programs and criticizing George McGovern as soft on drugs and pornography. He said a victory by McGovern "would be a disaster for the rule of law in America." After the election campaign, Kleindienst was called on by Nixon and the President's closest associates for continued assistance in putting out Watergate fires.

PART III

The Washington Post

1

ON SATURDAY, JUNE 17, 1972, at about 8:30, I wasn't yet out of bed when my boss, Harry M. Rosenfeld, the metropolitan editor of the *Washington Post*, phoned. Five men had been arrested during the night at Democratic headquarters. Rosenfeld had hardly anything in the way of details, nothing about bugs or camera equipment or surgical gloves or hundred-dollar bills. But with the presidential election less than five months away, it was a damned peculiar event, extraordinary on its face. Before getting out of bed, I called two reporters, and had them come in to work on their day off. One of them was Bob Woodward, who had been at the *Post* nine months.

Before the day was out, I had ten reporters working on the Watergate story, including a member of our Virginia staff, Carl Bernstein. We ran three articles in our Sunday editions: the main story on the break-in, which appeared prominently on page one; a story on the security guard, Frank Wills; and one piecing together what we could on the men who had been arrested.

In the following days and weeks, the *Post* made several stunning disclosures. On June 20, for example, even as the White House was disassociating any re-election aides from the break-in, we reported the ties between the arrested men and Howard Hunt. We disclosed that the Miami men were not just right-wing Cubans but that they had done mundane work for Nixon's campaign, such as seeking accommodations for large groups at the upcoming Republican convention in Miami. But the *Post*'s coverage was scattershot, and hardly better than that of our main competitors, *The New York Times* and the *Washington Star*.

At the time of the break-in, the *Post* was preparing to send more than forty reporters, editors and photographers and other staff members to the Democratic national convention. Some reporters on the national staff were fascinated by the Watergate bugging, but they weren't able to pay much attention to it. There was a full plate of election coverage for every political reporter and editor. The bugging story could very well lead nowhere; it was iffy at best: tantalizing but not substantial enough to take precedence over the routine election coverage.

But the *Post*'s managing editor, Howard Simons, saw how extraordinary the Watergate story was and acted to prevent us from falling behind in our coverage of it. In the second week of July, Simons called me into his office. He pointed to an article in that day's *New York Times* and expressed anger that we hadn't had it. Simons said he wanted me to see to it that our coverage did not drift, and he asked how I would go about it. I said we should make formal what had become a working arrangement anyway, and assign Bob Woodward and Carl Bernstein to investigate the story full time, and that I would work closely with them. Simons approved the procedure. We didn't talk about where the investigation might lead. We had no idea, and we didn't speculate.

Toward the end of July, Bernstein told me he wanted to go to Miami, where a local prosecutor, Richard Gerstein, a Democrat running for re-election, had begun his own Watergate investigation.

The New York Times stories we had been noticing appeared to come from Gerstein's office, and Bernstein had talked to the chief investigator there by telephone. He had the feeling that a face-to-face visit would be more worthwhile.

The investigator in Miami was Martin Dardis, a man in his late forties or early fifties, a former New York State trooper who, like many in the large Dade County state's attorney's office, had gone south after World War II. Dardis was to tell me later, in February, 1974, how, by simple methods that might be used to catch piggy-bank thieves, he had traced money recovered at the Watergate to the Nixon re-election campaign.

Dardis said his office had seen Watergate as a major crime immediately and began investigating because four of the arrested men had Miami addresses. He found no real crime in his own Dade County jurisdiction, he said, but he "kept after things."

When serial numbers on the hundred-dollar bills found at Watergate were traced to the Republic National Bank in Miami, Dardis went there and asked if any of the arrested men had accounts at the bank. He was told that Bernard Barker had two.

On July 6, 1972, Dardis subpoenaed Barker's telephone records and bank accounts. He found that $114,000 had been deposited in one of them on April 20, 1972, in the form of five cashier's checks. Four of the checks, totaling $89,000, had been issued by Banco Internacional of Mexico City to the Mexican attorney, Ogarrio, whose signature appeared on them. The fifth was written on the First Bank and Trust Company of Boca Raton, Florida, payable to Kenneth Dahlberg.

Barker had rapidly withdrawn the funds, in cash: $25,000 on April 24, $33,000 on May 2, $56,000 on May 8.

As Dardis started making inquiries about Dahlberg, he was told that Frank Sinatra and Dahlberg knew each other, and that both had been in Boca Raton recently. For a while the investigator thought Sinatra might have financed the break-in, a notion that was farfetched but suggested that Dardis had the imagination to cope with his assignment.

One day a *New York Times* reporter, Walter Rugaber, began calling on the investigators in Miami, chasing down the foreign money. When Bernstein went to Miami, the state attorney's office had been working closely with Rugaber and was reluctant to get involved with another newspaperman.

On Monday, July 31, 1972, the *Times* carried a front-page story by Rugaber, datelined Mexico City, that for the first time traced the $89,000 deposited in Barker's account to Ogarrio. The article never mentioned the $25,000 Dahlberg check. When it came to explaining the significance of his findings, Rugaber could only offer conjecture. At the bottom of the article he wrote, "The appearance in the case of the finance lawyer [Ogarrio] and the Banco Internacional drafts has fed speculation in Washington that the Republicans, in an effort to assure anonymity to contributors, had established a conduit for money through Mexico."

That day Bernstein called repeatedly from Miami to say that Dardis—"this wild man," Bernstein called him—had kept promising to meet with him but was putting him off. Late in the afternoon Bernstein called back. Dardis had let him see Barker's telephone toll-call records. He had copied them down and read them to Woodward and me. Some had appeared in the *Times* earlier but there were many new ones. We took them all down and began checking them out.

We had dinner and came back to work, prepared to stay in the office quite late. Woodward took his toothbrush and toothpaste from his desk, went to the bathroom and brushed his teeth.

About 8 or 8:30 Bernstein called again. He had now seen Barker's bank records and told us of the Mexican checks that the *Times* had written about that morning. "There's another check here. I don't know if it's important or not, but it's for $25,000. It's from a man named Kenneth H. Dahlberg."

Reporters who had covered the Nixon campaign in 1968 might have recognized Dahlberg's name immediately; he was an important fund-raiser then and again in 1972. But Woodward and I had never heard of him. I called for clips from our library and we had clerks or copy help look up Dahlberg in *Who's Who* and various other directories.

The only clipping was a faded picture and caption from 1967. It showed a man named Kenneth H. Dahlberg with Vice-President Hubert Humphrey at an award ceremony in connection with some heroism dating back to World War II.* It wasn't much help.

Moments later we got better information. There was a Kenneth H. Dahlberg listed in Boca Raton, a member of a bank board there, and there was a Kenneth H. Dahlberg who lived in Minneapolis. We now didn't know whether there was one Dahlberg or two, but we had a lead.

Woodward got through to Dahlberg in Minneapolis and immediately established that he kept a second home in Boca Raton. There was only one Dahlberg. They talked for a few minutes. Dahlberg said he was a fund-raiser for Richard Nixon but that he didn't have "the vaguest idea" about the $25,000 check. "I turn all my money over to the committee." He wouldn't go into details beyond that and hung up. But he had already told us plenty.

---

*In one of the nicer Watergate stories, it was later revealed that during World War II, Dahlberg, a flier who had shot down fifteen Nazi planes, had been rescued after crash-landing in Belgium by Dardis, who was a PFC. Dahlberg at first mistook Dardis for an enemy and drew a gun. When they met in 1972 in the course of the Watergate investigation, they realized they knew each other. Dahlberg, joking, reportedly said to Dardis, "I should have shot you."

A campaign fund-raiser.

It meant that the money in Barker's account had probably originally been a campaign contribution. It appeared more clearly than ever that the Watergate burglars were part of the Nixon re-election drive.

The Watergate bugging financed by the re-election committee. No story had been that strong. It was a breakthrough.

I began writing background material for an article from my desk, ten feet from Woodward's, as he made other telephone calls. He was talking to Clark MacGregor, who had replaced John Mitchell as Nixon campaign director, when a call came in on his other line. I answered. It was Dahlberg, calling back to ascertain that the *Post* had a reporter named Bob Woodward. I assured him that we did.

Dahlberg sounded uncomfortable, said thank you, and started to hang up. We had more questions for him, but I felt he might be put off if a second person asked them. I made some conversation to keep him on the line until Woodward could pick him up.

Dahlberg opened up further with Woodward the second time around. He said the first call had taken him by surprise, that he had just been through an ordeal and wasn't sure Woodward was really a newspaper reporter. He had been jolted by the kidnapping of a neighbor of his, Minneapolis socialite Virginia Piper, who had been held captive for two days the previous week until her husband paid a reported one-million-dollar ransom, thought to be the highest payment ever made to kidnapers in the United States.

Then Dahlberg went into the $25,000 check.

"In the process of fund-raising I had accumulated some cash," he told Woodward, "so I recall making a cash deposit while I was in Florida and getting a cashier's check made out to myself. I didn't want to carry all that cash into Washington."

In early April, he said, he gave the check either to Hugh Sloan, the treasurer of the Nixon finance committee, "or to Maurice Stans himself," the chief Nixon fund-raiser and head of the committee. Dahlberg maintained that he had no idea how the check found its way into Barker's bank account. He said the FBI had asked him about it three weeks earlier.

Woodward and I put the story together very quickly. Howard Simons had stayed late that night on another major story; I told him what we had and asked for proper display.

When the newspaper came out, the Dahlberg story had a two-column front-page headline, but it was almost lost under the massive display given the other story. In an eight-column banner headline in our largest type, it said: Eagleton Bows Out of '72 Race; McGovern Weighs Replacement.

It is almost beyond doubt that the Eagleton debacle ended whatever possibility McGovern had of winning the 1972 presidential election. I once asked McGovern adviser Frank Mankiewicz if anything aside from Eagleton played an important role in the campaign. He said that was equivalent to asking, "Aside from that, Mrs. Lincoln, what did you think of the play?"

But in the end, while such determinations can never be made with absolute certainty, the Dahlberg story that night was probably the one that had a greater impact on the course of events in the United States for many years to come. That story immediately set in motion an inquiry by the General Accounting Office of Congress, the first body to cite illegalities in the Nixon campaign. It also sparked the so-called Patman investigation, which was eventually blocked after White House intervention in October, 1972, but which apparently led Senator Edward M. Kennedy to conduct a quiet, three-month investigation of his own as chairman of the Judiciary Committee's subcommittee on Administrative Practices and Procedure. On the basis of Kennedy's findings, the Democratic leadership of the Senate decided to hold hearings on Watergate. The result was the creation of the Senate Select Committee on Presidential Campaign Activities, the Ervin Committee, through which the nation learned of the White House tapes, the specific cause of the drive to impeach Nixon.

In the most significant ways, the Dahlberg article may be used to describe one role of the press at its best in the entire course of the Watergate scandal. The press managed to set in motion certain inquiries by government agencies that inexorably had to be resolved in one fashion or another. At the outset, some of these inquiries were successfully aborted by those directing the coverup or by politicians cooperating with them. But later, the press and the media en masse became watchdogs, scrutinizing all proceedings and serving as a constant reminder to politicians and others dealing with Watergate that they were being watched, that they had to behave carefully or run the risk of being discredited.

It seems quite possible that had there been no Dahlberg

check story, there would have been no Ervin Committee, no revelation of the existence of the tapes, and little pressure exerted to force those who knew of the coverup to come forward.

2

IN 1971, CONGRESS enacted the first major campaign finance legislation in forty-six years, seeking to amend a system that had become more loophole than law, and it created the Office of Federal Elections to enforce the legislation. The new body was placed under the aegis of the General Accounting Office, which conducts investigations for Congress. A career civil servant, Phillip S. (Sam) Hughes, was named director. Hughes had had a long career in the marble halls of bureaucratic Washington. He had helped draw up the GI Bill, which provided returning World War II servicemen with free schooling and low-cost home loans and life insurance. For part of the Eisenhower Administration, he had worked under Maurice Stans at the Bureau of the Budget.

On August 1, 1972, Hughes read the *Washington Post*'s article describing the $25,000 Dahlberg check. Two Democratic Senators, Proxmire of Wisconsin and Cannon of Nevada, read it too and requested a General Accounting Office audit of Nixon campaign financing. But Hughes had already decided to conduct one.

The *Post*'s article sparked others on Capitol Hill to action as well, including Democrat Rep. Wright Patman, a seventy-nine-year-old Texan who had shown interest in the Watergate affair from the beginning. As chairman of the House Banking and Currency Committee, Patman assigned members of the committee's staff to determine whether there had been any banking violations in the transfer of the Dahlberg check and the Mexican money from their points of origin to Bernard Barker's bank account.

Both inquiries, Hughes's and Patman's, are hardly remembered today, ten years later. But both were life-threatening to

Nixon at the time, and he responded accordingly, using his Justice Department to bury Hughes's findings, and collaborators in Congress to thwart Patman.

The Office of Federal Elections had no subpoena power and was therefore limited in its ability to press for interviews with people who knew about Nixon campaign financing. Often the fact that the GAO has a mandate from Congress to investigate is sufficient to insure cooperation, but this time it wasn't.

Hughes was given access to some CRP records, and he spoke to Kenneth Dahlberg. But he got outright refusals on his requests to interview Maurice Stans and Hugh Sloan. He said he got little or no help from Earl Silbert, who pointed out that information given a grand jury is secret. Nevertheless, in three weeks, just as the Republican National Convention opened in Miami, it was known that Hughes had made some findings that were expected to be damaging to the Nixon campaign.

On Tuesday, August 22, 1972, the day Richard Nixon was renominated for the Presidency, Hughes was ready to put out his report. Suddenly, an hour before it was to be made public, he was asked to delay its release and was summoned to Miami by his former boss, Stans. Hughes suggested to his colleagues that the trip be made public, realizing that otherwise he might subject himself to unfavorable publicity. But when in doubt, the GAO, like so many government agencies, leaned to secrecy, and Hughes's flight went unannounced.

By Wednesday night, when he returned to Washington, Hughes's meeting with Stans had been discovered and there was sharp reaction to it.

Lawrence O'Brien charged that the delay was part of the "most outrageous conspiracy of suppression that I have witnessed in a generation of political activity . . . an example of the frantic Republican effort to conceal, lock up, or otherwise submerge a growing scandal that reaches into the White House itself."

In retrospect, this was another instance in which Democratic Chairman O'Brien seems to have been exactly correct in his assessments of Watergate. At the time, however, in the midst of the election campaign, he was ignored by almost all but those who never would vote for Nixon anyway.

O'Brien said that "this kind of coordinated coverup can only mean that President Nixon, John Mitchell, and Maurice

Stans believe that the facts, if known, would seriously jeopardize the entire Republican re-election campaign."

Wright Patman charged that the delay "raises major questions about the objectivity of Hughes's report and that Hughes's conference with Stans gives "the Republicans a golden opportunity to cover their tracks."

But Hughes's trip to Miami did more than bring the Republicans and Hughes an embarrassing headline during the convention. In Miami, Hughes finally cornered Hugh Sloan, who went to the convention although he was no longer functioning as an official in the re-election drive. Sloan told Hughes that the Dahlberg check and the Mexican money had gone into a cash fund kept in two safes at re-election headquarters, one in his office and one in Stans's.

Noting that "some individuals who may have knowledge of the matters involved have not been available to discuss the subject with us," Hughes's report cited half a dozen or more "apparent violations" of the campaign disclosure laws. He referred them to the Attorney General for criminal investigation. He cited four other "possible violations" and forwarded them to the Justice Department for investigation as well. The Justice Department set the matter aside until after the election. Then it pressed charges only against the re-election committee as a body and not against individuals.

Hughes's report was issued August 26, 1972, as the GOP convention ended. It contained a statement by Dahlberg that the $25,000 had been a contribution by Dwayne Andreas. The Patman staff, armed with that information, began looking for a possible quid pro quo for such a large contribution. They discovered that Andreas and Dahlberg were members of a group that earlier in August had received a federal charter for a new bank in a suburban Minneapolis shopping center.

The charter had been awarded by the Federal Reserve Board 88 days after it had been applied for, which was said to be an extraordinarily rapid approval. The timing showed that the application for the charter had been placed shortly after Andreas made his $25,000 contribution. Patman investigators questioned why the application was processed so speedily in 1972 when the shopping center the bank was to go in was not scheduled to open before 1974.

On August 30, 1972, four days after the issuance of the Hughes report, three members of Patman's staff met with Maurice Stans and an attorney for CRP, Kenneth Wells

Parkinson, one of the lawyers who had sat in on FBI interrogation of CRP employees.

At the meeting, Stans denied any knowledge of the transfer of campaign contributions through Mexico. But the following day a Nixon fund-raiser from Texas told Patman investigators that Stans had approved routing the funds through Mexico as a means of laundering them. Faced with this contradiction, Patman got in touch with Stans again and received a letter from him dated September 5, 1972, in which Stans said he now recalled being "informed by our Texas chairman of a possible contribution of $100,000 in U.S. funds in Mexico."

Patman had assigned Democratic staff members to his preliminary investigation, and they were making sharp, politically explosive findings. Some felt that Patman, who was first elected in 1929 and had watched the latter stages of the Teapot Dome scandal as they were played out, was too old to have the energy to pursue the matter fully, to give it the personal attention and drive a younger man could. Nevertheless, Patman, a populist in the 1930's mold, decided he had enough information for a full-fledged probe. He announced his intention to hold hearings, possibly televised ones, and to ask his committee to approve issuance of subpoenas for balky witnesses.

At the White House, Nixon and his aides watched the work of Sam Hughes and Wright Patman with anger. Publicly, Stans attempted to counter the GAO report by charging that any CRP financial irregularities were purely technical ones brought on by difficulties in interpreting the new campaign laws, which had taken effect in the middle of his fund-raising drive. He charged that the McGovern campaign was guilty of more extensive and more serious violations than was CRP.

Stans also criticized Patman staff members for what he called "the most shocking example of partisan misbehavior and discourtesy that I have encountered in all my years in public life." He said they were guilty of "deliberate falsehoods, misrepresentations and slanted conclusions—all politically motivated."

Privately, the tape of a presidential conversation during that period, one for September 15, 1972,* shows that Nixon,

---

*This was Dean's first meeting with Nixon after the bugging arrests, except for a brief moment in August. The quotes that follow were taken from a transcript made by the House Judiciary Committee.

Haldeman, and Dean were deeply involved in plans to bury Hughes's damaging GAO report and to block the Patman staff from any further findings.

"The GAO report that was referred over to Justice is on a shelf right now," John Dean told Nixon. "They've got violations of McGovern's, they've got violations of Humphrey's, they've got Jackson violations and several hundred congressional violations. They don't want to start prosecuting one any more than they want the other. So that's——"

"They damn well not prosecute us unless they prosecute all the others," Nixon interrupted.

Dean said he had been told that the GAO audit had been requested by House Speaker Carl Albert, an Oklahoma Democrat. Albert was known to have personal problems; earlier in 1972 he had received unfavorable newspaper publicity after a minor automobile accident when witnesses said the congressman had been very drunk and belligerent.

Haldeman, hearing that Albert might be responsible for the GAO audit, said, "Well, God damn the Speaker of the House. Maybe we better put a little heat on him."

"I think so too," Nixon said.

"Because he's got a lot worse problems than he's going to find down here," said Haldeman.

"That's right," said Dean.

"I know," said Nixon.

The President then made reference to a "police department note" dealing with Albert. Exactly what this note was is unclear. It seems probable that it had to do with one or more of Albert's personal problems. Regardless of what was in it, it is striking that Nixon—and not Haldeman or Dean—should be the one to first refer to its existence.

Nixon repeatedly maintained that he was too busy with important affairs of state to take an active part in his own political campaign of 1972.* He blamed the Watergate break-in and the subsequent coverup on "overzealous" men who never would have gone so far had the President only had the time

---

*On July 2, 1974, Alexander Butterfield told the House Judiciary Committee, which was then studying impeachment of Nixon, that the President "absolutely" ran his 1972 re-election campaign from the White House. "Anything having to do with strategy would emanate from the President and be carried to the [re-election] committee via Haldeman and Strachan," Butterfield testified in a closed session of the impeachment panel.

to run his own campaign, as he had in the past. Yet here, on September 15, 1972, was an example of Nixon bringing to the attention of his aides something far, far removed from affairs of state. *He* was telling *them* of a police department note that might be used for political purposes.

"What we really ought to do is call the Speaker," Haldeman said, "and say, 'I regret to see you ordering the GAO down here because of what it's going to cause us to require us to do to you.' " Nixon agreed.

There is no evidence that pressure was ever applied on Carl Albert. Nevertheless, this piece of conversation and others that run through the transcripts of Nixon tapes that have been made public reveal basic aspects of Nixon's political style. This kind of pressure, discussed for Carl Albert, was a fundamental part of that style. Political blackmail was often discussed for the handling of difficult problems. But it was seen only as a last resort. Nixon preferred to employ more routine political methods.

At the same September 15 meeting, the subject of the Patman Committee came up. Dean said:

> We're looking at all the campaign records of every member of that committee because we are convinced that none of them have probably totally complied with the law either. And if they want to get into it, if they want to play rough, some day we better say, "Well, gentlemen, we think we ought to call your attention that you haven't complied with A, B, C, D, E, and F, and we're not going to hold that a secret if you start talking campaign violations here."

Exhibits entered with Dean's testimony before the Senate Watergate Committee in 1973* show that CRP did indeed look at the campaign reports of each member. Dean has suggested the plan was dropped because of the fear that the Republican members of the committee, who could be expected to vote against the hearings anyway, might be as embarrassed by their failing to comply with the A, B, C's as the Democrats would be.

The September 15 conversation shows, however, that Nixon was not happy with this blackmail plan to begin with.

---
*Senate Watergate hearings, Book 3, p. 1183 *ff*.

He did not respond favorably to Dean's mention of it, did not even discuss it, and suggested a much more common political approach. He wanted Gerald Ford, who was then House Minority Leader, to exert pressure on William R. Widnall, a New Jersey Republican member of the committee who had been in Congress for more than twenty years and who Nixon said was a "very weak man."

"Jerry should talk to Widnall. After all, if we ever win in the House, Jerry will be the Speaker; just brace him. . . . Jerry has really got to be led on this."

Then Nixon urged that members of the White House congressional liaison staff, especially one named Dick Cook, speak to members of the Patman Committee, and Haldeman volunteered to brief Cook on the problem.

"Oh, I think Ehrlichman should talk to him," Nixon said. "Ehrlichman understands the law, and the rest, and should say, 'Now, God damn it, get the hell over with this.' . . . This is, this is big, big play. I'm getting into this thing, so that he—he's got to know that it comes from the top."

But, said Nixon, "I can't talk to him myself."

Such lobbying is far from what anyone would describe as political blackmail. Nixon was discouraging blackmail. His favored method of operation, as he demonstrated here and frequently afterward, was to elicit cooperation in a normal manner.

Nixon suggested routine lobbying through routine channels—his White House congressional liaison staff and House Minority Leader Ford. Nixon's statement that "this is big, big play" shows how strongly he wanted to block the Patman hearings. But while Dean saw a possible need for rough political tactics, Nixon, with his experience in the House, the Senate, and the Executive Mansion, saw no need for such actions. They were not necessary, even on this crucial matter. Simply make it clear to key committee members that the President wants, and the votes could be expected to fall in place. It is hard to see how Nixon's behavior in this instance is in any way different from how his predecessors might have worked with Congress. Legislation is seldom achieved by twisting arms or by deep, secret threats. Politics on Capitol Hill involves washing other people's backs, not breaking them. It is a matter of doing favors in return for favors. No one knew this better than Nixon.

It is impossible to exaggerate the importance of this political reality. Nixon's instincts invariably led him to seek help from those who might be regarded as friendly and to shrink from confrontations or threats.

Dean suggested that John Connally, the powerful Texas Democrat who was so close to Nixon, pay a call on Patman and "talk turkey" to him. Nixon vetoed that. Patman, whose name was on the White House's "enemies list," was not one of those politicians who could be dealt with in a normal manner of live and let live. He might publicly denounce Connally's visit as intervention by Nixon. "Connally can't be sent up there," Nixon told Dean.

Dean mentioned that one committee member, Republican Garry Brown, had written a letter to Attorney General Kleindienst questioning whether hearings might jeopardize the rights of the men who were suspects in the Watergate criminal case.

"Brown's a smart fellow," Nixon said. "He's from, he's from Michigan . . . and some tie into Ford. He's very, he's a very smart fellow. Good."

"Good lawyer and he's being very helpful," Dean said. "He is anxious to help."

"Tell Ehrlichman to get Brown in and Ford in and then they can all work out something," Nixon said. "But they ought to get off their asses and push it. No use to let Patman have a free ride here."

In the summer of 1973, when John Dean made public the enemies list with the names of 21 organizations and more than 200 people on it, it became natural to think of Nixon politics as the politics of revenge. The enemies list was part of a plan to "use the available federal machinery to screw our political enemies," as Dean explained it. The concept, involving fundamental abuse of government power for the basest ends, was obviously repugnant and offended many Americans. But it would be a mistake to reason that Nixon considered Congress as loaded with his enemies. Exactly the opposite is true.

Very few senators and congressmen were considered enemies. The list included mainly representatives of the media, civil rights or citizens group activists, labor leaders, celebrities, academics, businessmen, and antiwar leaders. There were only ten U.S. senators on the list and, aside from the black members of the House, only six congressmen.* Those whose names were not on the enemies list were not necessarily considered friends. But most assuredly, with few exceptions they were considered politicians who could be reasoned with in a normal manner. So one implication of the enemies list, with so few senators and congressmen on it, was that 90 senators and 417 congressmen were not exactly enemies.

Perhaps nothing better illustrates the relationship between Nixon and those supposedly partisan politicians, the Democrats on Capitol Hill, than the public testimony of White House aide Gordon Strachan at the Senate Watergate hearings on July 23, 1973. Strachan said that the White House had a list of one hundred Democratic members of the House and Senate who were running for re-election in 1972 "who would not receive very strong opposition from Republicans. . . . The goal was not to give a tremendous amount of support to Republicans that would oppose these congressmen."

In 1972, a total of ten Democratic senators and 235 Democrats in the House ran for re-election *nationwide*. If Strachan's figure was correct—and he was questioned about it repeatedly by Senator Lowell Weicker—then Nixon was lending encouragement or support of one kind or another to 42.5 percent of the opposition party's incumbent candidates. The Democrats favored, Strachan said, were selected for having supported Nixon's Indochina policies or because they had won the backing of labor interests that were also aiding Nixon.

Weicker was so upset at Strachan's testimony that he reflected on "Republicans doing in Republicans" and asked rhetorically, "Did we have any sort of an election contest . . . was there a contest in 1972 for the House or for the Senate?"

Throughout the Watergate scandal, Nixon sought assistance from more or less friendly members of both parties. And from the moment Wright Patman announced his plans to investigate Watergate, through the most intensive stages of the Senate Watergate Committee hearings and the later drive

---

*The senators were all Democrats: Bayh of Indiana, Fulbright of Arkansas, Fred Harris of Oklahoma, Hughes of Iowa, Kennedy of Massachusetts, McGovern of South Dakota, Mondale of Minnesota, Muskie of Maine, Nelson of Wisconsin and Proxmire of Wisconsin. The representatives were Abzug of New York, William Anderson of Tennessee, Brademas of Indiana, Drinan of Massachusetts, Kastenmeier of Wisconsin, Patman of Texas, and every member of the Black Caucus.

for his impeachment, the President time after time received at least some cooperation from leaders of both parties.

Watergate was first and foremost the scandal of Richard Nixon, but it was a scandal that could have ended quickly if not for the help powerful men on Capitol Hill extended to their President.

3

WRIGHT PATMAN STRUGGLED through September and into October, 1972, in an attempt to gain subpoena power and hold hearings on Watergate. It was a losing battle, but while he was fighting, he must have struck terror in the hearts of those behind the coverup.

In September he announced that he would hold a committee meeting on October 3 to seek subpoena power to interview more than forty people. Among them were Dwayne Andreas, Alfred Baldwin, John Caulfield, Kenneth Dahlberg, John Dean, Gordon Liddy's secretary Sally Harmony, Fred LaRue, Jeb Magruder, Robert Mardian, and John Mitchell. Had these people been forced to testify under oath before the election of 1972, not only could they have caused embarrassment to the Nixon campaign, but it is conceivable that the entire Watergate coverup, which centered on the payments of hush money by LaRue, would have been revealed.

It was clear by the time Patman issued this list that there would be no trial in the criminal or the civil cases before the election. Hearings by Patman were the only official inquiry that the Nixon forces had to contend with. But how could Patman be stopped?

Aside from lobbying members of the committee in the traditional way, the White House went to the Justice Department, as it often did, for help. They got it from Henry Petersen in the form of a response to a letter that Michigan Congressman Garry Brown had sent to Richard Kleindienst asking whether Patman's hearings would interfere with criminal proceedings.

Petersen wrote to Patman, saying that the Justice Department "is seriously concerned that public hearings on matters related to the Watergate case at this time may not only jeopardize the prosecution of the case but also seriously jeopardize the rights of the defendants. It is distinctly possible that matters which adversely reflect on the defendants, and which would not be admissible at the criminal trial, will become known to the public and to potential jurors as a result of the proposed congressional investigation."

The problem of prejudicing the rights of defendants is a genuine one, even in open and shut cases such as the break-in and bugging at Watergate. Certain civil libertarians therefore joined in opposition to Patman's plans to hold hearings. But there are indications that Petersen had other motives in writing his letter—for example, he discussed the matter with John Dean. Dean's testimony and the tape of the September 15, 1972, conversation between Dean, Haldeman, and Nixon show that the White House wanted the Patman hearings blocked for fear of what might be disclosed, not on civil liberties grounds.

Petersen's letter seems one more example of his willingness to keep the "political element" out of the case when pressured to do so.

Patman ignored the letter from Petersen. But other members of his committee, Republicans and Democrats alike, seized on the opportunity to appear to be civil libertarians and quash the investigation at the same time.

One of the Democrats to vote against holding the hearings was Frank Brasco of New York, who in 1971 had been the beneficiary of John Mitchell's largesse. Brasco had been accused of receiving payments in return for using influence to obtain a postal service contract for a firm with reputed Mafia ties. Mitchell intervened to block a proposed grand jury investigation into Brasco. On October 3, at the committee meeting, Brasco made an emotional appeal not to hold hearings on the grounds that "politics should stay out of justice."*

In a slashing account of the maneuvering behind the vote that day, writer Marjorie Boyd described in the April, 1973, issue of *Washington Monthly* how "all the Republicans met in the office of senior Republican committee member William Widnall, and then went on to the committee meeting en masse, a splendid martial display of party discipline." It was

---

*In 1973, after Elliot Richardson became Attorney General, the Brasco case was reopened. Brasco was indicted and went to trial in New York in 1974. A mistrial was declared, but in July, 1974, he was convicted.

Widnall, of course, whom Nixon had singled out for special attention.

The final vote was 20 to 15 against the hearings, as six Democrats joined the fourteen Republicans to defeat Patman.

Mrs. Boyd's article went into detail on several of the Democrats who voted with the Republicans. She said that one southern Democrat, Robert G. Stephens of Georgia, had persuaded three others, Tom S. Gettys of South Carolina, Charles H. Griffin of Mississippi, and Bill Chappell, Jr., of Florida, to vote against the hearings. Mrs. Boyd wrote:

> Although it would be hard to prove any connection to the vote on the Watergate probe, the government has been exceedingly generous to Stephens' Georgia district (since then). Three days after the committee vote, the director of the Athens Housing Authority announced that he had "worked out a solution" with the Department of Housing and Urban Development to end an impasse in the construction of a $2 million, 11-story apartment building for the elderly in downtown Athens.

Mrs. Boyd outlined the sudden approval for local legislation sponsored by Stephens after similar legislation had been vetoed by Nixon.

> Stephens stoutly denies that he received any pressure on the Watergate vote from the Administration or Republicans in Congress. Asked about his vote to kill the Watergate probe, he said, "When you give a fellow a vote, you don't hesitate to take any proposition you may have to him, and you have a right to expect a hearing. It's always understood; it's not a thing you ever speak about."

Florida Congressman Chappell, Mrs. Boyd wrote:

> emphasized that he was not against an investigation of Watergate but was only interested in protecting the rights of the defendants awaiting trial. He said that while he could not support the investigation Patman proposed, he would be willing to go along with closed hearings without subpoena power....
>
> A week before the vote, Chappell had been over to the White House for a private talk with Nixon and had

his picture taken with the President for use in the campaign. George McGovern was as popular as swamp fever in Chappell's District.

Mrs. Boyd went on to describe how, years earlier, a secretary to Chappell had charged that the congressman had illegally diverted part of her salary to make secret payments to someone who had allegedly written speeches for him. "After a five-month investigation, the Justice Department quietly announced that 'the facts do not warrant criminal prosecution,'" Mrs. Boyd wrote.

She described Congressmen Gettys and Griffin as men who "admire Stephens and are accustomed to following his lead," and pointed out that their votes were in fact announced on October 3 by Stephens.

The vote of the last Democrat, Richard Hanna of California, Mrs. Boyd wrote, was "a mystery. He told his hometown paper that he was angry at Patman over his failure to push a key housing bill through Congress—a less than compelling reason for being opposed to such an important hearing."

The private conversations of Richard Nixon show how hard he and his aides worked to block the hearings, and it is easy to blame Nixon for sabotaging them. Certainly, it was part of his continuing obstruction of justice. But the fact is the Patman hearings could not have been blocked without active assistance from members of the Patman Committee. The people ultimately responsible were the Republicans and Democrats on the committee who saw advantage to be gained in doing a favor for the President. They, not he, had the power to block Patman.

As Patman counted the votes against him on October 3, 1972, he said, "I predict that the facts will come out, and when they do I am convinced they will reveal why the White House is so anxious to kill the committee's investigation. The public will fully understand why this pressure was mounted."

He was right, of course. But no one could have forced the members of the committee to vote the way they did. They chose to.

A few days later, Patman made a second try at holding hearings, without subpoena power. He invited Mitchell, Stans, Clark MacGregor, and Dean to appear before the committee on October 12. All said they would not attend. In a hint of things to come, Dean sent word that his appearance would violate the principle of Executive privilege.

Patman denounced the four, calling their refusal to appear "a sad spectacle—a massive coverup . . . I'm convinced that it was dictated by the White House." He said their decision not to appear was "an insult to every single American who believes in free, open elections. It is an arrogant act, an amazing act for those who are supposed to be seeking the votes of the American people."

On October 12, Patman surveyed the empty chairs that had been reserved for the witnesses and blamed Nixon for their absence, saying the President "has pulled down an iron curtain of secrecy to keep the American people from knowing the facts."

But the witness chairs weren't the only empty ones. Only seventeen committee members responded to Patman's called meeting, too few for a quorum. Patman called a meeting for later in the day. Only fourteen members showed up then. Patman was through.

4

THE MONTHS OF September and October, 1972, as frustrating as they were for Wright Patman, marked the high point of the *Washington Post*'s early coverage of the Watergate scandal. We began by continuing to drop occasional stories in the newspaper without knowing where they fit in an overall pattern. Somewhere toward the end, after the newspaper became the subject of a vicious public attack by the Nixon Administration, some of us stopped, looked back at what we had written, and realized that we were onto a scandal of vast proportions. Even then we had no idea how big the story was, or how much trouble we had been causing Nixon.

On the 15th of September, the day the original seven Watergate defendants were indicted, the White House tapes show that Nixon, Haldeman, and Dean privately discussed plans to seek revenge on the *Post*. As in many other conversations, it was Nixon, not his associates, who took the lead in planning an attack. "The main thing is the *Post* is going to have damnable, damnable problems out of this one," he said; "the game has to be played awfully rough."

What is so striking about this conversation—given that such sentiments by Nixon are no longer surprising—is its timing. After September 15 the *Post* was to make findings that proved terribly damaging to Nixon. But before then our coverage had hardly gone beyond the August 1 Dahlberg check story. In retrospect, it became clear that the Dahlberg article was of extreme significance because of the forces it set in motion—the GAO, the Patman Committee, and later inquiries. From the Nixon, Haldeman, and Dean conversation, it appears that no one had a keener, more immediate understanding of that than they did. Nevertheless, all three had an air of confidence.

Nixon had seen Dean only once after the bugging arrests—for a few minutes in August on a matter concerning the President's personal finances. Just before Dean walked in on September 15, Haldeman told Nixon how well the young aide had been performing, describing him as "one of the quiet guys that gets a lot done," who makes sure "that you don't fall through the holes."

"Well, you had quite a day today, didn't you," Nixon said as Dean entered his office. "You get Watergate on the way, huh?"

They spoke of how the inclusion in the indictment of two former White House aides, Hunt and Liddy, had taken the edge off possible charges of a whitewash—"the thing Mitchell kept saying," Haldeman noted.

Nixon minimized the bugging incident, suggesting that it was part of routine politics. "Goldwater put it in context, he said, 'Well, for Christ's sake, everybody bugs everybody else. We know that....'

"It's true," Nixon went on. "We were bugged in '68 on the plane and bugged in '62, even running for governor. God damnedest thing you ever saw."

Dean said that he could anticipate that "not a thing will come crashing down to our, our surprise" by the time of the election fifty-four days away.

Nixon responded that "as you know, a lot of this stuff went on.... But the way you, you've handled it, it seems to me, has been very skillful, because you—putting your fingers in the dike every time that leaks have sprung here and sprung there."

Nixon said, "This is war. We're getting a few shots and it'll be over, and we'll give them a few shots and it'll be over."

Shortly before the indictments, Woodward and Bernstein had begun to develop an approach that was once more to escalate the scandal. CRP seemed clearly responsible for at least the financing of the break-in. The ranking officials, of course, were denying that, putting the blame on "over-zealous" underlings. The reporters acquired a list of CRP employees and began attempting to interview many of them one by one.

They were rewarded almost immediately. One secretary, in tears, told Bernstein she was terrified. She described FBI interviews with CRP attorneys sitting in, spoke about destruction of papers immediately after the bugging, said she was afraid to meet with Bernstein.

Other lower-level workers shared her alarm. They didn't know what the bugging was about or what CRP's ties to it were, but they knew something was very, very wrong. One woman had asked the FBI to interview her secretly because she felt inhibited by the CRP attorneys; days later, we were told, she was called in and asked why she felt the need to meet alone with the FBI.

5

ON THE 16TH of September, only one day after Dean had told Nixon that he anticipated no surprises, Bernstein and Woodward were able to write that funds used for the Watergate spying had been "controlled by several assistants of John N. Mitchell," men who still held "policy-making positions on a high level in President Nixon's re-election campaign."

The following day, a Sunday, they wrote that two officials, Jeb Magruder and Herbert Porter, had each withdrawn "more than $50,000 from a secret fund that financed intelligence-gathering activities against the Democrats." Magruder, reached on the telephone by Woodward, denied receiving any money from a secret fund. It was probably the first time he had been asked about Watergate by a reporter, and his voice was shaky. Porter could not be reached for comment.

Woodward and Bernstein were now talking frequently to Hugh Sloan, who had resigned in July as campaign treasurer. Armed with pieces of information from him and from lower-level re-election workers, the reporters were often able to get their findings confirmed by people close to the Watergate investigation. On September 20, they reported assertions that two of Mitchell's chief aides, Mardian and LaRue, had "directed a massive house cleaning" at CRP in the days following the bugging arrests. "Financial records were destroyed and staff members were told to 'close ranks' in preparing a public response to the incident."

The article said that "some employees, particularly those who were aware that documents had been destroyed in their offices, said they were offered advice from superiors on how to respond to inquiries from FBI agents and others investigating the Watergate case.

"Other employees received unexpected promotions in the weeks following the break-in, according to colleagues. . . . Steps were taken to insulate the Nixon campaign staff from the press. Sally Harmony, who had served as Liddy's secretary, became office manager Robert Odle's secretary and told a reporter, 'I'm under strict instructions from the committee not to talk to anybody. You'll have to call the press office if you want to know something.'"

To articles like this, CRP's official response was that the *Post*'s sources "were a fountain of misinformation." But by the end of September, Woodward and Bernstein took the trail of Watergate funding all the way up to John Mitchell. Bernstein called the former campaign director at home late on the night of September 29 to ask his comments on a report that he controlled the "secret fund" while he was Attorney General. Bernstein read aloud the first several paragraphs.

"All that crap you're putting in the paper!" Mitchell said. "It's all been denied. Katie Graham's gonna get her tit caught in a big fat wringer if that's published. Good Christ! That's the most sickening thing I've ever heard."

Bernstein said he wanted to ask Mitchell a few questions.

"What time is it?" Mitchell asked.

"Eleven-thirty. I'm sorry to call so late," Bernstein said.

"Eleven-thirty. Eleven-thirty when?"

"Eleven-thirty at night."

"Oh."

Bernstein told Mitchell that a spokesman for the re-election committee had issued a statement about the story but that he wanted Mitchell's response to some specifics.

"Did the committee tell you to go ahead and publish that story? You fellows got a great ball game. As soon as you're through paying Ed Williams and the rest of those fellows, we're going to do a little story on all of you."

Mitchell hung up. A short while later, a CRP official called and asked Bernstein not to run Mitchell's statements, saying it was unfair to catch Mitchell off guard after he had been sleeping. Bernstein suggested that the official call Bradlee at home. He did, fruitlessly. The story ran, with only one expression omitted.

It was less than two weeks after the indictments, just over five weeks before the presidential election. By pursuing CRP and the trail of the money in Barker's bank account, we had suddenly taken Watergate far beyond anyone's expectations. But even before the Mitchell telephone call, we were starting to move in an entirely different direction. We were on the trail of Donald Segretti.

6

LONG BEFORE WATERGATE, I knew that Bob Woodward had extraordinary drive and skill, and that he had several most unusual contacts. On May 15, 1972, hours after George Wallace was shot in a Laurel, Maryland, shopping center just sixteen miles from the center of the District of Columbia, we at the *Post* still had not learned the name of the man who shot the Alabama governor. Woodward mentioned to me that he had "a friend" who might be able to help. It was the first time I remember hearing Woodward speak of his "friend."

In September and October, as we began to get deeply into the Watergate scandal, "my friend," as Woodward called him, or "Bob's friend," as the rest of us referred to him, came to play a mysterious and crucial role. Four editors—Bradlee, Simons, Rosenfeld, and I—often asked the names of sources used by Woodward and Bernstein. The first time Woodward came to me with something from his friend, he asked if it would be possible not to tell me his friend's name. Woodward said he would tell me if I insisted, but that he would rather not. It was the only time he had made such a request. I didn't ask, and to the best of my knowledge, neither did Bradlee, Simons, or Rosenfeld, then or later. Over the months, Bob's friend became more and more important to us, and Howard Simons gave him a new name: "Deep Throat."

Deep Throat seemed to know everything about Watergate, but he seldom volunteered information. Woodward could never count on seeing him at any given time, and they seldom met at all. Generally, Deep Throat confined his help to telling Woodward whether information we had was correct or to explaining what seemed to be the philosophy behind the Watergate spying without getting into the individuals responsible for it. He was more a guide than a traditional news source, letting Woodward know when he was on the right track and steering him from dead ends or from exaggerating the importance of certain leads.

Deep Throat, whoever he was, was thoroughly disgusted by Watergate, and while the White House and various politicians accused the *Post* of overplaying the story, he always assured Woodward that there was more, much more, and not to be misled. When so many members of the press were ignoring Watergate, this was no small succor. And sometimes, at moments when Deep Throat was particularly angry, he gave more than just general assistance, as he did when Woodward asked him about Donald Segretti.

On September 28, Bernstein got a call from a man who identified himself as a government lawyer. The man spoke about a campaign of spying and sabotage against the Democrats that might in some way be linked to Watergate. Bernstein began checking the lead by calling Alex Shipley, an assistant attorney general in Tennessee, whose name the man had given him.

Shipley had known Donald Segretti in the army, where both had been attorneys. Shortly before Shipley's discharge, while he was stationed in Washington, Segretti asked if he would be interested in doing some political work. Shipley quoted Segretti as saying, "We'll go to a Kennedy rally and find an ardent Kennedy worker. Then you say that you're a Kennedy man too, but you're working behind the scenes; you get them to help you. You send them to work for Muskie, stuffing envelopes or whatever, and you get them to pass you the information. They'll think that they are helping Kennedy against Muskie. But actually you're using the information for something else."

Shipley said he asked Segretti, "Well, who will we be working for?" and that Segretti said Nixon. "I was really taken aback because all the actions he had talked about would have taken place in Democratic primaries. He said the main purpose was that the Democrats have an ability to get back together after a knockdown, drag-out campaign; what we want to do is wreak enough havoc so they can't."

Shipley said Segretti would not reveal who was funding the sabotage, but that he would be paid, and also taken care of with a job after the election. "I said, 'How in hell are we going to be taken care of if no one knows what we're doing?' and Segretti said, 'Nixon knows that something is being done.

It's a typical deal'; Segretti said, 'Don't tell me anything and I won't know.' "

Shipley said he turned Segretti down. Through Shipley, Bernstein found out the names of other lawyers who had been approached, and they told much the same story.

By this time, Woodward and Bernstein, who were resourceful reporters to begin with, had developed techniques for getting information that were unknown to most newspapermen. They could often get telephone, hotel, and travel records. Like the superior investigators they had become, they could make sources think they knew much more than they did; they could cajole, bluff, or plead their way to eliciting information. As they amassed information, they often were able to get confirmation or denials, and sometimes a little more, from certain federal investigators.

They found that Shipley's account of his meetings with Segretti matched travel and hotel records for Segretti, and that Segretti had criss-crossed the country ten times during the election campaign, visiting many states at the time of the Democratic presidential primaries in them. Things seemed to be falling into place. But what was the connection to Watergate?

In California, we had a stringer—that is, a free-lance writer who worked for the *Post* on special assignments—try to find out what he could on Segretti. The stringer, Bob Meyers, paid a visit to Segretti at his bachelor apartment in Marina del Rey. He found a tiny, slightly built, soft-spoken young man whose lifestyle seemed aimed more at the swift singles life in that part of Los Angeles than at political sabotage. Meyers told Segretti what we were finding out about him, and Segretti denied it, saying, "This is material for a good novel; it's ridiculous."

On Sunday, October 8, Bernstein and I were in the office at the *Post*. We had become obsessed with Watergate. The more we heard about Segretti the weirder the story became—perhaps it was all fiction. We laid out the information we had over and over, as we had for days past, matching it against Segretti's denial. We had been on his trail for two weeks, but we didn't understand where the information was taking us. In the simplest terms, we were afraid of the story. It might be wrong.

We kept going around and around, and finally I suggested that we were taking the wrong approach by discussing it so much. "Why don't we put it on paper, see what it looks like, and talk about it then," I said. Woodward was in New York, having for once taken a weekend off. Feeling a little guilty, I called him, told him what we were doing, and asked him to come back to Washington. He said he didn't feel we had enough information to write a story; I said he might be right but I wanted to see what we did have.

That evening Bernstein wrote and Woodward got off the air shuttle and headed for a meeting with Deep Throat. All three of us were in the office very early Monday, and we were terribly excited as we discussed what we had with Harry Rosenfeld. Overnight, our understanding of Watergate had taken a quantum leap as a result of Woodward's meeting with his friend. We now understood the relationship between the bugging incident and Segretti's sabotage. Much earlier, Deep Throat said, the FBI had come to the conclusion that Watergate was simply one incident in an overall series of campaign spying and sabotage. Segretti was part of that campaign; there were more than fifty such agents, he told Woodward.

The reporters began to write what was to become the centerpiece in the *Post*'s collection of pre-election Watergate stories, accenting the totality of campaign spying on behalf of Nixon and pushing to the bottom of the story what Bernstein had written the previous evening on Segretti. We were well on our way to completion when a new and equally peculiar development emerged.

About the time Bernstein first heard of Segretti, another *Post* reporter, Marilyn Berger, who covered the State Department and diplomatic events, had met with Ken Clawson. For some reason, according to Berger, Clawson asked if she recalled the incident involving the Canuck letter that had been so damaging to the candidacy of Edmund Muskie back in February. He told her, she said, that he had written the Canuck letter. Berger kept the information to herself for a while, considering it to have been said in confidence. But she grew increasingly disturbed by it.

She mentioned the incident to David Broder, who told her to take it to Woodward and Bernstein. As we were nearing the end of the Segretti story, then, out came this new incident of campaign sabotage laid at the door of the White House. Segretti's activities had been aimed largely at sabotaging Muskie; the Canuck letter seemed to fit right in with "black politics" against the man who had topped Nixon in the voter preference polls month after month in 1971. Very soon there was a crowd of us around Berger, and it was Ben Bradlee, I believe, who suggested that she try to meet Clawson for lunch to see if he would repeat the story.

They ate at the fashionable Sans Souci, a favorite luncheon place for Henry Kissinger. Berger told Clawson that Woodward and Bernstein were working on a big story that was going to include the Canuck letter and that she had told them that "Ken said he did it."

In a memo written immediately after the lunch, she noted that Clawson "said he wished I hadn't said that," that he would "deny it on a stack of Bibles."

Woodward and Bernstein prepared to do two stories: one on Segretti and one on Clawson, with a long list of examples of sabotage against Muskie to be placed in one of them. Bradlee, saying no one had ever heard of Donald Segretti, ruled that we combine Segretti and Clawson and do one story. The lead written earlier, before we knew of Clawson's involvement, was the one that was kept. The story led our front page on October 10, 1972, exactly four weeks before the election. The headline said, "FBI Finds Nixon Aides/ Sabotaged Democrats." The story began:

> FBI agents have established that the Watergate bugging incident stemmed from a massive campaign of political spying and sabotage conducted on behalf of President Nixon's re-election and directed by officials of the White House and the Committee for the Re-election of the President.
>
> The activities, according to information in FBI and Department of Justice files, were aimed at all the major Democratic presidential contenders and—since 1971— represented a basic strategy of the Nixon re-election effort.
>
> During their Watergate investigation, federal agents established that hundreds of thousands of dollars in Nixon campaign contributions had been set aside to pay for an extensive undercover campaign aimed at discrediting individual Democratic presidential candidates and disrupting their campaigns.
>
> "Intelligence work" is normal during a campaign and is said to be carried out by both political parties. But federal investigators said what they uncovered being done by the Nixon forces is unprecedented in scope and intensity.

The article then went into detail on Clawson and Segretti. Clawson denied knowledge of the Canuck letter, and the White House would not comment on the story. The press office there referred the reporters to CRP, where a spokesman said for publication that the article was "not only fiction but a collection of absurdities." The following morning there was havoc at Ronald Ziegler's 11 A.M. White House press briefing as reporters demanded but did not get something more than just a refusal to discuss the story.

On Friday night, October 13, Woodward and I stayed at work until about 1 A.M., or until we were groggy, and Bernstein stayed in the office all night. Our first Segretti story mentioned that Segretti had told a friend he intended to use a law firm in Los Angeles, Young and Segretti, as a cover for his sabotage. In the intervening few days, our stringer in Los Angeles, Robert Meyers, found and interviewed Lawrence Young, an attorney who had been friendly with Segretti since their days together at the University of Southern California.

Segretti had confided in Young and made use of him in some ways, such as borrowing his telephone credit card. Now Young, who considered himself a liberal Democrat, repeated to Meyers what Segretti had told him: that presidential aides had shown Segretti copies of his interviews with the FBI and had briefed him on how to conduct himself before the Watergate grand jury; that Segretti had been paid from a trust account by a lawyer who was a high-placed friend of Nixon; that Dwight Chapin, the President's appointments secretary, had been one of Segretti's "contacts" in Washington and that Howard Hunt had been another.

The FBI had discovered Segretti through an examination of Hunt's telephone records. Ten days before the Republican National Convention in August, Young said, Segretti phoned him in "an absolute panic" because FBI agents had interviewed him about the calls from Hunt.

"He was worried because there was no prior warning that he would be contacted by the FBI," Young said. "He was afraid of being left out on a limb, sacrificed without any protection or coverage. He wanted some advice as to what he should do."

Young said that Segretti had met with Hunt in Miami several months earlier and had turned down a request by Hunt to organize "an attack" by demonstrators on the GOP headquarters at the Doral Beach Hotel. The attack was to have been staged to appear sponsored by supporters of the Democratic presidential nominee.

"Don said he knew Hunt by a different name, an assumed name, but that he knew he was Hunt. Hunt would always talk in a very whispery, conspiratorial voice, he said . . . and seemed to add even more intrigue than was already there," Young said.

We included these rich details—and also Young's description of Segretti's appearance before the Watergate grand jury on August 22, 1972—in the article. "The U.S. attorney [apparently a reference to Earl Silbert] interrogated him ahead of time in an office and thoroughly went into everything"—including Chapin's alleged role in the sabotage campaign, where Segretti was getting his money, and the names of such other persons involved in acts against the Democrats. Then, the article continued, the prosecutor told Segretti "not to worry, that those weren't the questions that would be asked."

Our basic reporting was complete by 8 or 9 P.M. Friday, but we worked at making the story more readable. Woodward called the White House for a response and got this statement from Chapin through the White House press office:

> As the *Washington Post* reporter has described it, the story is based entirely on hearsay and is fundamentally inaccurate.
>
> For example, I do not know, have never met, seen, or talked to E. Howard Hunt. I have known Donald Segretti since college days, but I did not meet with him in Florida as the story suggests, and I certainly have never discussed with him any phase of the grand jury proceedings in the Watergate case.
>
> Beyond that, I don't propose to have any further comment.

We were becoming accustomed to carefully worded statements that were meant to pass as denials, and we examined this one closely. The White House called everything we wrote "hearsay." This story had come from a friend of Segretti, whom we named, and had in it a sentence that said, "Federal law enforcement sources, apprised of what Young had told the *Post*, said Segretti had told essentially the same story to investigators." Certainly it was possible to charge us with reporting hearsay. But the assertions made were specific ones, and, as such, could have been checked by the White House, which had access to Justice Department reports.

The Chapin statement did not contest any of these key assertions. He never denied, for example, that he had served as Segretti's contact in a spying and sabotage operation against the Democrats—the main point of the story. Furthermore, the article never said that Chapin knew Howard Hunt, nor did it charge that Chapin was among the presidential aides who met with Segretti in Miami to discuss his grand jury testimony. Chapin was denying charges that had not been made.

For those reasons, the Chapin statement seemed more an indication that our story was correct than a denial. From 10 P.M. on we labored over details. Realizing that most of our readers wouldn't know who Dwight Chapin was—that I wasn't sure of his exact role myself—I asked Woodward to find out the relationship between Chapin and Nixon. We were able to make this the second paragraph of the story:

> The appointments secretary, Dwight L. Chapin, 31, meets almost daily with the President. As the person in charge of Mr. Nixon's schedule and appointments, including overall coordination of trips, Chapin is one of a handful of White House staff members with easy access to the President.

It was the closest we had come to Nixon.

7

JUST AS I had called Woodward back from New York on the eighth of October, someone in the White House summoned John Dean back from Florida a week later, on the fifteenth. Dean and his new bride, Maureen, had begun their honeymoon only two days earlier. But he was needed to help shape a response to the Segretti and Chapin stories we had printed, and sometime that Sunday he met in the Roosevelt Room at the White House with Ehrlichman, Ziegler, Chapin, speech writer Patrick Buchanan, and presidential assistant Richard Moore, who had helped prepare some of the carefully worded responses to articles we had written.

On Monday the Nixon Administration began a bitter, sustained attack on the *Post*. Its aim was obvious: to obfuscate the issues, to make the credibility of the *Post* appear to be an election campaign issue and to divert attention from the involvement of powerful men in the White House in base, illegal campaign activities.

That morning, October 16, we followed our Sunday story with a piece saying that Segretti had been paid to do his undercover work by Herbert Kalmbach, Nixon's lawyer. *Time* magazine, published on Mondays, also named Kalmbach as paymaster and reported in addition that a second aide to Haldeman, Gordon Strachan, had helped recruit Segretti. Strachan, Chapin, Segretti, and David Young had all been college classmates.

At the White House, Ziegler ignored the *Time* magazine report but attacked the *Post*, complaining once more about "hearsay" reporting, suggesting that the newspaper was hand-in-hand with George McGovern and saying that "the President is concerned about the techniques being applied by the *opposition* in the stories themselves." The *Post* was now being identified as the opposition.

That afternoon Clark MacGregor called what he announced would be a press conference, then told reporters he would not allow them to ask questions. Clark Mollenhoff of the *Des Moines Register and Tribune*, who had returned to reporting after working for Nixon in the White House in 1969 and 1970, began demanding that MacGregor respond to reporters. Perhaps the loudest member of the White House press corps, Mollenhoff shouted, "What credibility do you have? What documents have you seen? Because if you can't tell us, you have no right to stand there!"

MacGregor said, "That will be a matter you will have to determine in consultation with your editors." He then read from a three-page statement, repeating Ziegler's criticisms of the newspaper with the added charge that the *Post* had deliberately refused to investigate sabotage committed against the Nixon campaign. We had never heard of most of this alleged sabotage until MacGregor mentioned it. He finished reading, turned, and left the room with reporters screaming after him.

In the evening, Republican National Committee chairman Robert Dole, speaking before a group of black Republicans in Washington, said that "Mr. McGovern appears to have turned over the franchise for his media attack campaign to the editors of the *Washington Post*."

The attacks, so similar yet coming from so many places at once, seemed to have been well coordinated. They came at a very sensitive moment for the *Post*. As we had prepared to print the first Segretti story on October 10, a number of us at the newspaper felt we had reached a point of no return. The assertions we had given air to—that sabotage was basic re-election strategy, formulated in the White House—were as serious as any that had been placed at the door of a sitting President of the United States. All of us knew that the reputation of the *Washington Post* was at stake for venting such charges during an election campaign.

On October 24, 1972, I got to work before 9:30, somewhat early for an editor on a morning newspaper. Woodward was already at his desk, speaking on the telephone. When he saw me, he raised one hand, thumb up, and smiled. He covered the phone and said quietly, "We've got Haldeman."

A few minutes later he came into my office. He and Bernstein had been to see Hugh Sloan again. We had reported that only a few high Nixon officials had access to the cash fund that had been used to pay for the Watergate bugging and other campaign spying, and we had named some of them, including Mitchell. After our story linking Chapin to Segretti, people familiar with the structure in the White House kept telling all of us that Chapin would never act without approval in advance from Haldeman. The reporters kept looking for ties to Haldeman, and perhaps the secret fund was such a tie.

Their talk with Sloan had been in some ways elliptical. Still deeply dedicated to Nixon, Sloan was reluctant to volunteer information and often confined his assistance to either confirming or denying assertions posited by the reporters. They stayed with him a good while that night, and when they left, Woodward was convinced that Sloan had told them Haldeman had access to the secret spying fund. In addition, Woodward felt that Sloan had told the reporters he had testified to that effect before the Watergate grand jury—although Sloan had not said so in just those words.

When they left Sloan, the two reporters returned to the newspaper office and called an FBI agent who was familiar with the investigation. Only Bernstein spoke, with Woodward listening in on an extension phone and taking notes. They wanted to ascertain whether Sloan had named Haldeman before the grand jury. Bernstein told the FBI man that they had heard that the "Haldeman name came out" only in grand jury testimony, and that the FBI had missed it. The source said that Haldeman had been named both to the FBI and the grand jury.

"Are you sure it's Haldeman?" Bernstein asked.

"Yeah, John Haldeman," the FBI agent said, and the conversation ended.

Bernstein and Woodward said to each other, "*John* Haldeman?" Bernstein dialed the source back. "You said John Haldeman, but his first name is Bob."

"Yeah, Haldeman. I can never remember first names."

Woodward and I went over what he and Bernstein had put together for fifteen minutes or more. We realized that we couldn't afford a mistake. I was satisfied that the information from Sloan, when matched with the second source's, was strong enough for us to write from. Not only did they fit together, but it was also logical that Haldeman, who seemed to control everything, should control or have access to that fund. I mentioned to Bradlee, who was, as usual, the first or one of the first in the office, that we were working on a Haldeman story. "Okay," he said; "be careful."

I told Rosenfeld also. The reporters worked on their story through the day and had some difficulty with it. We had written perhaps half a dozen stories about this "secret fund" and those who had access to it in the past. They had been easier to handle because we hadn't tried to be so specific in our attribution. We had been satisfied to say the information we printed came from sources close to the investigation, or to federal investigators, or to sources at CRP, or to a combination of such sources. We had been confident of what we were printing, and, although we would have preferred in each instance to name our sources, we knew that was impossible. The sources demanded protection; their careers were in jeopardy with every damaging phrase we printed.

On the Haldeman story, however, we wanted to be as specific as we could on attribution because a major charge in the White House attack on us had been that we were printing hearsay. We were concerned that the criticism was cutting into our credibility with readers.

Trying to achieve just the right nuance—sentences that would show the report to be authoritative but not expose the sources—kept causing the reporters to have false starts, getting a little way into the story and then pulling the page from the typewriter and throwing it away. They had begun work early, but they weren't done by late in the afternoon. All of us were concerned about writing these very sensitive articles against daily newspaper deadlines, and occasionally we decided at the last minute not to run them so that we could have the benefit of another day to check additional sources and write more carefully.

By about 6 P.M. the reporters had settled on the attribution and had begun writing background matter, describing how Haldeman's access to the secret fund fit into the picture of campaign spying as we understood it. Howard Simons called Rosenfeld, Woodward, Bernstein, and me into Bradlee's office to go over what we had.

Sessions like this in the past had been fairly open, with any of the editors and reporters talking or asking questions or even passing a wisecrack. This time it was different. Bradlee began asking questions the way a prosecutor would.

"What did Sloan tell you?" he asked. "What were his exact words?" "Were those his words, or is that your interpretation of what he said?" "What did the FBI agent tell you that makes you so sure he was confirming Sloan?"

I don't remember any of us asking questions aside from Bradlee, and there was no small talk. When he was done, he asked the rest of us whether we felt we should run the story. We all said yes. "Okay, go," Bradlee said.

As we left Bradlee's office, Simons expressed a slight uncertainty. Often the first to suggest holding a story over night, this time he didn't go that far, but he wanted the reporters to try at least one more source for further confirmation. Bernstein said he would call someone in the Justice Department he was reluctant to speak to, but who might confirm or deny a story of such magnitude. A few minutes later Bernstein said he had got the further confirmation.

He told me he had pleaded with this source for help and the source refused, saying he could not deal with the press. But Bernstein persisted, and suggested a procedure whereby the source would not even have to say yes or no—he would either remain silent or hang up. One signal would mean our story was correct, the other that it was wrong. I listened with incredulity as Bernstein explained this arrangement. The source used the signal for confirmation, Bernstein said; the story was good.

"That's madness, Carl," I said. "That's no confirmation, that's crazy. Don't ever do anything like that." Bernstein and Woodward knew a lot more about the details of what they were reporting than I did. But here was Bernstein saying that he was able to confirm a story damaging to the President of the United States and his chief of staff through the silence of a balky source. Maybe that could work in the movies, but not in the *Washington Post*.

As disgusted as I was, the thought of suggesting that we hold up the story never entered my mind, for even without this last source, I was sure the story was authentic—and I had been from the moment Woodward left my office in the morning.

About a year later, when this one story from among all our Watergate stories had proven to be damaging to the *Washington Post*—the one that drew specific denials because it was flat wrong in specifics—I talked to that last source of Bernstein's and asked him what had gone wrong. "Carl got his own signals mixed up," he said. "I didn't give him the 'confirm' signal, I gave him the 'deny.' "

8

AT WORK ON October 25, 1972, we found out early that Hugh Sloan's attorney had called the *Washington Post* story wrong—that Sloan had never testified that Haldeman controlled the secret fund. The lawyer's denial was specific, and he was not a political spokesman; it sounded as though we had definitely made an error. If so, we were in trouble. The White House attacked us when we were correct; what would they do now if we were wrong?

As it developed, we had made at least three errors in the story. We were wrong on Sloan's testimony, we were wrong in making a statement that Haldeman had been interviewed by the FBI—he never had been—and we were wrong, I learned long afterward, in our listing of Haldeman's age as forty-seven. He was forty-six—two days short of being forty-seven. Haldeman had issued a cryptic denial that had been included in our story, saying, "Your inquiry is based on misinformation because the reference to Bob Haldeman is untrue." It was another carefully worded statement: which reference did Haldeman have in mind? The statement had given me the impression that our article had been correct. But critics of the *Post* jumped to the attack.

At 11:48 A.M., October 25, 1972, Ronald Ziegler held his daily news conference at the White House. It lasted fifty-two minutes; two-thirds of the transcript consisted of an attack on the *Washington Post*.

"Ron," a questioner asked, "has the FBI talked to Bob Haldeman about his part in allegedly managing a secret slush fund for political sabotage?"

"I assume you base your question on the *Washington Post* story this morning," Ziegler said.

"No, it has nothing to do with that, Ron."

[The transcript indicates laughter here.]

"What do you base your question on?"

"It just struck me as a good question."

That was the end of the levity. Ziegler said the story was "shabby journalism." He noted the denial by Sloan's lawyer, pointed out that Haldeman had not been interviewed by the FBI, said the story was based on heresay, and that it referred

> to a secret fund, a term developed exclusively, virtually exclusively, by the *Washington Post*, based again on hearsay and based again on information obtained from an individual that they again refuse to identify, anonymous sources. I am told that there is no such secret fund.
>
> You can quote me directly on my references to the *Washington Post*. I say this only because I want there to be no misunderstanding. I am not attacking the press at all. I have never done that in this position, but I am making some very direct observations about the *Washington Post* and suggesting that this is a political—and saying that this is a political effort by the *Washington Post*, well conceived and coordinated, to discredit this Administration and individuals in it.

Ziegler was asked who told him there was no secret fund, and he wouldn't answer. He was asked whether he was denying the existence of the fund that the GAO had reported, or whether he was "quarreling with the word 'secret.'"

"I am not going to address the GAO fund," he said.

Finally, after considerable urging, Ziegler said John Dean was the person who told him there was no secret fund. In answer to a question on why the *Post* might be trying to discredit the Administration, Ziegler singled out Ben Bradlee as an individual who was dedicated to fighting Nixon.

Later in the day, Clark MacGregor and Senator Dole took after the *Post* again. Dole said that Katharine Graham, the *Post*'s publisher, had told someone at a party that she hated Nixon. Dole would not identify his source. Mrs. Graham denied making such a remark and also denied harboring such feelings.

At the *Post*, the reporters and editors met in Bradlee's office to go over the problem. Obviously the story was wrong. But was it wrong only in fairly minor details, or was it wrong in its central allegation? Woodward and Bernstein attempted to call Sloan but could only get to his attorney, who was not helpful. Woodward mentioned the possibility of naming our sources—but Bradlee and Simons dismissed the idea. Even had the sources lied deliberately, we couldn't use their names in the paper; it would break our pledge to them and it would be notification to all other sources that the *Post* could not be trusted to keep a confidence. If the sources had suckered us, we were trapped.

Woodward and Bernstein left the office, seeking the FBI agent who had confirmed the original Sloan report. They found him in the company of other people, but Bernstein, angry and upset, ignored them and asked him, "Did you mix up Haldeman and Ehrlichman?" The source nervously denied giving Bernstein any information. Woodward said he had been listening to the conversation and produced notes that he had typed afterward. One of those present said it was illegal for a third person to listen secretly to a telephone conversation.

The confrontation was becoming fierce. A year later, one of the other people at the meeting told me that the FBI agent was livid and in a rage, that his suit jacket flew open and the holster holding his gun was unbuttoned. "I was really afraid he might draw the gun," this person told me, "and I felt I had to calm him down. I was ready to restrain him by force if I had to."

The two reporters were ordered not to leave the building, and the men they were talking with disappeared for a moment. Bernstein called me at work. He was distraught and drained, and perhaps frightened. "Did they arrest you?" I asked. "No," he said. "Then get the hell out of there," I said. But the reporters wanted one more try at the source and his superiors.

"We are clearly wrong on the name," Bernstein told me before he got off the phone. "Nobody said it, but it's clear."

We had come a long way. We had been enterprising, aggressive, and careful, and now we were heartsick. Another reporter, Peter Osnos, wrote the denial story, featuring prominently Ziegler's slashing attack on the *Post*. It was displayed as the lead story in the newspaper, just as the original Haldeman story had been.

Long after we were through working we sat around, too bone-weary to get up and leave the office. Then, finally, Bernstein got through to Hugh Sloan. He asked Sloan what exactly was being denied: was it that Haldeman did not have access to the fund, or only that Sloan had not testified about Haldeman to the grand jury. Sloan said the denial "is strictly limited to correcting a factually incorrect statement." Would he say that for the record? No, he couldn't.

So we had not been wrong after all on the main thrust of the story, according to what Sloan told us, but we couldn't explain to our readers the exact nature of our error. We were under attack and unable to defend ourselves properly.

A few days later, just under two weeks before the election, we ran out of sensational Watergate stories. We had several small pieces but nothing of the kind we had become accustomed to. Woodward and Bernstein continued to work day and night but got nowhere. The other reporters on what had become an expanded Watergate staff were more or less occupied in simply putting on record what officials and politicians were saying about the bugging incident. The closer we came to Election Day, the more sensitive we would have been about last-minute accusations—but we didn't have any.

On November 7 Richard Nixon recorded one of the greatest election triumphs in the history of the nation, winning more than 60 percent of the vote and losing only in Massachusetts and the District of Columbia. At the *Post*, his victory meant a time to expect retaliation.

A reporter at the *Washington Star* told a friend at the *Post* that Charles Colson had called him into his office shortly before the election and promised that during the next four years the Administration would bury the *Post*. "Come in with your breadbasket and we'll fill it," he quoted Colson as saying. Confirmation of such a plan seemed to come when the President's first statements on what he intended to do in the next four years were reported in a lengthy, exclusive interview with Garnett Horner of the *Star*.

Some government officials in various agencies stopped notifying *Post* reporters of meetings and press conferences that they would in ordinary times have begged the *Post* to attend. When questioned, one high-level official said he had simply forgotten to call; another said, "You know how it is."

Colson, speaking before newspaper editors in New England less than a week after the election, sounded off at the *Post* and at Bradlee, a fellow Massachusetts native.

Ben Bradlee now sees himself as the self-appointed leader of what Boston's Teddy White once described as "that tiny little fringe of arrogant elitists who infect the healthy mainstream of American journalism with their own peculiar view of the world."

I think if Bradlee ever left the Georgetown cocktail circuit, where he and his pals dine on third-hand information and gossip and rumor, he might discover out here the real America and he might learn that all truth and all knowledge and all superior wisdom doesn't emanate exclusively from that small little clique in Georgetown and that the rest of the country isn't just sitting out here waiting to be told what they're supposed to think . . .

Weeks of testimony were presented before a grand jury consisting of twenty-three individuals who had no connection whatsoever with the United States government, and the grand jury in September indicted seven men, all of whom are now entitled to a fair trial under the judicial process.

An independent investigation was conducted in the White House which corroborated the findings of the FBI that no one in the White House was in any way involved in the Watergate affair. . . . That might normally have been the end of the Watergate story.

But, Colson said, the *Post*, which had perceived that McGovern was "in deep political trouble" before McGovern did, "with each passing day attempted to link the political shenanigans directly to the President of the United States, finally reaching Bob Haldeman." Colson then homed in on the errors the *Post* had made weeks earlier in the Haldeman story, exaggerating them.

Several days later, Bradlee said to me, "I haven't gone to a Georgetown cocktail party in two years."

The attack was on. All during the election campaign, letters to the editor at the *Post* had been a mixed bag, many laudatory but some highly critical of the Watergate stories. Weeks began to pass after the great Nixon election victory and we had no further exposés. Letter writers asked what had happened, wasn't this proof that the charges made against us were true?

That period was particularly painful for Bradlee and Katharine Graham. Though Watergate later came to be recognized as something of a triumph for the press as an institution, hardly any of its members had made genuine contributions to the story by then, and only the *Post* was being singled out for repeated criticism. From the time of the bugging arrests only *The New York Times*, the *Los Angeles Times*, and occasionally the *Washington Star* were to play any enduring role in breaking stories. *Time* magazine, with a reporter who had superb contacts at the Justice Department, was perhaps the leading disseminator of Watergate scandal news aside from the *Post*. Just before the election, CBS ran two segments on the Walter Cronkite news program that were mainly a compilation of material that had appeared in the *Post* earlier. Elsewhere, investigative reporting on the emerging scandal was virtually nonexistent. So when the time for abuse and retaliation came, starting before the election, it was the *Post* that once again was out in front—on the receiving end.

In the January–February, 1973, edition of *Columbia Journalism Review*, Ben H. Bagdikian,[*] a longtime media critic, noted that of 433 reporters based at Washington news bureaus with staffs of ten or larger, "fewer than fifteen were assigned full time to Watergate—some for only two weeks. . . . It is possible that more man-hours of investigative journalism were put into the 1962 rumor that John F. Kennedy had been secretly married in 1947 than were assigned to investigate the Watergate Affair."

Bagdikian cited bias in favor of Nixon as one reason for failure to investigate the scandal, noting that 93 percent of the newspapers that endorsed a candidate in 1972 had endorsed Nixon. His article, entitled "The Fruits of Agnewism," also charged that "the Nixon Administration's three-year war against the news media has succeeded. There has been a retrogression in printing newsworthy information that is critical of the Administration and a notable decline in investigation of apparent wrongdoing when it is likely to embarrass the White House."

The press was bad and television was much worse. Bagdikian noted that ABC and CBS had assigned no reporters to the scandal as it emerged, and NBC only one, after the Republican convention at the end of August, 1972.

---

[*]Bagdikian was a news executive at the *Washington Post* in the late 1960's and early 1970's, leaving shortly before the Watergate arrests of June, 1972.

So there was the *Washington Post*, out on a limb by itself. At work, Bernstein and Woodward spent as much time as ever on Watergate but continued to get no news. We had hoped that sources would open up after the election, but instead they got more close-mouthed. In the life of the Watergate story, six weeks may not seem like a long time. But it was a very slow, painful prelude to winter.

Then, the first week in December, our court reporter Lawrence Meyer brought to the office a certain pre-trial motion that had been submitted to Judge Sirica by Earl Silbert and the other Watergate prosecutors. In it was mention of a special telephone that had been used by Howard Hunt while he was a White House consultant. The phone was not connected to the White House switchboard, and calls made on it were billed to a secretary at her home in Alexandria, Virginia.

Woodward and Bernstein called the secretary, who had moved to Milwaukee, and she confirmed this account, saying the telephone was used exclusively by Hunt, that she was reimbursed by someone in Ehrlichman's office for the bill each month. An official at the Chesapeake and Potomac Telephone Company who had handled the White House business for twenty-five years said he knew of no similar arrangement there for anyone, ever.

The story indicated that some of Hunt's sabotage or spying had been conducted over this telephone while he was a White House employee. The fact that Ehrlichman's office manager, whoever that was, had approved the peculiar billing of business calls to a secretary's home telephone was very suggestive. The article was not among the front rank of Watergate disclosures, but it was solid enough to tell our readers that we were back in business.

The White House attack on the *Post* continued unabated. In one of the most bizarre episodes, a sixty-eight-year-old, white-haired matron, social events reporter Dorothy McCardle, began to be excluded from gatherings at the White House. The policy for years at the Executive Mansion had been to have a "pool" of reporters cover such events, not allowing everyone admittance because there wasn't enough room. But the local Washington press had been exempt from the pool arrangement since White House parties were considered local news.

Now Dorothy McCardle was singled out to wait in the press room for her colleagues to tell her what she had missed and feed her a few quotes. It seemed the most blatantly transparent kind of retaliation against the *Post* for its Watergate coverage, and many people thought it made the White House look stupid. It served to bring forth an extraordinary reaction from our competitors across town, the *Washington Star*.

All along, some reporters and editors there had objected to being recipients of White House largesse if it was part of a campaign of retaliation against the *Post*. When it became clear that Mrs. McCardle was being victimized, the *Star* printed an editorial suggesting very sharply that it would not serve as a White House tool for revenge against the *Post*. Mrs. McCardle was soon allowed back.

The most serious attack on the *Post* was one that the House Judiciary Committee later said it would investigate as possible grounds for impeachment of Nixon. Back in September, 1972, when Nixon said the *Post* would have "damnable, damnable problems," he, Haldeman, and Dean discussed challenges to *Post*-owned broadcasting stations. Three and a half months after that, as the deadline fell for challenges to license renewals at the Federal Communications Commission, only four challenges had been filed against TV stations in the entire nation. Three of them were against station WJXT in Jacksonville, the fourth against WPLG in Miami. Both Florida stations were owned by the *Post*, and both were considered among the most progressive in the nation, especially in terms of local news programming. People in the telecommunications business who had no relationship to the *Post* were startled by the challenges.

It was on notes like these that the year 1972 came to a close. The Nixon Administration, apparently confident that it had weathered Watergate, looked forward to the Inauguration on January 20, and Nixon himself to his second term in office, a term whose end, he assumed, would coincide with the 200th anniversary of the founding of the Republic.

Nixon later was to say that he had sat down on Christmas Eve, 1972, writing out some cherished goals for his four more years. He said he had written of his desire for a world of peace, an America of equal opportunity, jobs for all who can work and generous help for those who couldn't, a climate of decency and civility, and a land in which each person could be "proud of his community, proud of his country, proud of what America has meant to himself and to the world."

PART IV

Sirica, Gray, and McCord: The Turning Point

1

ON MONDAY, JANUARY 8, 1973, some 250 potential jurors were gathered in the U.S. District Courthouse in Washington. The Watergate trial was about to get under way. On the first day Judge John J. Sirica excused more than 150 people who said that a protracted trial would cause them personal hardship. On the second morning Sirica asked those remaining to stand if they had heard, read, or seen anything about the Watergate case, and only eight people remained seated. The judge asked one of them, "You didn't hear about the Watergate case?" She said, "No."

"You didn't read about it or hear about it on the radio?"

"No."

"Incredible," Sirica said.

He then proceeded to select twelve jurors and six alternates before the day was out, and had marshals accompany them home for some belongings and return them to the courthouse. They were sequestered on upper floors in modest rooms with glazed windows they could not see through for the following three weeks, the length of the trial.

Two defense attorneys charged that Sirica had ignored standard procedures in selecting a jury so rapidly, without giving them an adequate chance to ask questions. They said his actions would be grounds for appeal if their clients were convicted. But Sirica did things his own way and refused to be disturbed by such criticism; he had established quite a record for receiving criticism long before the trial began.

Sirica's reputation was that of a very tough sentencer, something of a publicity hound. In a court noted for its thoughtful and progressive jurists, he was regarded near the bottom in depth of legal knowledge, more a Sancho Panza than a Solomon. The son of an Italian immigrant, Sirica had the looks, manner, and speech mannerisms of a bus driver.

By 1972, Sirica's court had begun following new guidelines recommended by Chief Justice Warren Burger on the handling of major cases. Included was a procedure through which the chief judge was to assign the best available jurist, replacing the ordinary practice of selecting a judge at random, by lot. Sirica proceeded to assign himself to Watergate, saying it would be a time-consuming case and that while other judges had a backlog to contend with, he didn't. He had appointed himself to the last sensational case in his court, a bizarre murder that captured the attention of a blasé city. So it was not a total surprise that Sirica took Watergate. He liked the big ones. Nevertheless, because of the political overtones, one of the first questions asked about Sirica's conduct had to do with why he took the Watergate case.

On October 4, 1972, Sirica issued a broad, possibly unprecedented order prohibiting all law enforcement agencies, the defendants, witnesses, potential witnesses "including complaining witnesses and alleged victims, their attorneys and all persons acting for or with them in connection with this case" from making statements about the matter to anyone outside the court.

The motion requesting the order had been filed by defense attorneys and approved by prosecutor Earl Silbert, with both sides doing their best to end all Watergate publicity at the time. Sirica, who was ill when the order was prepared, signed it at home. It was so sweeping yet so vague that the judge couldn't explain exactly who was restricted by it and was himself uncertain of its legality.

Lawrence Meyer of the *Post* called the judge to ask whether the order meant that George McGovern could no longer discuss Watergate in campaign speeches. "That's a good question," Sirica said. "I tried to make it as broad as I could. I hadn't thought about it. I frankly hadn't given that a thought. I'll have to deal with that at some time, I suppose, but I'd rather not answer that question now."

Sirica agreed that the order might create problems where "we get into free speech and all that business," but he said that "was something we have to meet at the proper time. I have no comment. It may be raised, it may never be raised."

Compliance with Sirica's order would have forced the *Post* and other news agencies to stop reporting all Watergate developments except those that took place in court. By not talking to investigators, witnesses, or potential witnesses, reporters would be left to talk only to themselves. They could write columns of opinion, but they couldn't investigate.

Two days later, under widespread criticism, Sirica modified his order, striking the restrictions on witnesses, potential witnesses, and alleged victims. This action was proper, but it made the judge subject to the charge that he was erratic and hadn't really known what he was doing in the first place.

In December, 1972, Sirica jailed the Washington bureau chief of the *Los Angeles Times* when that newspaper refused to turn over to the court the tapes of an interview two of its reporters had conducted with Alfred Baldwin, the man who had monitored the Democrats' telephones from the Howard Johnson's across from the Watergate. The editor, John Lawrence, was the second person Sirica had jailed for contempt, the first being attorney Douglas Caddy, who had refused to testify before the grand jury.

Both the newspaperman and the attorney had noted an appeal of Sirica's ruling to a higher court before he ordered them incarcerated, and there were many who felt that Sirica had acted improperly. Neither man was detained more than a few hours, but, especially in the case of Lawrence, there was a sense that Sirica was unnecessarily exacerbating tension, highly felt at the time, over the rights of a free press.

The courtroom was Sirica's bus, and he did what he wanted with the passengers. His conduct of the Watergate trial in January, 1973, was every bit as arbitrary as his handling of pretrial activities. Had the trial of the Watergate Seven been a sensational civil rights case instead, Sirica would probably have been criticized as much as was Chicago federal judge Julius Hoffman for his handling of the Chicago Eight, which involved nationally known antiwar and civil rights leaders.

But the Watergate was not such a trial, and many who otherwise would have lashed out at Sirica for his bluster on the bench or his disregard for normal courtroom procedures were hushed by his obvious sincerity, his disgust at the coverup, and his incontrovertible leading role in bringing to light the enormity of the Watergate scandal.

On January 10, prosecutor Silbert laid out his opening arguments, basing his theory of prosecution in part on the concocted story presented to him months earlier by Jeb Magruder. Gordon Liddy had been allotted $250,000 for legitimate intelligence-gathering, Silbert said, and had received

$235,000 by the time of the bugging arrests in June, 1972. The government could account for only $50,000 of that; what happened to the rest was a mystery, Silbert said.

As he talked, the seven defendants and their attorneys sat around a large table. Liddy, with his back to the judge, took notes on a legal pad, occasionally rocking in his swivel chair, with a wide grin, his trademark, stamped on his face. Howard Hunt and Bernard Barker sat next to each other, with one sometimes leaning toward the other to whisper. Eugenio Martinez, who claimed to have been a wealthy businessman in pre-Castro Cuba, was calm and neatly dressed. His well groomed, graying hair helped give him an appearance of distinction. Sturgis, a Norfolk-born man who had sought adventure in Cuba, fighting with Castro and then against him, seemed emotionless, occasionally surveying the crowd in the large, ceremonial courtroom. Virgilio Gonzalez, the locksmith and "safe man," as he called himself, appeared the most apprehensive. James McCord, like Liddy, followed the proceedings closely but with some apparent detachment, almost as though Silbert was describing the actions of other people, not him.

In addition to the Watergate incident, Silbert laid out six other actual or planned acts of political spying against Democrats that had been run by Liddy or Hunt, including the placing of an agent in McGovern headquarters. He told how Hunt had tried to recruit former CIA agents to help, outlined the nature of testimony that could be expected from the many witnesses to be called, and displayed charts as visual aids, using a long pointer, like a schoolteacher, to show where the Democrats' headquarters were, and where, across the street, the telephone calls were monitored.

Silbert attempted to examine the motives of the defendants, saying that "obviously it was a political motive, political campaign. The operation was directed against the Democratic Party, particularly Senator George McGovern, because of his alleged left wing views." He said the interests of the defendants may vary, "the motivation of defendant Hunt and defendant Liddy may have been different from the motivations of the four defendants from Miami, and they in turn may have had a different motivation than defendant McCord." He then showed that McCord and the Miami men all were in financial need, with McCord having problems that were "very serious." Silbert made no attempt to further define the motives of Hunt and Liddy.

The main surprise in the opening argument was the introduction of the spy placed in the McGovern campaign, a young man named Thomas Gregory, who had first been accepted in Muskie headquarters as a volunteer and who was directed by Hunt, in April, 1972, to transfer to McGovern. Through Gregory, Silbert said, he would show that plans had been made to bug McGovern headquarters and that information on McGovern's campaign was passed regularly from Gregory to Hunt. Hunt paid Gregory $175 a week, in cash, at meetings in a drugstore or a hotel near CRP headquarters, only a couple of blocks from the White House.

Silbert's presentation was precise and formidable, as far as it went. He had introduced elements showing that Watergate was part of a wider campaign of political sabotage on behalf of Nixon, but he failed to explain how a figure as low in the chain of command as Liddy could be "the boss," as Silbert described him, or to what use the illicit information was put. Sirica had already warned that he would want to know whether higher-ups were involved, and Silbert did not address the question.

There had been rumors that one or more of the defendants wanted to plead guilty, and when Silbert was done, William O. Bittman, the attorney for Hunt, rose to ask that his client be allowed to plead to three of the six counts against him, conspiracy, burglary, and illegal wire tapping. Sirica noted that his practice generally was not to accept anything but a plea of guilty to all counts.

Bittman—the best known of the Watergate lawyers for his past work as a Justice Department attorney who handled the successful prosecutions of Teamsters leader Jimmy Hoffa and Lyndon Johnson's Senate aide Bobby Baker—pointed out that Silbert had agreed to accept the plea as presented. Sirica said he would consider the request.

Also on the first day, attorney Henry Rothblatt, representing the Miami men, likened them to foot soldiers, saying they acted in the belief they were serving both the United States and the cause of a free Cuba. Making an emotional appeal, and interrupted several times by Sirica who told him to "get to the point," Rothblatt said that Barker had given up his Cuban citizenship to join the American Army after the attack on Pearl Harbor. At that point Barker, an American born in Cuba who did indeed immediately enlist in the Army, leaned toward Hunt and whispered, "I was never a Cuban citizen."

The following day, while Thomas Gregory testified, Hunt changed his plea to guilty on all six counts, leaving Sirica no choice but to accept it. He faced a maximum thirty-five-year sentence and the certainty that he would be recalled before the grand jury for further questioning. Hunt, speaking to reporters after his plea, said that because of "the unexpected and tragic death of my wife just a month ago, I felt that I could not sustain the experience of a long trial. I felt that I should be with my children. I felt further that by pleading guilty, my plea of guilty might be taken into consideration at the time of sentencing later on and result in a perhaps, hopefully, lesser sentence."

Hunt was asked whether his testimony before the grand jury would result in the implication of higher-ups or the existence of a wider conspiracy. "I would testify to the following, gentlemen," he said: "to my personal knowledge there was not."

On the next day, Friday, January 12, the Watergate trial was thrown into a shambles. It was widely rumored that the four Miami defendants were attempting to follow Hunt's lead and plead guilty, and that their attorney, Rothblatt, had refused to enter the plea for them. No trial proceedings were held at all, as Judge Sirica met several times during the day in his chambers with the defendants and their attorneys, recessing the trial until Monday.

During the weekend, the press once again played a dramatic role in bringing to light otherwise hidden elements in the scandal. In the strongest story to appear in *The New York Times* in many months, reporter Seymour Hersh became the first to spell out publicly the details of hush-money payments to the four Miami men. Their attempt to plead guilty was suddenly seen in a new light—the trial, instead of opening up the Watergate scandal, had become the next step in the coverup.

On Monday, the Miami men formally entered their guilty pleas, and Judge Sirica, frustrated and angry, excused the jury and called the men before him. "I indicated more than once, and I am going to say it again, I want each of you to listen carefully. This jury is going to want to know somewhere along the line what purpose did you four men go into that Democratic headquarters for? You understand that question?"

"Yes, sir," Bernard Barker answered for the four.

"They are going to wonder who, if anyone, hired you to go

"I want you all to stonewall it, let them plead the Fifth Amendment, cover up, or anything else," Richard Nixon said privately to his closest associates on March 22, 1973. Publicly, on April 17, 1973, when this picture was taken, the President said, *"I condemn any attempts to cover up in this case, no matter who is involved."* (The WASHINGTON POST)

CHARLES W. COLSON: "*Colson would do anything,*" Nixon once said. *He is shown here with his wife as he pleaded guilty in June, 1974, to obstructing justice in the trial of Daniel Ellsberg.* (ASSOCIATED PRESS)

JOHN MITCHELL: "*I still believe that the most important thing to this country was the re-election of Richard Nixon,*" *the former attorney general said long after the coverup was exposed.* "*I was not about to countenance anything that would stand in the way of that re-election.*" (The WASHINGTON POST)

JOHN D. EHRLICHMAN approved a recommendation for a covert investigation of Daniel Ellsberg in 1971 by writing on a memo: "If done under your assurance that it is not traceable." On July 12, 1974, Ehrlichman was convicted of conspiracy and lying to a grand jury and the FBI in connection with a break-in at the office of Ellsberg's psychiatrist. (The WASHINGTON POST)

H. R. HALDEMAN: "You can say you've forgotten, too, can't you?" Haldeman asked Nixon and John Dean on March 21, 1973. Later, in testimony before the Senate Watergate Committee, Haldeman said about 150 times in answer to questions that his memory failed him. (The WASHINGTON POST)

JOHN DEAN,
shown here with his wife, Maureen, told Nixon on April 17, 1973, that "when history is written and you put the pieces back together, you will see why it happened. Because I triggered it. I put everybody's feet to the fire because it just had to stop."
(THE WASHINGTON POST)

JOHN J. SIRICA,
the chief U.S. District Court judge who liked to take the big cases himself, and who became a key figure in exposing the great coverup.
(ASSOCIATED PRESS)

SAM ERVIN:
"I think the Watergate tragedy is the greatest tragedy this country has ever suffered. I used to think that the Civil War was our country's greatest tragedy, but I do remember that there were some redeeming features in the Civil War in that there was some spirit of sacrifice and heroism displayed on both sides. I see no redeeming features in Watergate."
(The WASHINGTON POST)

ALEXANDER P. BUTTERFIELD said he felt the Senate Watergate Committee should know about the White House taping system but was concerned about embarrassment to the President and to the nation. (The WASHINGTON POST)

*G. GORDON LIDDY
laughed and rocked back
and forth in his chair
at the original Watergate
trial in January, 1973,
then fell into a stance of
silence, a grin almost
fixed on his face.*

DONALD H. SEGRETTI: It was the uncovering of political saboteur Segretti that led the Washington Post *to expose the Watergate bugging as only one incident in a large campaign of political spying and sabotage conceived by Nixon aides.*
(The WASHINGTON POST)

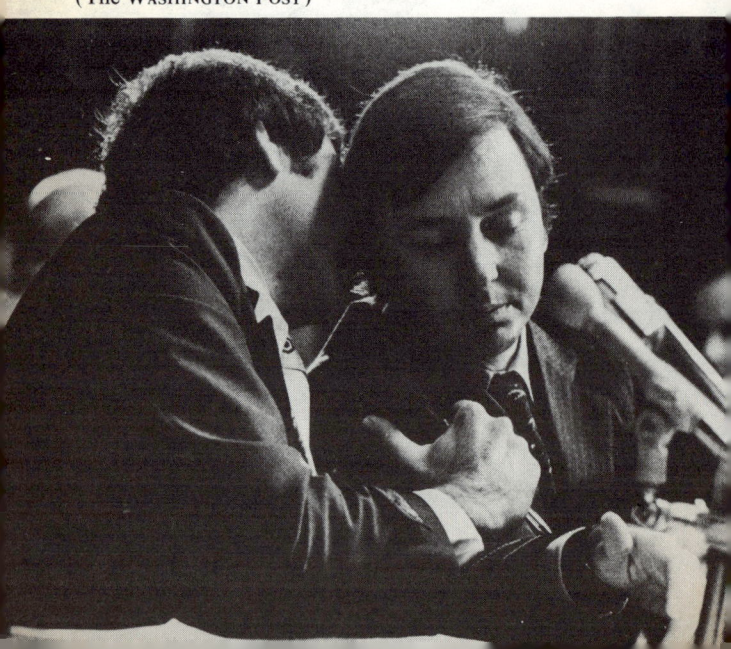

E. HOWARD HUNT, JR., shown here walking by his daughter, Lisa, asked Judge Sirica for mercy two days after getting $75,000 that has been described as "hush money" from the White House. (The WASHINGTON POST)

Shown at work at the Washington Post *are, left to right, Barry Sussman, Bob Woodward, and Carl Bernstein.* (WALTER BENNETT)

***L. PATRICK GRAY III**
was responsible for actions
that helped expose the
Watergate scandal, but had
to resign as acting director
of the FBI in shame for
having destroyed documents
given him by Ehrlichman
and Dean.* (The
WASHINGTON POST)

***RICHARD G.
KLEINDIENST:**
After years of loyalty and
devotion to Nixon,
Kleindienst, in one of his
last acts as attorney general,
apparently forced the
President's hand on the
Ellsberg case and blew the
Watergate scandal wide open.*
(The WASHINGTON POST)

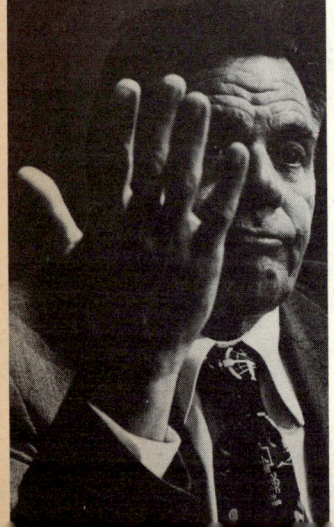

***HENRY E. PETERSEN,**
assistant attorney general
of the United States, a man
caught in the middle,
told Nixon on April 27,
1973, that he had cautioned
investigators: "We have to
draw the line. We have no
mandate to investigate the
President. We investigate
Watergate."*
(The WASHINGTON POST)

in there, if you were hired. I am just assuming they will be asking themselves these questions. They are going to want to know if there are other people, that is, higher up in the Republican Party or the Democratic Party or any party who are mentioned or who are involved in this case and should be in this case, you understand that?"

Sirica questioned each of the defendants, beginning with Martinez. "I want you to start from the beginning and I want you to tell me how you got into this conspiracy, how did it happen that you got involved? Do you understand what I mean?"

"Yes, I understand."

"Tell me in your own words what you did, how did you get mixed up?"

"I believe the facts that you have read in the charges are true and are just to the truth."

"That is a blanket answer," Sirica said. "I want to know specifics."

"I am sorry," Martinez said.

As he refused to be more responsive, Sirica moved to Gonzalez and then Sturgis, and neither was more helpful. They said they joined the break-in team thinking they were helping liberate Cuba.

To particularly dangerous questions, they sometimes answered in chorus. "Was there any statement made to you by Mr. Barker or anybody, Hunt or anybody else that you would be taken care of if you got into trouble or anything like that?"

"No, sir," they said.

"You deny that?"

"Yes, sir."

Sirica went around and around with Barker, seeking an explanation for all the money that had passed through his bank account. "Where did you get this money, these hundred-dollar bills that were floating around like coupons?" the judge asked. "Didn't you think it was strange, that amount of money coming through the mail without being registered or anything. . . . Where did you get that money that you used to pay those men's expenses?"

"Your Honor," Barker said, "I got that money in the mail in a blank envelope."

"I am sorry, I don't believe you," Sirica said and gave up. "All right. This is all I think I have to ask now."

The proceedings against the remaining two defendants,

Liddy and McCord, continued for another two weeks. In the middle, on January 20, an unseasonably mild Saturday as the trial had ended its second week, Richard Nixon was sworn in for his second term of office.

That morning the *Washington Post* had a special twenty-two-page section, entitled "The Nixon Years," and the word Watergate was never mentioned—a moratorium of sorts. The Inaugural Committee served as a temporary haven for Jeb Magruder, Herbert Porter, and several others on the election committee who were involved in Watergate, related spying, or perjury in covering up the scandal, as J. Willard Marriott, the chairman, Nixon's friend, provided them jobs. Magruder's position was director of the Inaugural.

In the traditional ceremony at the Capitol, Nixon, with Vice-President Agnew at his side, called on all citizens "to renew our faith in ourselves and in America."

"From this day forward," he said, "let each of us make a solemn commitment in his own heart: to bear his responsibility, to do his part, to live his ideals—so that altogether, we can see the dawn of a new age of progress for America, and together, as we celebrate our 200th anniversary as a nation, we can do so proud in the fulfillment of our promise to ourselves and to the world."

The President concluded his message on a religious note, saying, "Let us go forward from here confident in hope, strong in our faith in one another, sustained by our faith in God who created us, and striving always to serve His purpose."

As the parade moved that afternoon from the Capitol to the White House, the sidewalks along the way were lined with temporary stands and the event was televised in its entirety. At the U.S. District Courthouse, on Pennsylvania Avenue not far from the Capitol, Watergate jurors were for once allowed to look out of windows and watch as the President went by in triumph. They had heard nothing in court to lead them to believe that the events they were considering might ultimately lead to his ruin.

On January 30, after sixteen days of trial and testimony from sixty witnesses, Liddy and McCord were found guilty. Their attorneys said they would appeal, and McCord's lawyer, Gerald Alch, criticized Sirica, saying he "did not limit himself to acting as a judge—he has become in addition a prosecutor and an investigator." Not only did Sirica indicate that the defendants were guilty, Alch said, "but that a lot of other people are guilty. The whole courtroom is permeated with a prejudicial atmosphere."

That criticism rolled off Sirica's back. He was absolutely disgusted with the failure of his trial to answer any important questions. The judge saw one last ray of hope in upcoming Senate hearings on Capitol Hill. It had been during the month of January that Senator Kennedy completed his own quiet inquiry, and he and Senate Majority Leader Mansfield had decided definitely to hold a formal investigation. Kennedy was seen as a man who would appear too partisan to conduct an inquiry, and Sam Ervin, the elderly North Carolina Democrat, was chosen to preside.

Sirica passed the burden of uncovering the truth to Ervin in these words: "I would frankly hope, not only as a judge but as a citizen of a great country and one of millions of Americans who are looking for certain answers, I would hope that the Senate Committee get to the bottom of what happened in this case."

2

THROUGH FEBRUARY AND much of March, 1973, despite the threat of damaging Senate hearings, Nixon and his aides could see their way out of the Watergate in the not too distant future. They had survived two great hurdles, the election of the past November and the Watergate trial in January. If Nixon was tarnished, it was mainly in the eyes of those he felt would always be his enemies anyway—certain liberal elements of the citizenry, the media, and some members of Congress—and he had in the past been able to turn such opposition to his own advantage.

After the Inaugural, the White House went through a housecleaning of sorts, with those most tainted by Watergate removed. Dwight Chapin, who once was almost like a son to Nixon, had been publicly tied to Donald Segretti and was forced to leave government for an executive position at United Air Lines. Officially it was denied that Watergate, or Segretti, had played any part in Chapin's departure, but as one White House official said at the time, "any second grader" really knew better.

Jeb Magruder, who had considered running for attorney general in California, was given a high-paying position in the Commerce Department. The thought of finding even a higher position for him was abandoned because it was feared Magruder's perjured testimony might be revealed at Senate confirmation hearings, which were a requirement for those placed in most of the highest Executive branch positions.

Gordon Strachan, Haldeman's aide who had been liaison between Haldeman at the White House and Magruder at CRP and who had destroyed incriminating material from Haldeman's files, left to become general counsel to the United

States Information Agency, the government organization that dispenses publicity about this country in foreign lands.

Egil Krogh, who had headed the "plumbers," had remained untouched by unfavorable publicity. But Krogh had become balky about spying on his colleagues even before Watergate; he had lied to a grand jury in saying he did not know the Miami men who worked for Howard Hunt, and, in personal anguish, he left the White House to become Undersecretary of Transportation, at an annual salary of $42,500. At his Senate confirmation hearings Krogh said he knew nothing about Watergate.

Charles Colson—the one man so many people still suspected as having played a great part in the original Watergate bugging—announced plans to enter a private law practice as a partner in an existing Washington firm. With Colson's contacts, the firm of Colson and Shapiro* was expected to make a fortune during the second Nixon Administration. One of the first new clients was the Teamsters Union, which dropped the firm of Williams, Connolly and Califano. No doubt it was a particularly delicious retainer for Colson.

In the White House on February 28, 1973, John Dean, meeting with President Nixon for the second day in a row, said that "Chuck is going to be of aid when he is out there not connected with the White House, coming through with bits of tidbits."

Nixon emphatically agreed: "Sure, sure! In my view . . . I don't care what you think: Colson can be more valuable out than in, because, basically in, he has reached the point that he is too visible—"

"A lightning rod," Dean said.

"And outside he can start this and say that I am a private citizen and I can say what I (expletive deleted) please," Nixon said.

In meeting alone with Nixon, Dean was reaching a new plateau in his career. Through the many months of coverup, Dean had reported to Haldeman or Ehrlichman. He had kept many balls in the air at once—always a step ahead in the FBI's investigation or that of the grand jury, coordinating Nixon's lawyer Kalmbach and others in the secret payments

---

*David Shapiro was a successful attorney in his own right, and one who had defended civil rights causes and people who were the subject of witchhunts in the early 1950's during the era of McCarthyism. After Colson joined him, Shapiro became deeply involved in trying to extricate his new partner from the Watergate mess.

to buy silence from the Watergate defendants, helping shape the White House response to press reports, and serving as a calming influence to those who became flustered from time to time. Dean had proven to be exactly what Haldeman told Nixon he was the previous September 15—"One of the quiet guys that gets a lot done . . . the kind that enables other people to gain ground while he's making sure that you don't fall through the holes."

The Nixon transcripts show repeated statements of appreciation by the President for the fine work Dean had done in containing the coverup—many of them made even after the young counsel turned against the President and became his chief accuser. Now, at the end of February, 1973, Dean began what was to be a series of some thirty meetings and telephone calls with Nixon during a three-week period, almost all of them initiated by Nixon.

Dean was only thirty-four years old and he had made a wildly rapid advance. His role in containing Watergate had elevated him from the position of a competent messenger boy—a man with a title but little real responsibility—to that of a true presidential adviser on what he and Nixon knew to be the most important problem in the White House. Dean knew more about the coverup than Haldeman or Ehrlichman; he had become indispensable, or so it must have seemed.

As Dean entered the President's confidence, he had no first-hand knowledge of the President's personal role in the coverup until then, except for what Nixon had said in their September, 1972, conversation. When Dean later turned against Nixon, there was a gap in his testimony about Nixon's own role from September 15, 1972, until February 27, 1973.

By dealing only through aides in whom he had total trust, Nixon was free of fear that he would be caught in the coverup. People could suspect him of wrongdoing but they couldn't prove it. All that changed after Dean was taken into Nixon's confidence.

The Nixon-Dean meeting of February 28, 1973, was the first conversation between them during that period to be made public. It is clear that Nixon had been working earlier to prevent damaging Watergate disclosures from being revealed. As the conversation opened, Nixon wasted no time telling Dean what was on his mind. He was concerned about the Ervin Committee and he said, "I wanted to talk with you about what kind of a line to take." Nixon's deep fear of

Watergate was evident, even at a time when the coverup was running most successfully. In the past week or ten days he had met secretly with Senator Howard Baker, the ranking Republican on the Ervin Committee, in an attempt to arrive at some working arrangement with the committee, or at least to get a feel for what could be expected.

Nixon had agreed to what Dean said was a request by Baker that Attorney General Kleindienst serve as a go-between for the White House on the one side and Baker and perhaps Sam Ervin on the other. The President told Dean he didn't trust Kleindienst to work without White House guidance and instructed his counsel to "have it clearly understood that you will call him and give him directions and he will call you, et cetera, and so on."

Nixon's first concern was to prevent the committee from interrogating White House aides, and he laid out for Dean the elements of his strategy. As always, Nixon began from the premise that most people on Capitol Hill of both political parties were more his friends than his enemies and that accord might be reached through mutual agreement. He showed repeatedly that he was not leery of approaching Ervin with demands that anyone seeking a thorough investigation would immediately refuse. For example, Nixon said to Dean that "another possibility is the one that Ehrlichman has suggested. If you could have an agreement that the Chairman and the ranking member could question basically the same under very restricted . . ."—the sentence trails off but its thrust was that Nixon was hoping that Ervin would agree to a plan through which he and Baker, but no other senators and no committee staff, would handle the interrogation of present or former White House aides. Traditionally, the most knowledgeable people on Senate committees and the ones who make investigations a success or a failure are the staff members, not the senators. Such an agreement obviously would have crippled the Senate Watergate probe.

Nixon did not gain that agreement from Ervin, but he did win other concessions from him. Originally, for example, *all* senators on the committee could review files on Watergate being held by the FBI and the Justice Department, two Executive-branch agencies that dealt in investigation or prosecution of crimes. But Ervin, without even calling for a committee vote, agreed to a request by Kleindienst that only he, Baker, and Samuel Dash, the chief counsel, and Fred Thompson, the minority counsel, be allowed to see FBI files.

Concerned with privacy, Ervin said in explanation, he didn't want innocent people damaged by having FBI files leaked.

This agreement infuriated Lowell Weicker, who put out a blistering press release in which he said that it "cannot be permitted to stand because it would emasculate the function and effectiveness of the other Watergate Committee members."

The second element in the Nixon strategy, then, as he laid it out to Dean on February 28, was to find a way to enable the committee to help the White House without giving the appearance of helping. "I think we ought to cooperate in finding an area of cooperation," Nixon said. One method, discussed by Nixon in this conversation and by Haldeman and others at different times, was for the White House to adopt a very hard line on certain issues, such as who would be allowed to testify, and then effect a compromise, hopefully giving Nixon pretty much what he wanted and allowing the committee to appear to have faced up to the President at the same time.

With this in mind, Nixon instructed Dean to send Kleindienst to Ervin and Baker with a proposition on limiting testimony of White House aides that he knew they could not accept. The strategy, as initially conceived, was for Nixon himself to adopt an even harsher public stance at the same time. This, Nixon said, would make Kleindienst's "position be reasonable in the public mind. That is what we have in mind."

It was such routine politics that had been so successful for Nixon in blocking the Patman hearings before the election in 1972. Once again, because Nixon came to be so closely associated with the politics of enemies lists and retaliation, it is sometimes difficult to think of him indulging in anything so simple as commonplace bargaining. But the politics of cooperation—a favor for me and a favor for you—was the cardinal rule.

The tactic was to be employed, much more fervidly, when Nixon, the prospective defendant in an impeachment proceeding, began openly courting his probable jurors, inviting congressmen and senators of both political parties to the White House and taking them on little excursions along the Potomac in the presidential yacht. It was only then that people in great numbers realized that something was inherently wrong in the politics of cooperation as it had been practiced for so many years, for such cooperation among politicians meant that somewhere along the line the public interest was necessarily thwarted.

A striking illustration of this came during the February 28 conversation as Nixon and Dean briefly touched on one of the pesky situations they still faced in the Watergate coverup—the civil suit brought by Lawrence O'Brien and the Democrats. Through the practice of taking depositions from John Mitchell, Charles Colson, and others, the attorneys for the Democrats occasionally came up with damaging findings. Dean told Nixon that he hoped the suit could be settled out of court because the Democrats as well as the Nixon forces had problems.

"Hell yes, that is right—they've got problems, and we've got problems." Only through the politics of cooperation would it have been possible to settle such a suit out of court.

Through the summer and fall of 1972, before the election, and then continuing until and after the Watergate trial, this civil suit had served as an ongoing, effective means of exposing some of the facts of the scandal. Witnesses had been forced either to make occasionally damaging revelations, or to refuse to answer questions and give the appearance of harboring incriminating information, or to resort to perjury. Charles Colson, who had indicated publicly that he had hardly known Howard Hunt, testified in a deposition that they were social friends who had known each other for a long time. John Mitchell said under oath that he had seen McCord only once or twice, which later could have been the basis of a perjury charge against him.

Since the Watergate trial had been such a failure, the civil suit was the only forum in the criminal justice system for a continued airing of the case. It seems incredible that Nixon and Dean could have expected Democrats to settle the suit out of court. But the politics of cooperation made strange things possible. By April, 1973, at a time when settling that suit could conceivably have led to the complete rescue of Nixon, the new chairman of the Democratic National Committee, Robert Strauss, confirmed that as a result of secret meetings with John Mitchell, he had agreed to settle the suit for $500,000. It was only the glare of newspaper publicity that blocked a settlement then.

Nixon understood this role of the press, too—that its true danger to him was that by constant scrutiny the press could prevent individual elected officials and political groups from indulging in the normal politics of cooperation. Nixon was never frightened by personal attacks in the press; he knew they would subside eventually and that it was within his ability to nullify them somewhat by returning the pressure. "Colson's sure making them move it around, saying we don't like this or that," Nixon told Dean about the press and TV on February 28, 1973, and Dean said that such pressure was having "a sobering effect. We will keep them honest."

So while it was never stated exactly in these terms, at least not in a conversation that has been made public, the Nixon view of how to handle Watergate in early 1973 was to work as closely as possible with the Ervin Committee and to attempt to reduce pressure on the committee from the press and the public. Dean expressed a certain confidence that this could be accomplished, saying, "We have come a long road on this thing already. I had thought it was an impossible task to hold together until after the election until things started falling out, but we have made it this far and I am convinced we are going to make it the whole road and put this thing in the funny pages of the history books rather than anything serious."

But the President himself, while satisfied that he was moving in the right direction, was not so certain that all obstacles could be overcome, for there were Nixon enemies lurking—especially one, Senator Kennedy of Massachusetts. Dean told Nixon he was convinced that Ervin "has shown that he is merely a puppet for Kennedy in this whole thing. The fine hand of the Kennedys is behind this whole hearing. There is no doubt about it. When they considered the resolution on the floor of the Senate I got the record out to read. Who asked special permission to have their staff man on the floor? Kennedy brings this man Flug* out on the floor when they are debating a resolution. He is the only one who did this. It has been Kennedy's push quietly, his constant investigation. His committee did the (unintelligible) subpoenas to get at Kalmbach and all these people."

"Uh, huh," the President said.

"He has kept this quiet and constant pressure on this thing," Dean said. "I think this fellow Sam Dash, who has been selected counsel, is a Kennedy choice. I think this is also something we will be able to quietly and slowly document.

---

*James Flug, who was in charge of Kennedy's quiet Watergate investigation from October, 1972, through January, 1973.

Leak this to the press, and the parts and cast become much more apparent."

"Yes," Nixon said, "I guess the Kennedy crowd is just laying in the bushes waiting to make their move."

So Nixon and Dean discussed the next step—the possibility of leaking to the press information they hoped to get from a former high-ranking FBI official that would be damaging to the Kennedys. The official, William Sullivan, who had conducted wiretaps on newsmen and aides to Henry Kissinger in the early years of the first Nixon Administration, was said to have knowledge of previous abuses of government that could be linked to John F. Kennedy and his brother Robert. Viewing the White House tapes as a whole, it appears that Dean first brought up the possibility of using Sullivan to make it appear that any improprieties by Nixon were no different from those of the Kennedys, and that afterward Nixon kept pushing Dean to have Sullivan's story made public.

In their conversation of February 28, 1973, Nixon and Dean discussed other aspects of the Watergate scandal and additional ways of making inroads with the Ervin Committee.

The opening of confirmation hearings for L. Patrick Gray as permanent FBI director was scheduled for later that morning, and Nixon pointed to possible help from him. "Gray has to shape up and handle himself well," Nixon said, pointing out that Gray could be useful in working with Lowell Weicker. Gray, like Weicker, was from Connecticut. Weicker was an unknown to Nixon, a Republican who had received support and funds from the Administration in his 1970 election campaign.

"I think Pat has had it tough," Dean said. "He goes up this morning, as you know. He is ready. He is very comfortable in all the decisions he has made, and I think he will be good."

"But he is close to Weicker, that is what I meant."

"Yes, he is."

"And so, Gray—"

"Has a lead in there—yes," Dean said.

"One amusing thing about the Gray thing, and I knew this would come," Nixon said. "They say Gray is a political crony and a personal friend of the President's. Did you know that I have never seen him socially?"

The President also brought up the subject of Executive clemency for the convicted Watergate conspirators. "You know, when they talk about a thirty-five-year sentence, here is something to think about. There were no weapons! Right? There were no injuries! Right? There was no success! Why does that sort of thing happen? It is just ridiculous!

". . . I feel sorry for those poor guys in jail, particularly for Hunt with his wife dead," Nixon said. "Do they expect clemency in a reasonable time? What would you advise on that?"

"I think it is one of those things we will have to watch very closely," Dean said.

"You couldn't do it, say, in six months?"

"No, you couldn't," Dean said.

Nixon told Dean he would remain publicly silent on the Ervin Committee hearings if they progressed, according to his fondest hopes, in a commonplace, unrevealing manner. "Of course, if they break through—if they get muckraking," the President said—he would be forced to change his plans. "But the President should not become involved in any part of this case. Do you agree with that?" It was the Nixon politics of insulation; Dean certainly agreed. The President had already met secretly with one senator, was instructing his aides to deal with at least two others, and had said that a fourth, Senator Edward J. Gurney of Florida, could be expected to serve the White House well by instinct, without consultation.

As always, this insulation was crucial for Nixon. When Dean made his comment that Watergate would go on history's funny pages, the President disagreed, saying it would be regarded as "somewhat serious, but the main thing, of course, is also the isolation of the President."

In their February 28 conversation, Nixon also sought and received assurance that investigators had not asked his lawyer Herbert Kalmbach for material regarding his private affairs. Later, these private affairs—the President's tax dereliction, the financing of his estate at San Clemente and his property in Key Biscayne, a trust fund for his daughter, lavish assistance from his friends Bebe Rebozo and Robert Abplanalp, were to further degrade and humiliate the President in ways more immediately understandable to the public at large than any other single element in the Watergate scandal.

As for the bugging itself, Nixon, who was to say that he could have understood it had there been a need, described to Dean his incredulity on first hearing of the arrests at Democratic headquarters. "I thought, what in the hell is this? What is the matter with these people? Are they crazy? I thought they were nuts! A prank! But it wasn't! It wasn't very funny. I think that our Democratic friends know that, too. They know what the hell it was. They don't think we'd be involved in such—"

"I think they do, too," Dean said.

"Maybe they don't. They don't think I would be involved in such stuff. They think I have people capable of it. And they are correct in that Colson would do anything."

In what today reads as a dramatic forecast for Dean of the loneliness in the role he was to assume, Nixon spoke about how terrible life is for informers. There is little reason to think the President was issuing a subtle warning to Dean. This part of the conversation seems instead to reflect Nixon in one of his more expansive moments, harkening back to one of the high points of his career, the House Un-American Activities Committee hearings on communism in government in 1948 when Nixon was a thirty-five-year-old congressman.

Nixon told Dean about Whittaker Chambers, an ex-Communist and a writer for *Time* magazine when he testified against Alger Hiss in the hearings that were so instrumental in Nixon's rapid rise in national politics. Hiss was later convicted of perjury and imprisoned.

Nixon described Chambers as "the greatest writer of his time, about thirty years ago, probably *Time*'s greatest writer of this century—they finished him." He said Chambers was treated as a pariah because of his testimony against Hiss, and that "the informer is not one in our society. Either way, that is one thing people can't survive."

The Nixon-Dean conversation was a wide-ranging one that lasted for an hour and eleven minutes, as the President and Dean were first really coming to know each other. One can almost see the young counsel flush with embarrassment after making a remark—that congressional staffs are inadequate—and arousing the President's ire for it. "Don't try to help them out!" the President said, with the transcript indicating an expletive deleted.

"I'm not suggesting any reserve money for them," Dean apologized, and then, as if in an aside, he said, "I ought to keep my observations to myself."

But time and again in this conversation Nixon returned to the most important matter at hand, the need to keep his aides from appearing before the Ervin Committee. The talk ended with Nixon urging Dean to explain to Kleindienst that he was "the man who can make the difference," that "Kleindienst owes Mitchell everything," and that Mitchell could not withstand scrutiny. "Baker's got to realize this, and that if he allows this thing to get out of hand he is going to potentially ruin John Mitchell. . . . What the committee is after is somebody at the White House. They would like to get Haldeman or Colson, Ehrlichman."

"Or possibly Dean," the President's counsel said. "You know, I am a small fish."

"In your case, I think they realize you are the lawyer and they know you didn't have a (adjective deleted) thing to do with the campaign," Nixon said.

"That's right," Dean said.

"That's what I think," said the President. "Well, we'll see you."

Politics was chess. It was filled with threats, decoys, sacrifices. It could be played politely or like war, and after a few moves the best players had almost all their pieces in position, ready to attack or to protect the king at the same time. Nixon the master had gone over the entire board with Dean the pupil. But even the greatest chess players are sometimes taken by surprise.

3

> Mr. Chairman, we in Connecticut are proud of Pat Gray, and so am I. We in Connecticut respect Pat Gray, and so do I. . . . There is no question in my mind that as Director of the FBI Mr. Gray will perform his tasks on a completely nonpartisan basis. In all the years I have known Pat Gray he has never questioned the civil rights of individuals and the protection of constitutional guarantees. My feeling is that only the criminal has much to fear from Patrick Gray, and that the law-abiding citizen has nothing to fear from Pat Gray. . . . He has my unqualified support.

THE SPEAKER WAS Democratic Senator Abraham Ribicoff of Connecticut; it was the start of confirmation hearings on Gray's nomination as permanent FBI director on February 28, 1973, about half an hour after Nixon told Dean that Gray "has to shape up."

The second and last speaker on Gray's behalf as the Senate Judiciary Committee's hearings opened was the junior senator from Connecticut, Lowell Weicker, who also urged that Gray be confirmed, saying, "I believe he is a man of absolute integrity, and I believe he is a man of intellectual capacity, and I know that he believes not only in the words of the Constitution and the laws of this nation, but the spirit, and I think that is even more important nowadays."

In his own opening statement Gray spoke of his admiration for J. Edgar Hoover, of the need to open the FBI to increased press scrutiny, of his desire for continuity and change at the same time. He said he had pioneered in hiring the first seven women FBI agents and, also in keeping with the times, that he had relaxed the rigid dress and grooming standards for agents. The FBI had embarked on an equal opportunities program "to recruit more black Americans, Asian Americans, Spanish-speaking Americans, and American Indians." Gray pledged to fight organized crime and to guarantee that all civil rights complaints were heard fairly. He made no mention of his or the FBI's handling of the Watergate investigation.

The first senator to question Gray was committee chairman James Eastland of Mississippi, a Democrat who had received Nixon's open support in his last successful election bid. Eastland complimented Gray on his opening statement and broke the ground for what Gray knew would be his two most difficult areas: the problem of politicizing the FBI through its chief, and Watergate. From May 15, 1972, through the November election, Gray had made more than twenty speeches across the country. While some may have thought his speeches political, Gray told Eastland, the President had given Gray only one order when he appointed him acting director, and that was to stay out of politics. Gray said he felt he had.

As for Watergate, Gray said he was so proud of the FBI's investigation that "I am prepared to offer, and I have been prepared from the inception, that any member of the U.S. Senate, this committee, or any member of the U.S. Senate who wishes to examine the investigative file of the Federal Bureau of Investigation in this matter may do so, and I will provide knowledgeable, experienced, special agents to sit down with that member and respond to any question that member has."

Gray expressed the hope, however, that the Judiciary Committee "not get into the Watergate substantively," leaving that responsibility to the Senate Watergate Committee. Sam Ervin, chairman of the Watergate Committee, was also a member of the Judiciary Committee, and he told Gray that the timing of the nomination compelled him to ask questions he would rather have held off on.

Then, armed with an old *Washington Post* clipping of October 15, 1972, Ervin asked Gray what he knew about the assertion that a White House aide had shown Donald Segretti copies of FBI interviews.

Gray's answer was unresponsive. He said, "I think we only interviewed Segretti once, but I have to check that. Let me just check this record here. I know we interviewed him on the

26th of June and am just trying to see whether there was another date on which we interviewed him.

"My recollection, first, is that we only interviewed him on the 26th of June. I don't know whether we interviewed him a second time. We didn't look into that allegation at all as to whether or not he was shown any FBI interview statements."

Sam Ervin had a lot of questions on his mind; other senators wanted to ask Gray about issues far removed from Watergate, such as the safekeeping of FBI records, allegations that the FBI kept files on congressmen, the infiltration of FBI agents in radical groups, fingerprinting records, the motivation behind the recent FBI arrest of writer Leslie Whitten, an assistant to columnist Jack Anderson.

"Then you can't give me any information on that question," Ervin said, apparently ready to go on to his next line of inquiry.

It would have been easy for Gray to say, "No, sir, I can't." But he didn't. He would not let Ervin change the subject. Gray said, "I can give you information on it but I can't tell you whether or not he has shown those statements—that is what I cannot tell you. To give you that information I am going to have to take time to tell you how we progressed on this investigation."

Ervin did not push for any lengthy explanation. He simply asked Gray to confirm that showing someone the account of his FBI interview "wouldn't be a likely procedure to be permitted by the FBI, would it?"

"Of course not," Gray said.

"So you, at the present time, can neither affirm nor deny that statement," Ervin said. "I take it that you give the committee your reassurance that if any such event happened, that is, if any copy of the FBI interview was given to Mr. Segretti, it was not given by you or with your knowledge or consent."

"It was not done with my knowledge or consent, that is true," Gray said. Again, he could have concluded his answer there. "But I can go into it further if you want me to explain how it possibly could." On such slender threads, such unexpected and largely unnoticed moments in the actions of marginal figures, bit players of the world, does history ride.

"Yes, I would like to have that," Ervin said.

And at this point, on the very first day of his confirmation hearings, Patrick Gray effectively put to an end his own future in Washington and began to spin out, unsolicitedly, FBI findings that for the first time confirmed the most damaging assertions that had been printed in the *Washington Post* and elsewhere the previous summer and fall, adding additional details that had never been made public. For openers, Gray revealed that in mid-July, 1972, John Dean had asked him to provide "a letterhead memorandum because he wanted to have what we had to date because the President specifically charged him with looking into any involvement on the part of White House staff members." Gray said he began forwarding material to Attorney General Kleindienst to be given to Dean on July 21, 1972.

"So you see the possibility here, Senator, and I think what is being driven at is this, the allegation is really being directed toward Mr. Dean having one of these interview reports and showing it to Mr. Segretti."

No one other than Gray had brought up Dean's name. Until February 28, 1973, Dean had lived publicly at the periphery of Watergate—a White House aide who had reportedly investigated the bugging incident for the President, never seen, seldom if ever in mind.

Gray said that after reading the *Washington Post* article of the past October, he asked Dean whether he had shown the FBI report to Segretti and Dean said he hadn't. At that point, Gray said, he let the matter drop.

The role of John Dean began to intrigue other senators on the Judiciary Committee. Philip Hart of Michigan, a former prosecutor in Detroit, asked, "When Mr. Dean said to you, 'No, I did not do it, I didn't have the FBI reports with me,' did you ask him if he knew who might have had them with him?"

"No," Gray responded, "because the thought never entered—"

"Did you ask him whether anybody had done it?"

"You know, when you are working closely with the office of the presidency," Gray said, "the presumption is one of regularity on the conduct of the nation's business, and I didn't even engage in the thought process that I would set up a presumption here of illegality and I didn't consider it."

Gray said, however, again volunteering information that had not been sought, that after the *Post* story, he asked whether Segretti's political actions should be investigated, and "that opinion came back, no."

Hearing that, Robert C. Byrd, the Senate Majority Whip and one of the most powerful Democrats in the nation, questioned who it was that determined the scope of the Watergate investigation. Gray said the decision to limit the inquiry to the interception of oral communications, and to refrain from getting into more sensitive political areas, had been made by him "in conjunction with the Assistant Attorney General of the Criminal Division, and U.S. Attorney."

"Were you required to clear the scope of the investigation through the Justice Department?" Byrd asked.

"Yes, sir; we work very closely with them on that."

"But were you required to clear the scope of the investigation through the Justice Department, or was this a determination that you would make yourself?"

"No, I do not think it was a determination at all," Gray responded. "I could make a determination, but I would have to investigate what the Department of Justice told me to investigate."

Byrd asked whether Gray had ever discussed the investigation with anyone at CRP.

"No, sir."

"With Mr. John Mitchell?"

"No, sir."

"Or with anyone from the White House?"

"Yes, sir."

"Who?"

"John Wesley Dean, counsel to the President, and I think on maybe half a dozen occasions with John Ehrlichman."

There was always a certain rumbling, earthquake nature to the forces that pushed breaks in the Watergate coverup into view, compelling investigators to deal with them. One cannot ignore an earthquake.

By March 1, the second day of the hearings, the conduct of John Dean had become as important in the proceedings as that of Gray, the man whose nomination was under consideration. "Let me ask you this," said Senator John V. Tunney, the California Democrat: "when you make information available to a counsel for the President, and it appears that the information that you have made available is leaked or made available to third parties who have no right to it, do you feel, as director of the FBI, that you have any responsibility to see that an investigation is done of that White House counselor?"

Tunney asked that Dean be brought before the committee to testify. "Mr. Gray," he said, "I have no reason in any way to doubt your integrity. I think that you have handled yourself here as a person who is speaking the truth. But one of the reasons that I feel strongly that we ought to have Mr.

Dean come down and testify to the committee, and perhaps Mr. Colson, is that I am shocked, quite frankly, at the possibility that something that you, as director of the FBI, send to the White House could be used by White House counselors to disseminate to a man like Segretti."

In a matter seemingly unrelated to Watergate, Tunney and other committee members heard Gray say that it was Dean who had requested that the FBI give him a memo, written by International Telegraph and Telephone Company lobbyist Dita Beard, which had played so keen a role in an earlier 1972 scandal—the pledge by ITT to help fund the Republican National Convention at a time when ITT was seeking favorable Justice Department action in a huge corporate merger.

Under questioning from Senator Kennedy, Gray confirmed reports dating back to the summer of 1972 that there had been destruction of documents at the Committee for the Reelection of the President in the wake of the bugging arrests—another charge that had until then remained mainly an allegation printed in newspapers and magazines.

Kennedy, possibly more knowledgeable than other members of the Judiciary Committee because he had conducted his own Watergate inquiry, began asking a series of questions about the effectiveness of the FBI's inquiries into Segretti. Agents had obtained records of Segretti's long-distance telephone calls, and Kennedy asked, "Would there be any names on there—would you remember?" It was another question phrased in a manner that might have allowed Gray to say no, or to turn it aside in some other way. Instead, Gray said he would provide the answer for the committee's record at a later time.

Kennedy asked, "Now, was Mr. Kalmbach interviewed?" Gray said he was. "Can you tell me what questions he was asked by the investigators?" Gray responded, "No, I would have to go to the 302s and give you that specifically, which I am perfectly willing to do." FBI 302 forms are the reports written by agents after interrogations.

On the same day, March 1, Gray revealed for the first time that John Mitchell had intervened to block agents from interrogating his wife after Gray had approved a request for an interview with her.

"We endeavored to interview Mrs. Mitchell, but Mr. Mitchell said that Mrs. Mitchell's stories and the things that were in the press were not so, and we were not going to interview Mrs. Mitchell. There was no need to interview Mrs. Mitchell, and that was that," Gray said.

It is impossible to determine what was going through Gray's mind during these hearings. A blunt man and basically honest under questioning, the effect of his testimony was at first to salvage the reputation of the FBI at his own expense and that of the White House. But there is little reason to believe that Gray wanted to hurt either himself, Dean, or Nixon. During the hearings, he was in constant contact with Dean, and Dean, generally an astute observer, told Nixon he felt Gray wanted to be helpful.

On March 6, after a punishing third day of questioning, Gray was in touch with Ehrlichman, asking him to keep secret the fact that Ehrlichman and Dean had given Gray documents from Howard Hunt's safe. Through a conversation immediately following this one, between Ehrlichman and Dean, it was clear that the White House had given up on Gray. But it seems equally clear that Gray felt he and the White House were cooperating with each other. Both conversations were taped by Ehrlichman and have been highly publicized.

"Been testifying today?" Ehrlichman asked Gray in the first call.

"Yeah, I'm having a ball," Gray said. "I'm being pushed awfully hard in some areas and I'm not giving an inch and you know those areas and I think you've got to tell John Wesley to stand awful tight in the saddle and be very careful about what he says and to be absolutely certain that he knows in his own mind that he delivered everything he had to the FBI and don't make any distinction between . . . but that he delivered everything he had to the FBI."

"Right," Ehrlichman said.

"And that he delivered it to those agents. . . . This is absolutely imperative."

"All right."

"You know, I've got a couple of areas up there that I'm hitting hard and I'm just taking them on the attack."

"OK," Ehrlichman said.

"I wanted you to know that."

"Good. Keep up the good work, my boy. Let me know if I can help."

Ehrlichman then telephoned Dean, telling him that Gray "says he's hanging firm and very tough and there's a lot of probing around."

"Yeah, he's really hanging tough. You ought to read the transcript. It just makes me gag," Dean said.

"Really?"

"Oh, it's awful, John."

Dean told Ehrlichman that the Judiciary Committee might make no determination on confirming Gray until they heard testimony from White House officials, including Dean. Since Nixon had decided to refuse to allow aides to testify—and was having Dean prepare a paper on Executive privilege spelling out a legal basis for that refusal—Gray's nomination might be left hanging until the question of Executive privilege was resolved.

"Let him hang there?" Ehrlichman wondered, and completed his thought in a sardonic statement that will chill those who read about the Watergate scandal a hundred years from now. "Well, I think we ought to let him hang there. Let him twist slowly, slowly in the wind."

In response, Dean told Ehrlichman that those were also Nixon's sentiments. "I was in with the boss this morning and that's exactly where he was coming out. He said, 'I'm not sure that Gray's smart enough to run the Bureau the way he's handling himself.'"

As damaging as Gray's testimony was in the first few days, it was not until March 7, the fourth day, that the full sense of what a disaster he was for Nixon became truly apparent. In each of his preceding appearances, Gray had been asked some questions he could not immediately answer, and he had begun the practice of bringing in material on later days to be entered in the committee's record. Each morning, beginning March 1, Gray submitted documents such as correspondence regarding speeches he had made, or dates of FBI interviews with certain people, or even the summaries of specific FBI reports. Often these documents were not discussed at the hearings, they were simply entered in the record and forgotten.

On March 7, Gray introduced the material he had promised Senator Kennedy six days earlier in response to questions about FBI inquiries into Segretti and Kalmbach. It was ignored by committee members, who pounded him again on John Dean's role. But Bob Woodward, who was sitting in on the hearings although not covering them for the *Washington Post*, made copies of these documents, and that afternoon he and I studied them in sheer astonishment.

In answer to Kennedy's first question, which had to do

with Segretti's telephone calls, Gray's insert for the record said, in part:

> The greater majority of these calls did not appear to relate to the Watergate incident. We did learn that Mr. Segretti was in touch with the published telephone number of the White House on several occasions; with hotels in Miami, Washington, D.C., and Chicago; with Mr. Dwight Chapin's residence; and with Mr. Hunt, both at his office and his residence.

The second insert, dealing with Kalmbach, a lengthier one, said in part:

> Mr. Kalmbach said that in either August or September, 1971, he was contacted by Mr. Dwight Chapin and was informed that Captain Donald Henry Segretti was about to get out of the military service and that he may be of service to the Republican Party. Mr. Chapin asked Mr. Kalmbach to contact Segretti in this regard but Mr. Kalmbach said he was not exactly sure what service Chapin had in mind. . . . He said he did not press Chapin in this regard. He did contact Segretti and agreed that Segretti would be paid $16,000 per year plus expenses and he paid Segretti somewhere between $30,000 and $40,000 between September 1, 1971, and March 15, 1972. . . . He said the money he used to pay Segretti came out of campaign funds that were obtained from contributors prior to April 7, 1972. He said although he usually paid Segretti in cash, an occasional check may have been written.

Perhaps today, when the words "surprise" and "shock" no longer exist in the Watergate vocabulary, it is difficult to comprehend the significance of what Patrick Gray had so nonchalantly dropped into the public record. He had in a single stroke proven the authenticity of a number of the *Washington Post*'s most important pre-election stories—the ones that had brought the full wrath of the White House down on the *Post*.

For more than four months the Nixon Administration had attacked the *Post*, sought retaliation, and characterized its stories as without foundation, filled with "hearsay." Now, after the election and Nixon's grand triumph, after the inconclusive Watergate trial in January, at a moment when the coverup was succeeding so effortlessly as to be almost totally out of the public's mind, here was Patrick Gray, for no apparent purpose and certainly no personal gain, exposing all the lies beneath those carefully worded White House statements.

At the *Post* we wrote two stories that day, one on the Judiciary Committee's hearing, with its emphasis on John Dean, and the other on the inserts dealing with Segretti, Chapin, and Kalmbach. On the morning of March 8, 1973, Ronald Ziegler's White House press briefing was turned into bedlam.

Ron, will the President withdraw the nomination of L. Patrick Gray?

There's no plan to do that.

Dwight Chapin apparently was engaged in supervising political espionage; did it have anything to do with him leaving the White House?

Will you repeat the question?

[The question was repeated.]

I don't know how you draw the conclusion—

I draw the conclusion—

—that you base the premise of your question on, but Mr. Chapin's departure from the White House was announced and the reasons for his departure were stated at that time. . . . Gentlemen, let me make one observation to you before not answering your questions on this subject. We've been down this road many times and I looked at the stories this morning, and I have reviewed the stories and I have no further comment on them, because we've responded to them . . .

Do you consider it an invasion of privacy and sanctity of FBI files for raw and unevaluated information out of interviews to be turned over by Mr. Gray to Mr. Dean?

No, I don't. As you, I think should be aware, the counsel at the White House had an ongoing relationship with the FBI and always has.

Ron, since both Mr. Kalmbach and Mr. Chapin either do or have worked for the President of the United States and you are the President's spokesman, let me just ask you this direct question . . . just this very simple question: which man is lying?

That type of question . . . solidifies my intention to no comment.

On the morning of March 8, 1973, according to the White House, "the President met with Mr. Dean" from 9:51 A.M. to 9:54 A.M. in the Oval Office. Dean's own recollection of this meeting, as described in his testimony to the Ervin Committee, was the following: "I had a very brief meeting with the President on this date during which he asked me if something had been done to stop Gray from turning over FBI materials to the Senate Judiciary Committee. I told him I thought that the matter had been taken care of by the Attorney General."

In less than three weeks, the Watergate coverup was to be exposed to the public and a coverup of the coverup begun in the Oval Office. Patrick Gray's testimony was not the only rumble that warned of the earthquake, but it was the first. One day, while still testifying, Gray endorsed a contention by Senator Byrd that John Dean had "probably lied" to FBI agents. There was no way of predicting what Gray might say next, and on the following afternoon Nixon himself phoned Gray, possibly in fear that Gray, having exhausted the subject of John Dean, might launch into a discussion of the President.

4

ON THE TWENTY-FIRST of March, 1973, John Dean attempted to explain to Richard Nixon that the Watergate coverup had become more dangerous to the President than the crime itself, that some way had to be found to bring the affair to a close, not because of its illegality and immorality, but because it was about to collapse under its own weight.

The edited transcript of that conversation, made public on April 30, 1974, shows that Nixon time and again turned his back on Dean's pleas to stop the payment of blackmail to Howard Hunt. But it was not until later that several congressmen on the House Judiciary Committee, angered by Nixon's editing of those transcripts, revealed the final frantic order issued by Nixon to Dean and H. R. Haldeman on the need to pay Hunt: "For Christ's sakes, get the money."

The Watergate grand jury concluded that arrangements to pay Hunt were made immediately, apparently after a telephone call from Haldeman to John Mitchell. On March 1, 1974, Haldeman was indicted for perjury and obstruction of justice, and the President of the United States was listed as an unindicted co-conspirator, with this conversation cited in the indictment.

But the world did not know of the machinations in the Oval Office on March 21, 1973, and it was having a hard time coming to grips with the strange testimony of L. Patrick Gray III at his confirmation hearings before the Senate Judiciary Committee. On March 22, 1973, Senator Robert C. Byrd continued to use the hearings as a vehicle to inquire into the past conduct of John Dean, raising with Gray the possibility that Nixon had been betrayed by Dean much as other Presidents may have been betrayed by aides, or as Christ had been betrayed.

The Turning Point

On that note, Democratic Senator James Eastland, Nixon's friend, called a two-week recess in the Gray hearings—to "allow things to cool off a little bit," John Ehrlichman explained to Nixon that day. With the Gray hearings in abeyance there was no longer a daily forum to publicly examine possible White House interference in the handling of the Watergate investigation. Interest in the scandal had been renewed and heightened, but seemingly to no immediate purpose.

Then, on Friday, March 23, from a totally unexpected development, came the most substantial public revelation yet. It was a clear, brisk morning in Washington, the time for the sentencing of the seven Watergate conspirators by Judge Sirica. The judge had been unable to sleep all the previous night. Shortly before 10 A.M., as he went toward his court chambers, he had stomach pains and was quite concerned about them. But he stopped as he saw a reporter and said, "I'll have a surprise for you."

Sentencing was to be held in a second-floor courtroom, about one-fifth the size of the ceremonial room used for the trial in January, and the doors closed on an overflow crowd of newsmen and other spectators.

In the first row of the audience were Bernard Barker's dark-haired wife, daughter, and son-in-law, just as they had been during the trial. Also up front, in a corner, was a mild-looking, balding man who from time to time verged on falling asleep—Sam Dash, chief counsel to the Ervin Committee. In the last row was James McCord's wife with one of their three children, a teen-aged daughter.

Sirica had been unable to get to the bottom of the scandal. He was now to sentence Liddy, Hunt, and the others, and his job would be done. He had received thousands of congratulatory letters from across the country for his efforts to get at the truth, and though he had failed, he had much to be proud of. He was sixty-nine years old, and what might be his last case had been one of the most publicized trials in the nation's history. It had come at a time when the court system was under as severe an attack as most of America's other institutions, and Sirica, working in an impossible situation, had done as much as any single judge could do to restore confidence in jurists if not in the entire court system.

Sirica got right to his surprise. Three days earlier, he told the court, a probation officer had brought him a letter from McCord. The audience perked up. Sirica noted that it was not his practice to engage in private communication with litigants or defendants, and that he was therefore now making public the contents of the letter and would deal with McCord later. The letter said:

> Certain questions have been posed to me from your honor through the probation officer, dealing with details of the case, motivations, intent, and mitigating circumstances. In endeavoring to respond to these questions, I am whipsawed in a variety of legalities.

McCord explained that he saw strong reasons not to answer the questions: he stood to be called before the Senate Select Committee, he might be involved in a civil suit, there might be a new trial at some date, and, in all, his Fifth Amendment rights to keep silent meant that he did not have to respond to the judge. In addition, and more dramatically, the letter went on:

> There are further considerations which are not to be lightly taken. Several members of my family have expressed fear for my life if I disclose knowledge of the facts in this matter, either publicly or to any government representative. Whereas I do not share their concerns to the same degree, nevertheless, I do believe that retaliatory measures will be taken against me, my family, and my friends should I disclose such facts. Such retaliation could destroy careers, income, and reputations of persons who are innocent of any guilt whatever.

On the other hand, McCord wrote,

> to fail to answer your questions may appear to be non-cooperation, and I can therefore expect a much more severe sentence. . . . In the interests of justice, and in the interests of restoring faith in the criminal justice system, which faith has been severely damaged in this case, I will state the following to you at this time which I hope may be of help to you in meting out justice in this case:
> 1. There was political pressure applied to the defendants to plead guilty and remain silent.
> 2. Perjury occurred during the trial in matters highly material to the very structure, orientation, and impact of

the government's case, and to the motivation and intent of the defendants.

3. Others involved in the Watergate operation were not identified during the trial, when they could have been by those testifying ...

Following sentence, I would appreciate the opportunity to talk with you privately in chambers. Since I cannot feel confident in talking with an FBI agent, in testifying before a grand jury whose U.S. attorneys work for the Department of Justice, or in talking with other government representatives, such a discussion with you would be of assistance to me.

McCord had cracked. After an eight-month wall of silence, few if any had expected one of the conspirators to talk. But that McCord should be the first to finally do so seemed to make some sense. Liddy was a fanatic. Hunt was a spy. The four Miami men were only taking orders; they didn't seem to know much and they may have been more afraid to talk than not to. McCord, it was true, had been a CIA employee for nineteen years—but trained as a technician, not a spy. He had more of the middle class about him; he had married his sweetheart from college in Texas and had established roots in the Maryland suburbs of Washington.

McCord was a member of the community; he found time to attend reserve meetings and teach occasional classes on security, even electronic surveillance, at a local college. The pastor of the United Methodist Church in suburban Rockville, Maryland, had been a character witness at the trial and described McCord as a parishioner who had "done a great deal for our church. . . . Of all the people in our church, if you were to pick the half dozen best persons, I'd say he is one of them."

McCord was also a family man. He had a son who was a cadet in the Air Force Academy at the time of the arrests, the daughter in court with his wife, and a third child who was retarded. In breaking his long silence, McCord, from all appearances, had made a simple decision: he didn't want to leave his family and go to prison. Court proceedings had barely begun when Sirica, his stomach pains getting worse, called a twenty-minute recess. Reporters ran from the courtroom, jumped over guide ropes outside, quickly photostated copies of McCord's letter and telephoned the news to their editors. The judge stretched out on a couch in his chambers.

His clerk wanted to call a doctor or a nurse, but Sirica, afraid of what reporters would think, said, "Just give me Pepto-Bismol or something." A reporter from the Hearst newspapers wandered in and the judge threw him out. The pain was worse when the twenty minutes were over, and Sirica considered adjourning for the day. But in another ten minutes he began to feel better.

When court reconvened, Gordon Liddy, almost twenty pounds lighter than at his trial, drawn and haggard after a self-imposed 900-calorie diet while in jail awaiting sentencing ("The food is starchy," he had said), was called before Sirica. Entering the courtroom earlier, Liddy had made his traditional wave to the audience and saluted his co-conspirators. But there were few other such displays. Liddy was subdued.

It was 10:45 A.M. Liddy, his arms folded at his chest, stood before the judge. His lawyer, Peter Maroulis from Poughkeepsie, New York, where Liddy had been a prosecutor, asked Sirica for clemency, speaking of Liddy's contributions to society. Liddy was the first of the seven being sentenced, and the others listened intently. Bernard Barker, slightly slouched over the defense table, head in hands, suffered a twitching spasm at his mouth. Howard Hunt, who was to be the next one before the judge, sat motionless, his mouth stoic and his eyes forming a pained, how-did-this-happen-to-me expression.

In the audience a CBS reporter snickered as Maroulis described Liddy as the author of a film, *Stay Alert and Stay Alive,* used, Maroulis said, in a training program for police officers. As Maroulis spoke into a microphone, Liddy, a man used to arranging things, reached out and sharply tapped the microphone three times for sound. Maroulis completed his plea, pointing out that in a few moments Sirica would pass sentence and, as of then, Liddy a lawyer, would be barred for life from working at his profession. He asked the judge to consider that in sentencing.

Gordon Liddy was a strange, awesome man who had long since settled into a stance of silence. His constant grin made it appear that his mind was somewhere else, always pondering a happy secret. After the trial and before the sentencing he had begun to get into fights with black inmates at the District of Columbia jail. He feared no man, always held his own, and in a short time had gained great respect for his courage and for the fact that he had put his legal training to use, becoming the chief jailhouse lawyer.

One uneducated inmate astounded a prosecutor when he explained to a grand jury that no case could be pressed against him because he had "transactional immunity."

"Where did you hear that?" the prosecutor asked.

"My lawyer told me," the inmate said.

"Who's your lawyer?"

"Watergate Liddy."

Liddy's wife, a schoolteacher in the District of Columbia, said she regarded Liddy as a prisoner of war, that what he had done was in the service of his country.

But there was a darker side to Liddy. One of the Watergate prosecutors despised him, seeing in him the mentality and nature of a man who sends people into gas ovens. At his home in suburban Maryland, in a transient neighborhood largely comprised of military families living in modest houses, Liddy had shelves lined with books on Germany, including *Mein Kampf* and the postwar books with swastikas on their jackets, displayed where they would be noticed by visitors.

When Maroulis was finished speaking, Judge Sirica asked, "Do you want to speak, Mr. Liddy?"

"I have nothing to say, Your Honor," answered Liddy.

After then hearing prosecutor Earl Silbert describe Liddy as "the leader," the "person with the money," the "most blameworthy," Sirica pronounced sentence.

"From the evidence presented in the course of these proceedings," he said, "the court has reached the opinion that the crimes committed by these defendants can only be described as sordid, despicable, and thoroughly reprehensible." The statement the judge was reading from was titled "Sentencing: Liddy and McCord." It seemed clear that it had been prepared before Sirica received McCord's letter, since McCord was not being sentenced.

"Suffice it to say that the sentences which the court will now impose, are the result of careful thought extending over a period of several weeks," Sirica said. He sentenced Liddy on six counts dealing with burglary and wiretapping, ordering him confined for a minimum of six years, eight months, to a maximum of twenty years. Liddy was to stay "committed until his fine of $40,000 is paid or he is otherwise released in a court of law."

Maroulis asked if Liddy could serve his time in the Danbury, Connecticut, federal prison for convenience. To Sirica that was immaterial. He agreed and waved them off.

"Thank you, Your Honor," said Liddy. He went to his seat

and rocked occasionally but not with his usual ebullience. Even his grin was a bit narrower.

It was Howard Hunt's turn to stand before Sirica, and the courtroom was hushed. Defense attorney William Bittman described Hunt as a man who had devoted his "entire adult life" to his country and had accepted "all of his assignments without questioning them."

Hunt had played a principal role in the "successful overthrow of the Communist regime in Guatemala in 1954" and later worked for the U.S. government against Fidel Castro in 1960 and 1961. "In 1971, Mr. Hunt was contacted by a member of the presidential staff and asked to contribute his background in two specific areas of great significance to our country: combatting narcotics and the declassification of material of the highest national security significance." Hunt, Bittman said, had a motive in the Watergate bugging—to ascertain whether "foreign money was going to the Democrats." No individual had been damaged by Hunt's actions, the lawyer said, and he asked that Hunt be given a suspended sentence with a probationary period.

"Do you have anything to say, Mr. Hunt?" the judge asked. Hunt, who had just received the last installment of hush money from the White House, read in an even voice from a prepared statement.

> What I did was wrong, unquestionably wrong in the eyes of the law, and I can accept that. For the last eight months I have suffered an ever-deepening consciousness of guilt, of responsibility for my acts, and of the drastic penalties they entail. I pray however that this court—and the American people—can accept my statement today that my motives were not evil . . .
>
> Because of what I did, I have lost virtually everything I cherished in life—my wife, my job, my reputation. Surely these tragic consequences will serve as an effective deterrent to anyone else who might contemplate engaging in a similar activity.
>
> I am entirely conscious, Your Honor, that what is done to me from this time on is in your hands alone. The offenses to which I pleaded guilty were not crimes of violence. To be sure, they were an affront to the state, but not to the body of a man or to his property. The real victims of the Watergate conspiracy, Your Honor,

as it has turned out, are the conspirators themselves. But there are other prospective victims.

> Your Honor, I am the father of four children, the youngest a boy of nine. Had my wife and I not lost our employment because of Watergate involvement, she would not have sought investment security for our family in Chicago, where she was killed last December. My children's knowledge of the reason for her death is ineradicable—as is mine. Four children without a mother. I ask that they not lose their father, as well.

In making such a plea, Hunt was aiming it at a judge who had married at age forty-seven and who, twenty-two years later, was known to dote on his own two children. Sirica was said to be as soft at home as he was harsh on the bench. Hunt went on, saying that his "family desperately" needed him.

"I have lost everything, Your Honor—friends, reputation—everything a man holds dear—except my children, who are all that remain of a once happy family. . . . I have suffered agonies I never believed a man could endure and still survive. . . . My fate—and that of my family—my children—is in your hands."

Daniel Schultz, the young new attorney for the four Miami men, who had replaced Henry Rothblatt, then spoke briefly on their behalf. None of the men made a statement. Prosecutor Silbert said that their participation had been induced by Hunt and they "had been captives" of their first attorney who refused to plead them guilty. As for Hunt, Silbert said he did feel Sirica should consider his family situation in sentencing but pointed out that Hunt was "an organizer and a leader" in the bugging and that made "his conduct so culpable and blameworthy."

Judge Sirica was not moved by Hunt's appeal. During the days that Hunt, the writer of novels, had been preparing it, perhaps lingering before deciding to use the word "mercy" four times, Sirica also had been preparing. "I was ready," Sirica told me later on. "I worked very hard on this."

Sirica told the defendants that they would all serve maximum sentences unless they finally decided to talk. "You must understand that I hold out no promises or hopes of any kind to you in this matter, but I do say that should you decide to speak freely, I would have to weigh that factor in appraising what sentence will finally be imposed in each case.

Other factors will, of course, be considered, but I mention this one because it is one over which you have control."

The judge gave provisional sentences of 40 years and a $50,000 fine to each of the four Miami men, and 35 years and a $40,000 fine to Hunt, with final sentences to be pronounced in three months. He said that if he couldn't decide by then, there would be an extension. The message was simple. If the defendants still wanted to remain silent, they would pay dearly.

Hunt and the Miami men returned to their seats. Hunt sat expressionless, as he had all day. His plea for mercy hadn't worked; on Nixon's instructions he had just been paid off by the White House to maintain silence; he was fifty-four years old and faced with the threat of rotting in prison the rest of his life.

Court activities were not yet done. McCord was called before the judge for a discussion of his request to meet privately with Sirica. Nervously McCord held his eyeglasses between his fingers, clasping his hands first in front, then behind him. His eyes were lowered. From the rear of the courtroom, his wife strained forward.

Sirica spoke about McCord's startling letter. "This court has a strict policy not to consult with litigants or defendants," Sirica said. He told how the probation officer had come into his chambers on March 20, and how the judge had called in a court reporter because he wanted a record of their conversation. Finally he said, "In this particular case, if Mr. McCord wants to speak with me . . . it must be done in court with a court reporter. I will not enter into any agreement that my lips will be sealed."

Prosecutor Silbert then told the court that he intended to reconvene the grand jury and reopen the investigation in three days, on Monday, and asked that the prisoners be kept in the Washington area so that he could call them to testify. Sirica told Silbert not to be in a hurry. "Let the defendants think over what I've told them. Let them come back in a week."

The courtroom cleared, and there were press conferences outside, in little bunches around Liddy's lawyer, Maroulis, around other defense lawyers, and around Sam Dash of the Ervin Committee. "What Judge Sirica has done has given us a greater opportunity to get information that might not otherwise be known," Dash said.

Court was over for the day. The President was in Key Biscayne and deputy White House press secretary Gerald Warren issued a statement from there. "It is the consistent policy of the Nixon Administration not to comment on matters in this trial or any other pending trial. It is a policy that we will religiously follow while there is a judicial process in motion. I believe I would leave it at that."

The Justice Department, stung by McCord's charge that he could not "feel confident in talking with an FBI agent" or before the U.S. attorneys, also issued a statement, which was telephoned to newspapers by a spokesman for Attorney General Kleindienst. Given the nature of McCord's testimony, the statement was not very comforting. It said that if McCord's letter "contains information supporting these allegations or indicting any other violation of federal law, the Department of Justice will, of course, take appropriate action immediately." The statement seemed an example of political language as once described by George Orwell: "Designed to make lies sound truthful and murder respectful, and to give an appearance of solidity to pure wind."

PART V
Collapse of the Coverup

1

IT WAS NOT until the end of March, 1973, that the Watergate story began to publicly ensnare Richard Nixon. Even then, at first, the question was not what illegal acts Nixon might have conspired in, but rather how his presidency was or would be affected by the scandal.

After Judge Sirica's sentencing on Friday, March 23, Sam Dash and other Ervin Committee staff members met with McCord immediately and again on Saturday. On Sunday Dash called a press conference to announce that McCord had begun to implicate others in the Watergate bugging, but Dash would not say whom. Sunday night a report by the *Los Angeles Times* quoted McCord as saying that John Dean helped plan the bugging and that Jeb Magruder had known about it in advance.

This article and others in ensuing days from a number of news agencies introduced a new element to the Watergate saga: the striving among competing papers and the news magazines for a Watergate exclusive. The *Post* was to remain in the forefront of those reporting the scandal, but its days of being almost alone in Watergate coverage were over.

In his book, *The Center, People and Power in Political Washington*, the late Stewart Alsop likened the Washington press corps to beagles hunting rabbits, ". . . each beagle yelping like mad in order to convince the onlookers that he was really the first to pick up the scent. Sometimes the scent is actually that of a rabbit, but quite often the beagles, as they chase each other around in circles, giving tongue lustily, are simply smelling each other."

Alsop referred to reporters in packs, striving for the same story whether or not it was important, simply because it was fashionable. Watergate, which was obviously important, had suddenly become fashionable as well, and the reporter-beagles began their incredibly long and loud hunt. The rabbit was the President of the United States, and they chased him all over the capital. For days on end, masses of ten reporters or more would wait in the corridors of the U.S. District Courthouse, for example, keeping watch on the entryway to the grand jury quarters to see whether any Nixon aides were called to testify.

Television networks began stationing camera crews at the homes of people like McCord, Dean, and then Ehrlichman and Haldeman, and pictures were published or flashed on TV showing the wives of prominent men opening their doors in nightclothes to take in the morning newspaper.

Time magazine and *Newsweek* became caught up in a competition between themselves, expending more space on Watergate than on any single subject in the past. Eight-, ten-, twelve-page sections on the scandal became commonplace. Breaking their normal procedure of releasing their exclusive stories on Sunday, a day in advance of publication, these magazines began releasing Watergate news on Saturday in order to have their reports included in the big Sunday newspapers.

This fierce competition and the consequent constant glare of publicity would not have been possible without news leaks. Traditionally, before Watergate, a news leak was most often an attempt by a public official to put out a self-serving message or to float a trial balloon. Often the official would call a friendly reporter; the leak seemed newsworthy and was printed. At other times the official might subtly allow the reporter to believe he had uncovered the information. As the transcripts of Nixon conversations demonstrated, the President and his aides saw selected leaks as an important means of getting their message before the public, sometimes trying to spread scurrilous or misleading stories.

The *Post*'s early Watergate coverage, in my view, resulted from anything but leaks. From the beginning, what leaks we got, such as those from the White House suggesting that the bugging might have been the result of a right-wing Cuban conspiracy, were attempts to steer us away from the true story. Instead, our reportage consisted of hard footwork on the part of Woodward and Bernstein, who got little scraps of information from minor figures on the periphery of the scandal. Through persistence and imaginative questioning, the two reporters would piece together enough of a story to put a case before investigators or sources close to the investigation, who would either confirm or deny their findings. Occasionally such sources, like Deep Throat, would be of more help, but not often.

At the end of March, 1973, however, as the burden of the Watergate inquiry shifted from the criminal justice system to the Ervin Committee, news leaks of massive proportions occurred. Senators and committee staff members began feeding reporters much of what they were uncovering. These leaks most often amounted to nothing more than advance disclosure of testimony or the release of documents. Grounded in fact, they were not trial balloons or self-serving messages in the traditional sense of leaks. But they were extremely embarrassing to the Nixon forces, and once more, the President's men, instead of responding to the information revealed, began trying to obfuscate the issue by charging that the leaks were politically motivated. Ronald Ziegler, for one, attempted to discredit the Ervin Committee because of the leaks and thereby turn public attention away from the White House. But the leaks continued, and every day the scandal loomed larger. It would take a complete book to describe the atmosphere and events in Washington as the Watergate coverup began to collapse, exposing with it other illegal campaign maneuvers on behalf of Nixon and the unethical practices of the first Nixon Administration. But a review of some of the newspaper stories may give a feel of what it was like:

March 26: Senator Weicker said he had established independently that White House aides were involved in the Watergate bugging, and the Ervin Committee voted to permit live television coverage of its hearings.

March 27: Martha Mitchell telephoned *The New York Times* and said, "I fear for my husband. I'm really scared. I have a definite reason. I can't tell you why. But they're not going to pin anything on him; I won't let them."

March 28: Howard Hunt was given immunity from further prosecution and testified for four hours before the grand jury. (Later it was learned that Hunt lied repeatedly in this appearance before the grand jury.)

March 29: Republican Senators Charles McC. Mathias, Jr., of Maryland and Robert Packwood of Oregon demanded that a special prosecutor be appointed to investigate the scandal.

The *Washington Post* and several other newspapers reported that McCord had told the Ervin Committee that Mitchell approved plans for the bugging of Democratic headquarters, and the *Post* said that McCord claimed to have knowledge of other illegal wiretaps.

March 30: President Nixon said that White House aides would be allowed to testify before the grand jury, a move immediately seen and reported as an attempt to keep the investigation in the criminal justice system in hopes that the White House could control it. At the same time, Nixon offered to allow his aides to testify in closed sessions before the Ervin Committee.

Gordon Liddy was given immunity from further prosecution but refused to testify before the Watergate grand jury. (In a successful ploy unknown to reporters, prosecutors Silbert, Glanzer, and Campbell kept the silent Liddy sitting in a small room for hours and asked his attorney, Peter Maroulis, to notify the reporters outside that Liddy had cooperated. Instead, Maroulis stormed out and told the press that Liddy was remaining silent—exactly as the prosecutors hoped he would. Apparently John Dean, among others, viewed Maroulis's extreme protestations as an indication that Liddy had indeed begun to talk, and this belief added to the growing pressure on Dean. It has been regarded by some as a contributing factor in Dean's instructing his attorneys to begin speaking to the prosecutors, which they did three days later.)

April 1: Weicker, on a Sunday television interview program, launched into an attack on H. R. Haldeman, saying that in his position as White House chief of staff he was responsible for the bugging and other campaign violations whether he knew about them or not.

April 2: Senator Ervin said that White House aides were not "royalty or nobility" and had to testify under oath before his committee.

Senator Muskie charged that Nixon was exerting one-man rule over the budget, inflation, and the Watergate case.

April 3: Weicker said that Haldeman should resign. Liddy was held in contempt of court for refusing to testify to the grand jury and had an indefinite term added to his earlier sentence.

April 5: Patrick Gray asked Nixon to withdraw his nomination as permanent FBI director, and Assistant Attorney General Henry Petersen was seen as one possible replacement. But Petersen's role as the man in charge of the Watergate investigation, it was speculated, might rule him out. *The New York Times* said that Nixon was considering the nomination of Federal Judge W. Matthew Byrne, who was then conducting the trial of Daniel Ellsberg in Los Angeles.

April 6: The Wall Street Journal published the results of a nationwide poll, asserting that a majority of Americans felt President Nixon had been aware of the coverup before it was exposed.

April 10: Attorney General Kleindienst, appearing at an extraordinary joint session of three Senate and House committees, said the principle of separation of powers entitled Nixon to prevent all two and a half million Executive branch employees from testifying before Congress. The Congress could move against a President in only one way, Kleindienst said—through impeachment. Senator Ervin asked how Congress could impeach the President if he could keep all the witnesses from attending, and Kleindienst said Congress didn't need facts to impeach, only votes.

April 11: Bob Woodward and Carl Bernstein reported in the *Washington Post* that Mitchell aide Frederick C. LaRue had received $70,000, possibly for use as hush-money payments to the Watergate conspirators.

Senator Barry Goldwater urged Nixon to "clear up Watergate now," likening the scandal to the Teapot Dome affair of the 1920's.

April 12: Woodward and Bernstein reported that McCord had testified to the Ervin Committee that John Mitchell had been shown logs of the wiretaps at Watergate during the three weeks of the bugging.

Vice-President Agnew said he was "appalled" by Watergate, and growing numbers of Republican senators demanded that Nixon aides testify under oath before the Ervin Committee.

2

ON THE TWELFTH of April, we learned that the *Post* had been awarded the Pulitzer Prize gold medal for community service for its Watergate articles in 1972.

On Saturday, April 14, a good while before the *Post*'s Pulitzer was officially announced but with many newspaper people buzzing about it, thirty of us from the *Post* attended the annual dinner of the White House Correspondents' Association, a principal social event for journalists in the nation's capital.

More than sixty White House staff members were there, and more than fifty senators and congressmen. Watergate and the related scandals were a story only partly told. Nevertheless, so much rottenness had been exposed that there was little else to talk about. Of the 2,500 people in attendance, some were already known for the roles they were playing as the scandals unfolded: Judge Sirica, Wright Patman, Clark MacGregor, Edward Bennett Williams, Ronald Ziegler, Ken Clawson, Haldeman, and Ehrlichman. Others who might ordinarily have been at such a gathering had fallen by the wayside and were not there: Patrick Gray, John Dean, Jeb Magruder. And still others who were to play leading roles were on the guest list but were hardly noticed: Alexander Butterfield, who had left the White House to become chief of the Federal Aviation Administration, Bebe Rebozo, Rose Mary Woods, Elliot Richardson, Egil Krogh.

This day had been one of the most frantic of all at the White House. The transcripts of Nixon's taped conversations show that at 8:55 A.M. Nixon began sessions with Haldeman and Ehrlichman that were to last almost six hours off and on. In the morning, the transcripts show, they decided to summon John Mitchell from New York, and Ehrlichman met alone with the former attorney general in an attempt to have him shoulder responsibility for the Watergate debacle. Mitchell refused. Jeb Magruder and his two attorneys also met with Ehrlichman, laying out what Magruder had told prosecutors earlier in the day, including testimony damaging to John Dean.

Ehrlichman told Nixon early in the morning that an immediate decision had to be made on whether to keep Dean on at the White House, saying the President had to "bite the bullet on Dean, one way or the other, pretty quick." Nixon, apparently depressed, almost seemed to have given up hopes of continuing the coverup. He asked Ehrlichman whether a plan to keep the Ervin Committee from hearing witnesses who were under indictment was worth the effort. "John, is that better than just caving?" he inquired.

"We can cave anytime," Ehrlichman replied.

Nixon spelled out why the coverup was doomed. "It's just a question of putting together all the facts and any time someone—if the U.S. Attorney's office goes through the process that I've gone through, he'll have all the facts. And there it'll be. And you don't get it all from any one person. It's some from this one, some from that one."

A few moments later Nixon said he had made a decision on Dean: "He's to go." Ehrlichman questioned the advisability of that, and Nixon said he felt Ehrlichman had been recommending that Dean be severed from the White House staff. No, Ehrlichman said, what he had recommended was simply that a quick decision be made. But the decision he favored was keeping Dean on, in the hopes that he would be treated more favorably by the prosecutors as the President's counsel than as a private citizen. Such favored treatment would obviously have been beneficial to Haldeman and Ehrlichman, who were just becoming targets of the investigation.

At this point in the conversation, as they lingered over what to do about John Dean, the President, Haldeman and Ehrlichman broke off into a rare discussion of their own complicity in the Watergate coverup. The tapes made public by Nixon in 1974 cover more than thirty hours of conversation between Nixon and his associates. From time to time the transcripts reveal one or more of them engaging in illegal conduct, such as the moment on March 21, 1973, when Nixon ordered Haldeman and Dean to "get the money" for Hunt. But hardly ever did Nixon, Haldeman, and Ehrlichman appraise their own actions and knowledge as searchingly as they did for a few moments on April 14.

The President began by speaking in defense of Dean, saying that "Dean only tried to do what he could to pick up the pieces, and everybody else around here knew it had to be done."

"Certainly," Ehrlichman agreed.

Haldeman said Dean's involvement "was for what was understood here to be the proper system," and Nixon said, "The question is motive, that's right."

Ehrlichman, the only one of the three who reportedly had no knowledge that presidential conversations were taped, said, "There were eight or ten people around here who knew about this, knew it was going on. Bob knew, I knew, all kinds of people knew."

"Well, I knew it. I knew it," the President said.

Late in the day, after Mitchell had refused to take the blame for the bugging and Ehrlichman had talked to Magruder, the subject of conversation turned gloomier for Nixon and his two aides as they saw how testimony would lead to demands for the resignation of Haldeman and Ehrlichman. "You've got a really, a punchy decision, which is whether you want me to resign or whether you don't. That's one you've got to figure out," Haldeman told Nixon.

They discussed how such resignations could give the appearance that the President was cleaning house without indicating that the men who had resigned were guilty of any wrongdoing, and the President suggested that they might have "an attorney general added in" with the resignations, and also "a White House counsel, possibly."

"Pretty big bag, John," Haldeman said.

"The biggest," said Ehrlichman.

"Policy, that's the point," said Nixon.

Then they seemed to back away from the thought of resignations, and focused on a plan to allow aides to testify before the Ervin Committee. Enunciated by Nixon, the plan would include putting "a story out which will keep the enemy cool for awhile."

Unknown to them, around the time they were plotting, the Watergate prosecutors were telling Henry Petersen how strong their new findings were, how Dean and Magruder had confessed to a role in the coverup, and how they had implicated Mitchell, Ehrlichman, and Haldeman. The prosecutors had no information regarding improper activities by Nixon, and they discussed the need to inform the President that men close to him were now the target of their investigation.

At the White House Correspondents' dinner, Woodward and Bernstein were presented two awards for their Watergate coverage, a painful moment for the President's men. At the head table Ron Ziegler joined in the applause for the reporters, but lightly, his hands barely touching as he clapped. In an understandable break with tradition, the President and Mrs. Nixon entered after the awards were issued. On their arrival a band played "Hail to the Chief" and the massive black-tie crowd rose and cheered. Nixon was tanned and smiling. Although he seemed slightly ill at ease, I thought how much better he looked in person than in pictures. In one of his familiar gestures, he appeared to focus on someone in the front of the audience, extended his arm, smiled, and pointed in apparent recognition.

Nixon listened as a White House reporter, Ted Knap of the Scripps-Howard syndicate, made a few remarks with some amusing references to Watergate. The President also spoke briefly, stayed at the head table for a while, and left.

At 11:02 that night, while others were attending parties after the dinner, the transcripts of Nixon's taped conversations show that the President was back in the White House, telephoning Haldeman to once again go over details of what they had discussed all day. At 11:22, according to the transcripts, Nixon called Ehrlichman to discuss plans for the next day. Nixon mentioned that it was "terribly painful, of course, to go to that dinner tonight," but "I just feel better about getting the damn thing done."

At the dinner, Woodward and Bernstein had spoken briefly to Richard Kleindienst, who cryptically told them that Watergate was about to "blow up" and to have the courage of their convictions. One of the failings of newspapers, he said, was that they did good work and then backed away from it. He agreed to meet the reporters and discuss matters further on Sunday morning. But other events intervened.

Saturday night as the prosecutors had discussed with Petersen the need to bring their findings before Nixon, the most obvious way seemed to be through Kleindienst, the Attorney General. They hesitated out of fear that they couldn't trust Kleindienst, then decided that there was no other way. Petersen telephoned Kleindienst, and at 1 A.M. Sunday morning, Petersen, Silbert, and U.S. attorney Harold Titus, Silbert's boss, called on Kleindienst at his home in suburban McLean, Virginia. Until 5 A.M., out came the story of Watergate—the meetings in advance involving Mitchell, Dean, Liddy, and Magruder; the astonishment at the arrests of June 17, 1972; and the details of the coverup, involving massive payments of hush money and implicating Kalmbach, Haldeman, and Ehrlichman.

On Sunday morning Kleindienst went directly to the White House to inform Nixon, who knew a great deal more than the Attorney General did. In the afternoon Kleindienst asked the President to meet with Henry Petersen, marking the beginning of daily sessions between the President and Petersen.

Even as Kleindienst and Petersen were telling the President of the findings that Earl Silbert and his colleagues had assembled, Silbert was in the process of getting new information from John Dean, whose attorneys were battling to win him immunity from prosecution.

Dean had offered testimony against Mitchell in return for immunity, but the prosecutors refused. He offered testimony against Ehrlichman, and the prosecutors refused to grant him immunity for that as well. As he conferred with them in lengthy sessions, sometimes Dean would say things like, "Oh, and another thing that was done at the White House was . . ." Late that Sunday, in just such a manner, Dean began to describe the White House's campaign against Daniel Ellsberg. The impact of that was not to be felt for another ten or twelve days. In the meantime, the flow of Watergate disclosures continued relentlessly.

On Monday, April 16, the *Los Angeles Times* reported that a dramatic admission by the White House in regard to Watergate was expected at any time. Senator Ervin announced that his hearings would begin about May 17, and it was revealed that the President's personal attorney, Herbert Kalmbach, had been subpoenaed as a witness.

On the seventeenth of April, Nixon stepped into the briefing room at the White House and read a short statement to the press, one which he said "concerns the Watergate case directly."

> On March 21, as a result of serious charges which came to my attention, some of which were publicly reported, I began intensive new inquiries into this whole matter.
>
> Last Sunday afternoon, the Attorney General, As-

sistant Attorney General Petersen, and I met at length in the EOB [Executive Office Building] to review the facts which had come to me in my investigation and also to review the progress of the Department of Justice investigation.

I can report today that there have been major developments in the case concerning which it would be improper to be more specific now, execpt to say that real progress has been made in finding the truth.

If any person in the Executive branch or in the Government is indicted by the grand jury, my policy will be to immediately suspend him. If he is convicted, he will, of course, be automatically discharged.

I have expressed to the appropriate authorities my view that no individual holding, in the past or at present, a position of major importance in the Administration should be given immunity from prosecution ...

Nixon had conducted no investigation except one aimed at keeping him one step ahead of the court system and the Ervin Committee. The posture that no one should be given immunity from prosecution was high-sounding but aimed only at keeping John Dean from testifying, as the White House tapes show. Henry Petersen had urged the President not to mention immunity, since it was a tool to be used at the discretion of prosecutors and the Justice Department.

In a press conference following the statement, Ronald Ziegler was taken to task repeatedly by reporters, who, after so many months of denials and carefully phrased statements, wanted to know whether the President's brief talk meant that earlier denials of involvement by White House aides in the Watergate scandals would no longer hold.

"This is the operative statement," Ziegler kept saying. Finally, after a reporter provided the phrasing, Ziegler added, "The others are inoperative."

For several days it seemed possible that Nixon had stilled the growing clamor. The first reaction on Capitol Hill was sympathetic to him, as Republican leaders said the President had finally taken the lead and was now out front in bringing the scandal to an end. The Democratic National Committee, it was reported, was on the verge of settling its civil suit for $500,000—an indication that Democratic chairman Robert Strauss was willing to let bygones be bygones, although no one phrased it that way. On the 19th of April Kleindienst removed himself from further involvement in the Watergate investigation because of his close relationships with some of those under inquiry, and Henry Petersen, who was working closely with the President, was put in charge.

But the respite was brief. On April 19th it was reported that Magruder had told the Watergate grand jury that John Dean and John Mitchell had approved the bugging. Dean's secretary, in tears, called newspapers and wire services to read a brief statement in which Dean, who was so much in the news but who had yet to make a public appearance, said he would not allow himself to be made a scapegoat. The *Post* reported that representatives of the Democratic National Committee, in deciding to settle the civil suit, had conducted secret negotiations with Mitchell, although the former Attorney General was thoroughly discredited by then. The flow of news had started again.

April 20: *The New York Times* reported that Mitchell had told friends he heard plans to bug the Democrats three times but rejected them in each instance.

Nixon assured Cabinet members he would get to the bottom of Watergate, saying, "We've had our Cambodias before," a reference to his sending troops into Cambodia, in 1970, one of the most unpopular moves in the conduct of the war in Southeast Asia.

April 22: Nixon called John Dean to wish him a happy Easter Sunday and say, "You're still my counsel"—a stroking call, Dean later called it.

On *Meet the Press* Senator Edward W. Brooke of Massachusetts said it was "inconceivable" that Nixon did not know of the plans to commit the bugging in advance, and a Gallup poll stated that four Americans in ten felt the same way although no investigator or newspaper report had ever alleged that the President had prior knowledge of the bugging.

April 23: Congressman, Henry S. Reuss, who had requested the original Patman investigation before the 1972 election, demanded that Henry Petersen be removed from the Watergate investigation, pointing to Petersen's role in blocking the Patman hearings.

Henry Kissinger, in a major foreign policy address, brought up Watergate to say that the nation must ask itself if it could afford an "orgy of recrimination."

The White House disclosed that Nixon had met with two attorneys, John J. Wilson and Frank Strickler, who had been retained by Haldeman and Ehrlichman.

Collapse of the Coverup   167

April 24: The *Washington Star* reported that Herbert Kalmbach had kept a previously unknown fund dating back to January, 1971, and possibly earlier, with $500,000 available for political projects.

Ken Rietz, a former CRP official, resigned as an aide to Republican national chairman George Bush after Woodward and Bernstein revealed his ties to dirty tricks during the 1972 election campaign.

April 25: Vice-President Agnew told a group of students he would resign if developments in Watergate made him unable, as a matter of conscience, to continue in office. But Agnew also called a press conference to say, somewhat patronizingly, that he was fully behind Nixon. Agnew complained of rumor, hearsay, grand jury leaks, speculation, and the use of unidentified sources in news stories. The President's tapes show that three days later in an apparent reaction to Agnew's remarks, Nixon said to Henry Petersen, "I sometimes feel I'd like to resign. Let Agnew be President for a while. He'd love it."

The *Post* reported a new element in the Watergate-related scandals—attempts by the White House and CRP to manipulate public opinion through fraudulent and misleading advertising and an intensive telegram campaign. Just after the mining of Haiphong in May, 1972—an action that was considered the riskiest in the Vietnam War—CRP placed an ad in *The New York Times* suggesting that most Americans favored the mining. CRP did not identify itself in the ad as its sponsor, and, in violation of the campaign disclosure laws, did not report paying for the ad. The ad gave the appearance of having been sponsored by citizens of no particular political affiliation. At the same time CRP officials made telephone calls all over the country to ask that telegrams in support of Nixon be sent to the White House. With the results skewed, Ronald Ziegler, who on other occasions would not reveal how the mail was going, volunteered that public reaction, as evidenced in letters and telegrams to the White House, was 5 or 6 to 1 in favor of the mining.

On reading this article in the *Post* a nineteen-year-old former mail clerk at CRP came to the newspaper offices and described how CRP had rigged a local television station's poll of viewer attitudes toward the mining. Clipping sample ballots from the Washington newspapers and sending in postcards as well, CRP submitted between 2,000 and 4,000 entries in favor of Nixon's conduct. Only 8,000 responses were received in all, and the tabulation showed an exact 50-50 split, meaning that without CRP's intervention the poll would have indicated that public sentiment was actually against the mining, by at least 2 to 1.

Also on April 25, John Mitchell appeared before a grand jury in Pensacola, Florida, in a case involving antiwar veterans who had been arrested just before the Republican convention in Miami in 1972. The veterans complained that their arrest was aimed solely at keeping them from demonstrating at the convention. Mitchell, the personification of power and law and order in the Nixon Administration, was undergoing abject humiliation. This was one of three appearances on successive days for him as a witness before grand juries, as he testified also in New York and Washington.

April 26: Newspapers learned through Senator Weicker that Patrick Gray had destroyed two folders taken from Howard Hunt's safe and given him by Ehrlichman and Dean. One contained State Department cables doctored by Hunt to falsely implicate John F. Kennedy in the assassination of South Vietnamese President Ngo Dinh Diem in 1963. The other was a dossier Hunt had assembled on Senator Edward M. Kennedy.

George Bush, chairman of the Republican National Committee, warned that the White House handling of Watergate was compromising the entire Republican party.

In Los Angeles Judge W. Matthew Byrne sent the jurors home in the trial of Daniel Ellsberg, saying the government prosecutors had withheld evidence.

On April 27, Patrick Gray resigned, humiliated. And on the West Coast, Judge Byrne announced that Gordon Liddy and Howard Hunt had burglarized files at the office of Ellsberg's psychiatrist in 1971, while both of them were working in the White House.

April, 1973, had been a month in which all the plugs were pulled; there were absolutely no controls on disclosures. But as Judge Byrne stopped trial proceedings in the Ellsberg case, there were those in the White House who knew that what had gone before was nothing compared to what lay ahead.

3

IN THE COURSE of their investigation, the Watergate prosecutors and the FBI almost stumbled several times onto the White House campaign to malign Daniel Ellsberg. On June 28, 1972, Richard Helms intervened with Patrick Gray to postpone FBI interviews with CIA men who knew of the help the Agency had extended to Howard Hunt. On July 5 and 7, 1972, General Walters, who had replaced Robert Cushman as deputy director of the CIA, sent letters to Gray describing that assistance. On July 12, 1972, Walters gave Gray copies of the photographs the CIA had printed for Hunt, showing Gordon Liddy near the offices of Ellsberg's psychiatrist, Dr. Lewis Fielding. Gray has testified that he thought nothing of the photographs and put them aside.

Later these photos were given to the Watergate prosecutors, instilling fear in John Dean, who felt that investigators would immediately trace them, find out what they represented, and draw the connection between Watergate and the Fielding break-in. But, as with the Mexican checks that were so crucial in the first stages of the investigation, the prosecutors failed to grasp the significance of the photographs and did not investigate them. If those running the coverup in the White House were poker players afraid that everyone could see their cards, the prosecutors were sitting in another room entirely, forced to guess at not only what the cards were, but who was holding them as well.

One of the original three prosecutors, Donald Campbell, described to me in June, 1974, how he and his colleagues studied these pictures, hoping to find clues. One of the photographs showed Liddy standing in a parking area near Fielding's car. Another showed Liddy outside a stationery store.

170   784 DAYS THAT CHANGED AMERICA

There were pictures of the side of a building, doors, a residence. In several, Dr. Fielding's name could be seen.

"We sat on a couch and went over them, one by one, trying to figure out what they meant," Campbell said. As they looked at the photo showing Liddy and a car, "We thought, What is important here, the car tags? We had been down so many dead-ends by then."

Campbell said that the prosecutors gave up on tracking the photos because they didn't know what they were looking for. They concentrated on finding out what Hunt and Liddy had been doing in Los Angeles by other procedures that were ultimately unrewarding.

Working from hotel records, they checked telephone numbers dialed from Hunt's and Liddy's rooms. "But we got crazy things, like old ladies who only spoke Italian," Campbell told me.

"Donald Segretti's mother?" I asked.

"No. Relatives or friends of girls that Hunt, especially, liked to bring to his room," Campbell said.

The prosecutors also interviewed Egil Krogh and David Young, the White House plumbers who worked so closely with Liddy and Hunt, but neither of them would reveal the true nature of Hunt-Liddy Special Project #1.

In the pursuit of this matter the prosecutors apparently were once again thwarted by their superiors, Attorney General Kleindienst and his assistant, Henry Petersen. Earl Silbert had a dual concern with the photos taken by the CIA. He wanted to know what Hunt and Liddy had done in California, and, in late 1972, as the date of the Watergate trial neared, he wanted to be able to counter the claim that the defendants had broken into Watergate for the CIA, a possible defense for the crime that Silbert thought preposterous.

When Silbert requested from the CIA that it explain the nature of its assistance to Howard Hunt, Richard Helms and a legal adviser for the CIA went to Kleindienst and Petersen to keep the prosecutor at a distance.

According to Petersen's testimony before the Senate Watergate Committee, Helms and his counsel, Lawrence Houston,

> ... expressed some reservations about potential embarrassment to the CIA and that they were there with certain information as a result of questions generated by Mr. Silbert, they hoped it would not be necessary to disclose them.... There was one possible wholly unre-

lated valid CIA activity involved which they were most desirous of protecting. I assured them we would try and do that.

It was another example of Petersen's ready acceptance of instructions or requests from high officials to steer clear of areas of investigation that were too sensitive and would have broken the Watergate case wide open. Later, in June, 1974, Petersen owned up to having made one blunder in the Watergate investigation—his failure to track down the photographs which identified Fielding. Testifying before the Senate Judiciary Committee, which was then conducting hearings on Nixon's nomination of Earl Silbert as U.S. attorney for the District of Columbia, Petersen said that while Silbert had not pursued the photos either, "I'm not prepared to criticize Mr. Silbert for what I didn't have enough sense to tell him to do." Petersen failed to mention to the Judiciary Committee the meeting in which he and Kleindienst had promised to protect the CIA and not expose it.

So in March, 1973, the prosecutors had long since discarded attempts to find out what Hunt and Liddy had been doing in Los Angeles, while Richard Nixon and John Dean continued to worry about it, recognizing the Ellsberg venture as the key that could open the door on the vastness of the Watergate scandal. Their great fear was that Hunt would talk. That was the reason, more than any other, as the Nixon tapes show, that the President insisted on March 21, 1973, that Hunt be paid blackmail despite Dean's attempts to put hush-money payments at an end.

When Haldeman joined their conversation that morning, Nixon reviewed the problem for him, saying Dean was concerned "about Ehrlichman, which worries me a great deal. . . . This is why the Hunt problem is so serious, because it had nothing to do with the campaign. . . . Properly, it has to do with the Ellsberg thing."

Nixon asked, "What is the answer on that? How you keep it out? I don't know."

Dean had spent two hours in unsuccessful attempts to convince Nixon that the payments to Hunt had to end. The transcripts show how cautiously Dean kept trying to steer Nixon to that conclusion but how each time the President refused. Finally, with Haldeman present, Dean gave up trying. When Nixon asked for an answer on how to solve the Ellsberg problem, the young counsel offered one. As it later developed, Dean, who had tried in his way to sever Nixon from the Watergate and cut the President's losses with what was sometimes referred to as "a limited hang out," was to provide a suggestion that later became an integral part of the coverup as it continued.

"You might put it on a national security ground, basis, which it really, it was," he said. All three seized on the idea, the transcript of their conversation shows.

> *Haldeman*: It absolutely was.
> *Dean*: And just say that, uh,
> *President*: Yeah.
> *Dean*: That this is not, you know, this was—
> *President*: Not paid with CIA funds.
> *Dean*: Uh—
> *President*: No, seriously. National security. We had to get information for national security grounds.
> *Dean*: Well, then the question is, why didn't the CIA do it or why didn't the FBI do it?
> *President*: Because they were—We had to do it, we had to do it on a confidential basis.
> *Haldeman*: Because we were checking them?
> *President*: Neither could be trusted.
> *Haldeman*: Well, I think
> *President*: That's the way I view it.*

As it happened, it was to be Dean, feeling cast adrift and in a struggle to gain immunity from prosecution, who eventually told the prosecutors about the Ellsberg connection. On Monday, April 16, 1973, the day after Dean told Earl Silbert of the break-in at Dr. Fielding's, Silbert sent a memorandum to Henry Petersen describing the new disclosure and asking for guidance. The Ellsberg trial was then in progress in Los Angeles. The break-in had been unsuccessful in that the Hunt-Liddy team had not found anything that was eventually used against Ellsberg. In Silbert's view, as a technical, legal matter, it would be possible to draw a line and justify a decision not to notify the judge in the Ellsberg case, W. Matthew Byrne, Jr., of the break-in.

Petersen reportedly did not get the memorandum until Tuesday. On Monday afternoon, as Petersen went over some of Silbert's earlier findings with Nixon, seemingly reading to

---

*This segment of the taped conversation of March 21, 1973, is taken from the transcript prepared by the House Judiciary Committee.

the President from a notebook, he mentioned incidentally that Hunt had received help from the CIA—the camera, "a thing to disguise your voice, credentials."

Petersen explained to Nixon the prosecutor's early concern "that they might—the defendants might—try and defend by attacking the CIA. We asked the CIA people—we were told that they were simply responding to a routine request from another governmental agency to help out Hunt who was on a special assignment."

Nixon, who knew immediately it was the Ellsberg matter that Petersen was talking about, asked whether the other government agency was the White House, and Petersen said yes. The President, without going into detail, told Petersen "that was perfectly proper. He was conducting an investigation from the national security area for the White House at that point."

Petersen said that the request for CIA assistance had come from Ehrlichman. "Right," the President said. "That is not involved in this case, is it? (Inaudible) This came before."

Petersen said it could be relevant if Ehrlichman had facilitated Hunt's obtaining equipment used in the Watergate break-in.

Two days later, having received Silbert's memorandum, Petersen brought the matter to Nixon's attention again, this time identifying the Hunt investigation as the break-in at Fielding's office. Petersen was now meeting or speaking on the telephone to the President several times a day, keeping him informed of the prosecutor's findings and supplying him with information from the grand jury. Nixon, who had promised to keep the information confidential, would go over it in detail with Haldeman and Ehrlichman, boasting to them that he had Petersen "on a short leash."

No transcript of that April 18, 1973, conversation has been made public, but Petersen has testified that when he told Nixon of the Fielding break-in, the President snapped, "I know about that. That is a national security matter. You stay out of that. Your mandate is to investigate Watergate."

As in the early stages of the investigation when he worked closely with the prosecutors but bowed to pressure from Dean or Ehrlichman, Petersen was once again a man caught in the middle, this time taking orders from the President. He got in touch with Silbert and told him to drop the Ellsberg matter. Silbert did, but the prosecutors made it clear that they were growing increasingly disturbed with Petersen's role as a conduit to Nixon.

As days passed, Petersen, the good soldier, couldn't get the Fielding break-in out of his mind. On April 25 he told Richard Kleindienst about it and about the President's order that Petersen "stay out of that."

Kleindienst had traveled a long road with Nixon. Before Watergate, at his own confirmation hearings on becoming attorney general early in 1972, he had lied under oath to protect the President when asked if Nixon had interfered in a Justice Department investigation of a merger planned by ITT. Not only had Nixon ordered Kleindienst to see that the inquiry was stopped, he had called Kleindienst "a son of a bitch," demanding, "Don't you understand English?" as he issued the order. But Kleindienst told the Senate Judiciary Committee that Nixon had not intervened.

In the course of the Watergate investigation, Kleindienst, the chief law enforcement officer in the land, was the first to learn that White House aides might have been involved with the bugging, but he kept that information to himself at a time when it would have been vital news to investigators.

A proud man, he had tried to stay away from the Watergate probe, but off and on he succumbed to calls for assistance from Ehrlichman or Nixon. Told by Richard Helms that certain information that Silbert was requesting might prove embarrassing to the CIA, he worked with Petersen to avoid any problem.

During the election campaign Kleindienst had tried to convince the President that a special prosecutor should be appointed, but publicly, when Nixon refused, he ridiculed the idea; and he campaigned widely on Nixon's behalf, citing the President as a champion of law and order.

On April 10, 1973, fifteen days before Petersen came to him with the news of the Ellsberg break-in, Kleindienst made his appearance on Capitol Hill in defense of the widest possible use of Executive privilege by Nixon. The position he espoused brought him criticism from members of Congress and scorn from editorial writers—and a week after that, Nixon abandoned his hard-line stance, making Kleindienst appear that much more foolish.

As a reward for all his services, the Watergate prosecutors didn't trust him, and the Nixon inner circle often discussed firing him. On April 19, 1973, Kleindienst took himself out of the Watergate investigation totally, because of his friendship with John Mitchell and others who were targets of the prosecutors. Now, on the 25th, he had done as much for

Nixon as he was going to. He and Petersen agreed that the Fielding break-in could not be kept secret. According to Petersen's later testimony, the two decided that if Nixon did not change his mind, they would both resign.

Kleindienst went to see Nixon that day. Whether he issued the threat to resign has not been made public. But as a result of their meeting, Nixon agreed to allow the Justice Department to notify Judge Byrne of the break-in, and Silbert's memorandum to Petersen was sent to the West Coast. For Nixon, who knew how dangerous the Ellsberg matter was, it was a major, perhaps fatal capitulation. For Kleindienst, a highly loyal and emotional man, it marked the end of the road.

On April 26, Judge Byrne interrupted the Ellsberg trial, saying that the government had withheld evidence. On the 27th, Byrne revealed that Liddy and Hunt had burglarized Fielding's office. On the 29th, Kleindienst was summoned to Camp David and told by Nixon that he had to resign, against his wishes. On the 30th, Judge Byrne revealed that he had met twice with Ehrlichman and once with Nixon earlier in the month and had been sounded out as a possible successor to J. Edgar Hoover now that the hapless Patrick Gray was no longer being considered. Because of the White House's extraordinary attempts to malign Ellsberg, the dangling of the FBI director's job before Byrne was immediately seen as a bribe offer by Nixon to obtain a conviction of Ellsberg. The damage that Kleindienst had done by insisting that Byrne be told of the break-in was swift and heavy.

The night of April 30th, in what was to be the first "Checkers speech" of the Watergate years, Nixon went on TV with an American flag in his lapel and a bust of Lincoln at his side. He restated the resignations he had announced earlier in the day, lumping Kleindienst in with Haldeman, Ehrlichman, and John Dean, making Kleindienst suspect in many eyes despite the fact that the President called him "my personal friend for twenty years, with no personal involvement whatever in this matter."

In the rest of his talk, after announcing that Elliot Richardson would move from the position of Defense Secretary to be the new Attorney General, the President gave his version of how Watergate had occurred and issued an appeal for the nation to get on to more important matters.

Contrary to his entire career in politics, he said, he had let others run his campaign in 1972 because it was, in both foreign and domestic affairs, "a year of crucially important decisions, of intense negotiations, of vital new directions," particularly in working toward peace for America and the world.

"The easiest course would be for me to blame those to whom I delegated the responsibility to run the campaign. But that would be the cowardly thing to do."

He said that campaign excesses occurred on all sides, that both our great parties had been guilty of shady tactics in the past, that reform was needed, and that as for the President, Watergate had claimed too much of his time and he would now go on to "the larger duties of this office."

But Watergate, and Ellsberg, would not go away. On May 1, Judge Byrne made public a summary of an FBI interview with Ehrlichman three days earlier, in which Ehrlichman said that Nixon had ordered a secret investigation of Ellsberg that eventually led to the break-in. Ellsberg's defense attorneys demanded that the case against their client be dismissed.

On May 2, Earl Silbert interrogated Howard Hunt on the Ellsberg matter, and Hunt described the aid that the CIA had given him. On May 8, *The New York Times* reported that, contrary to an earlier claim by a Justice Department official, Nixon had at first tried to prevent the news of the Ellsberg break-in from being forwarded to Byrne.

On May 11, 1973, the case against Daniel Ellsberg and Anthony Russo was thrown out of court. In Washington, three congressional committees had begun inquiries into the CIA's role in assisting the White House's clandestine, illegal research on Ellsberg. What they found was that it was impossible to sever the Ellsberg case from Watergate.

The committees investigating were the Senate Appropriations subcommittee on Intelligence, headed by John L. McClellan of Arkansas, a Senate Armed Services subcommittee headed by Stuart Symington of Missouri, and the House Armed Forces subcommittee on Intelligence, headed by Lucien Nedzi of Michigan. McClellan, Symington, and Nedzi were all Democrats. Among the witnesses they called were Robert Cushman, Vernon Walters, Richard Helms, and the two CIA doctors who knew about the Ellsberg psychological profile. The hearings were all conducted in closed sessions, with senators and congressmen later revealing some of what had been said.

On May 14, Walters bridged the gap from Ellsberg to

Watergate. Until then, the public had heard only about CIA aid to Howard Hunt on the Ellsberg affair. But on that day Senator Symington revealed that Walters had submitted the memoranda he had written the previous summer, telling of his meeting with Haldeman and Ehrlichman on June 23, 1972, his subsequent attempts to keep Patrick Gray from investigating in Mexico and from interrogating Nixon fundraiser Kenneth Dahlberg, and the pleas from John Dean that the CIA pay bail bond for the Watergate suspects and continue to make other clandestine support payments to them.

Symington immediately took the view, at least publicly, that the CIA had resisted White House pressures, charging that Haldeman and Ehrlichman had "bypassed" Helms to get Walters's cooperation in the coverup. Such a posture, of course, seemed ridiculous—rather than bypass Helms, Haldeman and Ehrlichman saw to it that he was present as the plan was discussed.

On the 16th of May, Helms, brought back from his post as ambassador to Iran, appeared before the McClellan subcommittee, and, on the 17th, before Symington's. McClellan said that Helms had testified that Nixon's name had been invoked when the CIA was called into the Watergate coverup, that Helms and Walters felt "some things went too far and they put a stop to it." Symington said upon hearing Helms's testimony that "it is hard to believe" that Nixon didn't know of the CIA's role in the Watergate coverup.

Congressman Nedzi also said that it was difficult to conceive of Nixon not knowing of the coverup, although "anything is possible."

The testimony by Dean on the Fielding break-in had given Nixon every bit as much grief as the President had feared. Watergate was now a scandal about him, not about overzealous underlings, and the charges began to swirl madly as tales of secret conduct that had taken place over four years began to gush out publicly all at once.

On May 17, the Senate Watergate hearings opened, and on May 18, James McCord testified about offers of Executive clemency that had been made to him, putting Nixon that much more on the defensive. In addition, lying locked up and in the possession of Judge Sirica, were White House memoranda known as the Huston plan for domestic spying, given to the court by John Dean. The new acting FBI director, William D. Ruckelshaus, revealed that the logs of old wiretaps of four news reporters and thirteen Executive aides had been discovered in a safe in Ehrlichman's White House office, having been removed from the FBI's files.

Elliot Richardson announced the appointment of Archibald V. Cox, a Harvard law professor and former solicitor general under President Kennedy, as special Watergate prosecutor. Cox was said to know nothing about criminal law, but he had a reputation for being somewhat arrogant and totally independent, and one of his first statements was that he would pursue the investigation into the Oval Office, if necessary.

Making sure that she was heard from, Martha Mitchell telephoned a reporter to say that her husband was protecting Nixon. Mitchell himself picked up the telephone and complained that someone, whom he did not identify, was attempting to make him a fall guy in the Watergate scandal.

Sam Hughes of the Office of Federal Elections reported that the President's personal attorney, Kalmbach, had admitted to arranging payments to buy the silence of the Watergate conspirators, and that at least $460,000 had been spent to that end.

The liberal American sfor Democratic Action urged Nixon to resign, saying that the government was "under the shadow of the worst political scandal in American history." The assault on him was furious and coming from every direction as the Watergate hearings opened.

On Saturday night, May 20, Nixon, the object of such wrath as no President had ever known, took a quiet cruise on the Potomac toward Mount Vernon, accompanied by General Alexander Haig, Haldeman's replacement as White House chief of staff. On the following day Nixon worked alternately alone or with staff aides in the preparation of the May 22, 1973, statement that stood for many months as the most complete rendition of his own involvement in the Watergate scandal, the events leading to it, and the coverup that followed.

Consisting of four thousand words, it was the kind of statement Nixon had once asked Dean to prepare, one that purports to be a full account but really isn't. It dealt at length with the 1969 wiretaps, the 1970 Huston plan, the White House plumbers, and the Watergate. All, he said, with the exception of Watergate, were matters that involved sensitive national security concerns, the nature of which he addressed in only general terms.

In the statement, Nixon pledged not to resign, saying, "I

will not abandon my responsibilities. I will continue to do the job I was elected to do." He promised that "Executive privilege will not be invoked as to any testimony concerning possible criminal conduct, in the matters under investigation. I want the public to learn the truth about Watergate, and those guilty of any illegal actions brought to justice."

The statement was immediately recognized as Nixon's legal defense, the document that all subsequent charges were matched against in an attempt to sort out the truth in the scandal. Many observers read it over and over, looking for inconsistencies with the testimony of others or for remarks that in and of themselves suggested illegal activity, or lies, on the part of the President.

Parts of the statement, when compared to testimony by Haldeman, Ehrlichman, Richard Helms, and Vernon Walters, could be used as a prima facie case showing that Nixon had ordered the CIA into the Watergate coverup. In the first place, it would have been uncharacteristic for Haldeman to act independently of Nixon in taking so drastic an action as to use the CIA to block the FBI's investigation. More than that, however, Nixon took the responsibility in his statement for instructing his two chief aides to summon the CIA leaders to the White House. He stated that for national security reasons, he ordered the "coordination" of Walters with Acting FBI Director Patrick Gray to keep from exposing unrelated CIA activities or the existence of the White House plumbers.

While Nixon explained his order in the most favorable light for himself, the fact is that it led to the temporary aborting of a key aspect of the FBI's Watergate investigation—one that had the potential to destroy the President's political career—and it was read that way by many, including several members of Congress who said the statement was an admission of complicity in the coverup by Nixon, and reason enough to call for his impeachment.

PART VI
The Senate Watergate Hearings

1

ROOM 318 OF the Old Senate Office Building had grown shabby between the time fifty years earlier when the Teapot Dome hearings had been held in it and May 17, 1973, when the Senate Watergate hearings began. The paint on the ceiling of the cavernous room was badly chipped, the long window drapes were tattered. It had the appearance of a grand old downtown railroad terminal suddenly restored to use, mobbed with people but unrenovated. The lighting and the acoustics were poor. For those present there were a great many distractions—senators whispering to one another, their aides moving around, and seating arranged so that hardly any in the audience of 350 or so people could ever see the face of the witness.

But with a little cosmetics, the big eyes of the cameras created an entirely different setting for scores of millions of people throughout the world. Through close-up photography relieved by occasional pans of the audience or quick scenes of human interest, television turned the dingy into the brilliant and made the scandal of the century into the drama of the century. From the moment Sam Ervin, the chairman of the Select Committee on Presidential Activities of 1972, first banged his gavel, the Watergate hearings were imbued with the exciting sense of the hunt, long spells of deepening mystery broken by rich comic relief.

Ervin, a palsy-tongued orator, set the tone himself in an eloquent opening statement in which he spoke of the "atmosphere of utmost gravity" that had befallen the nation, of questions that "strike at the very undergirding of our democracy." If many of the allegations already made proved to be true, the North Carolinian said, then what the Watergate burglars "were seeking to steal was not the jewels, money, or other property of American citizens, but something much more valuable—their precious heritage, the right to vote in a free election. Since that day [June 17, 1972], a mood of incredulity has prevailed among our populace."

As he spoke these fine phrases, the Senator began stumbling over the word "incredulity." Six or seven times he attacked it, bumbling, his whole head involved in the act of speech, eyebrows lifting high and descending, ears twitching, his mouth sometimes moving without a sound coming out. Millions of people held their breath as Ervin's whole body and mind did battle with his tongue until finally the Senator gave up on the word and continued on.

No scriptwriter could have created a Sam Ervin. He was a throwback, a twentieth-century American equivalent of Samual Johnson, who had the same ability to regale an audience with grand incontrovertible statements of principle while lesser men haggled over what they had heard. It was Dr. Johnson who 210 years earlier had maintained, according to his diarist, Boswell, that the King can do no wrong, that "it is better in general that a nation should have a supreme legislative power, although it may at times be abused." But, added Dr. Johnson, "there is this consideration, that if the abuse be enormous, Nature will rise up, and claiming her original rights, overturn a corrupt political system."

Such was Ervin's philosophy exactly. He was never the one to favor revolution or expect perfection from government institutions; he was quite at home with the politics of cooperation and accommodation. He had practiced them all his life. At seventy-six years of age, he had no further political ambition and was from the outset probably less inclined than any man to strike at the President. But in his homey way, he began to savage Nixon, as when he asked Maurice Stans, "Do you not think that men who have been honored by the American people as you have, ought to have their course of action guided by ethical principles which are superior to the minimum requirements of the criminal laws?" Ervin, with clarity and conviction, would tolerate no quibbling from Stans, who pointed to earlier transgressions in American politics. "You know," Ervin said, "there has been murder and larceny in every generation, but that hasn't made murder meritorious or larceny legal."

With Ervin at the helm and a galaxy of Nixon aides as witnesses, the Watergate hearings became a spectacle unlike any other political event in the history of this or any other country. A nation became riveted to its TV screens. Some people would watch the hearings all day on the commercial TV networks and then again at night on public broadcasting stations. Television made Ervin an immediate folk hero, Senator Howard Baker a possible presidential candidate, and Watergate the central experience of an entire population.

On Friday, May 18, the second day of the hearings, James McCord described overtures of Executive clemency that had been made to him at overlooks on a scenic highway along the Potomac by an old friend, Jack Caulfield, one of the first Nixon White House secret agents. McCord told how a man with a heavy New York accent, later identified as Anthony Ulasewicz, an intermediary for Caulfield, had left word for McCord to go to a pay telephone booth near his home and, over that "safe" telephone, read McCord a message:

> Plead guilty.
> One year is a long time. You will get Executive clemency. Your family will be taken care of and when you get out you will be rehabilitated and a job will be found for you.
> Don't take immunity when called before the grand jury.

On Tuesday, May 22, the day President Nixon issued his statement in which he denied ever authorizing promises of Executive clemency, Caulfield testified that John Dean had told him to make such promises to McCord, and to say the offer "comes from the very highest levels of the White House."

The drama grew as the hearings continued through the testimony of Hugh Sloan, Maurice Stans, and Jeb Magruder. The actions and motivation of each witness were fascinating in and of themselves, but they also built up the theme, stressed so often by Baker, that the real question raised by the hearing was, "What did the President know and when did he know it?" And as the testimony of John Wesley Dean III loomed ever nearer, that theme reached a crescendo, for Dean, as everyone knew, was going to take on Richard Nixon.

John Dean—the man who was regarded by his colleagues as very, very bright, someone who thought things through to their end, ambitious but loyal to Nixon. What had made him become the President's chief accuser?

Dean himself maintained to the last that his aim had been to protect Nixon, to separate the President from the Watergate scandal even if it meant that Dean, Haldeman, and Ehrlichman would go to prison. But, Dean said, the others would not go along with such a plan, and, in Dean's view, they began to set him up as a lone scapegoat, a role he was not willing to accept.

Dean's departure from the coverup had its traceable beginnings in the confirmation hearings of Patrick Gray in March, 1973, which cast him as a likely Watergate villain just as he was entering the confidences of President Nixon. Dean's problems were exacerbated by the testimony of James McCord and by Dean's apparent fear that Gordon Liddy had talked as well. Earlier than his superiors, Dean had seen that the coverup could not continue. By the end of March or beginning of April, he knew that regardless of who above him was to be implicated, his own days were numbered. As Nixon, Haldeman and Ehrlichman failed to accept his views, Dean saw the possibility that he alone would be held accountable for carrying out orders issued by Haldeman and Ehrlichman. In his early meetings with the prosecutors, when immunity was his concern, he testified freely, telling them more and more and gradually working his way up to the roles of Haldeman and Ehrlichman. He did not discuss the President.

The prosecutors refused him immunity for a number of reasons, one of them being that Dean's actions had been reprehensible and that there came a point when a man's station in life was so high that he had to be held accountable for what he had done, lest the criminal justice system subject itself to ridicule.

The more the prosecutors refused immunity, the more Dean had to say. As Dean's attorneys warned Earl Silbert that they were prepared to put the entire Administration on trial, the extent of Dean's confessions came to the attention of Nixon, Haldeman, and Ehrlichman. They were warned by Charles Colson, for one, that Dean was spilling his guts.

..Nixon and his two associates had no idea how adamant the prosecutors were in refusing immunity for Dean. Nixon had come to fear Earl Silbert, in part because of what Dean had said about him. On April 14, for example, Ehrlichman told Nixon and Haldeman that Dean had warned that Silbert would not welcome overtures from anyone in the White House. "Silbert would ask you to wait a minute and he would step out of the room and he would come back to get you and walk you right into the grand jury," Ehrlichman said.

Not knowing how the prosecutors stood on immunity, it was Ehrlichman who insisted that Nixon specify on April 17, 1973, that no White House officials should be granted immunity. When Dean read Nixon's statement, he felt certain, correctly, that it had been aimed at him. Only a day earlier, Nixon had asked Dean to resign, giving him a letter to sign that Dean considered a virtual confession. It was another step toward convincing Dean that he alone had been abandoned by Nixon.

Furthermore, as Henry Petersen began meeting back and forth with the prosecutors and the President, he passed on to Silbert some disparaging remarks Nixon had made about Dean, which apparently helped heighten Dean's fears. Had Dean been closely associated with Nixon for more than a month and a half, he might perhaps have discounted Nixon's remarks to Petersen. The President frequently made cutting statements about people he was close to, either in a gossipy manner or as an apparent means of easing along a conversation. Such remarks provided few or no clues to the way Nixon might actually behave later on, and the fact was, that while Nixon was badmouthing Dean to Petersen, he was praising him to Haldeman and Ehrlichman, still seeming to regard the young counsel as a member of the team, or at least hoping he would stay that way.

From all the information available, then, it is conceivable that the decision by Dean to testify about Nixon was based on a misunderstanding.

For six weeks in May and June, John Dean was interrogated secretly by Ervin Committee chief counsel Sam Dash, with only Senator Ervin aware of the meetings. Dean's Senate testimony was scheduled to begin on Tuesday, the 19th of June. It was not until Saturday, June 16, that the committee staff, represented by chief counsel Dash, minority counsel Fred Thompson, and three others, met with Dean. The only senator present was Howard Baker. In a session that lasted five hours, Dean spoke about the early White House wiretaps and about the planning of Watergate. He inplicated Haldeman and Ehrlichman in the coverup. As for Nixon, he discussed in some detail the conversation of September 15, 1972, the day of the original Watergate indictments, and mentioned but did not describe his later meetings with the President.

In a game of cat and mouse, Dean described White House efforts to cope with the Ervin Committee, telling how a Nixon aide had contacted Senator Baker. He said Baker subsequently asked for a secret meeting with Nixon back in February, four months earlier—a meeting that others in the room except for Dash had never heard of until Dean mentioned it. Baker immediately explained that his reason for contacting Nixon was to discuss the President's hard-line position on Executive privilege. Dean then said that Baker's office sent word to the White House on several occasions that Baker was seeking guidance. Baker said he knew this to have happened only once, when a staff member requested that he be given organizational charts.

The following day, a Sunday, Baker appeared on the television interview program *Issues and Answers* and casually mentioned that he had met privately with Nixon in February, thereby taking the sting out of that part of Dean's later public testimony.

The question must arise as to why Dean gave Baker such an edge—why he mentioned this incident in closed session while keeping away from others. One answer may be that Dean, with his reputation for thinking things through, deliberately forewarned Baker to keep from antagonizing him, or to suggest he had more such goodies where that one came from, in the event Baker became very harsh in questioning.

On Monday, June 18, there was a certain tension in Washington as Soviet leader Leonid Brezhnev arrived for talks with Nixon a day before Dean's scheduled testimony. At the request of Senate Majority Leader Mike Mansfield and Minority Leader Hugh Scott, the Watergate Committee voted 6 to 1 to hold off for six days on having Dean testify. The lone dissenter was Lowell Weicker, who said he saw no reason why this particular exercise in democracy, which "might give an idea to Brezhnev of the strength of our kind of government," couldn't go on.

On Monday afternoon, leaks from Dean's private testimony began. It was revealed that Dean had "borrowed" $4,000 from 1972 campaign finances to pay for his honeymoon, and the implication was that he had misappropriated the money. The following day, Dean was asked to return for another executive session but refused, citing this leak. As if in reprisal for the attempt to sully Dean, one senator forwarded to reporters two pages of the seven-page summary of Dean's closed-door interview which contained Dean's references to Baker's contacts with the White House. The pages also included assertions by Dean that Nixon had wanted the Internal Revenue Service to turn off audits on his friends and that he had asked Dean to keep a list of those in the press who were causing him trouble, as well as Dean's conclusion that Nixon had known of the coverup by September 15, 1972.

Finally, on June 25, Dean was sworn in for what was to be a full week of testimony. With his striking blonde wife, Maureen, seated behind him, he began by stating his belief that the President was involved in the coverup but that "he did not realize or appreciate at any time the implications of his involvement, and I think that when the facts come out, I hope the President is forgiven."

Then, for more than six hours, Dean read from a 245-page prepared statement. Beginning with the atmosphere in the White House when he arrived in 1970, he described the concern about antiwar protesters, news leaks, the desire for political intelligence, "a do-it-yourself White House staff, regardless of the law." Watergate was an accident of fate made possible by such a climate, he said.

Dean described the meetings at Mitchell's office leading to the break-in, saying the second time Liddy proposed illegal tactics, Dean reprimanded him and returned to the White House to complain to Haldeman. Dean described his hearing of the Watergate arrests when he returned from Manila on June 18, 1972, and his immediate feeling that Charles Colson was involved when he was told of Howard Hunt having left a personal check behind. He told of the early days of the coverup; his role as go-between for Haldeman, Ehrlichman, and CRP; his talks with Patrick Gray, Richard Kleindienst, Henry Petersen; the summoning of the CIA into the plot to obstruct justice.

Stopping occasionally for a drink of water, his voice cracking once in a while but generally steady, showing no feeling one way or another, he told of his surprise on August 29, 1972, when Nixon said that a report by Dean showed conclusively that no one in the White House or the Administration, presently employed, had been involved in the bugging. Dean had made no such report. At that early moment, Dean said, he began to consult people he had confidence in—his assistant Fred Fielding, John Mitchell, Nixon aide Richard

Moore—to ask if they felt he was possibly being set up as a fall guy in the event the coverup later cracked.

There was in this passing remark a possible clue to why Dean later broke stride with Nixon in the coverup: he never trusted the President. He felt he himself was expendable. It was a theme developed by other men at other times. It was, in fact, very much in line with the public perception of Nixon the politician for many years: Would you buy a used car from this man?

Dean described his first discussion of Watergate with Nixon after the June, 1972, arrests, on the day of the indictments when the President, Dean said, expressed interest in and knowledge of methods of containing the scandal, Dean outlined the extensive and successful efforts to block the Patman hearings, he told of Donald Segretti, said it would take "another two-hundred pages" to describe how the White House planned its responses to the press reports of the scandal. He laid out Hunt's blackmail demands and efforts at the White House to circumvent the Ervin Committee. Then he began describing the series of meetings he had with Nixon beginning February 27, 1973, focusing most on the meeting of March 21, when he told Nixon of the cancer on the Presidency in the hopes "the President would tell me that we had to end the matter—now."

Dean also told of meeting later that afternoon with Nixon, Haldeman, and Ehrlichman—"a tremendous disappointment to me because it was quite clear that the coverup, as far as the White House was concerned, was going to continue."

In closing, he described his growing concern that he was being cast as a fall guy and his decision to "let the word out that I would not be a scapegoat."

Along with his testimony that first day, Dean introduced dozens of memoranda and other documents to or from the President, Haldeman, Ehrlichman, Colson, Dean himself, and others, dealing with plans to leak selected political information to the press, snooping on Senator Edward Kennedy, dirty tricks, subverting the Patman inquiry, and other matters.

No one could have immediately absorbed what Dean had said and introduced into the record. But the first day was only the beginning. On Tuesday, June 26, Dean, under questioning from Senator Weicker, described in some detail the Huston plan for domestic spying, which had by then been printed in *The New York Times*. Encouraged by Weicker to speak about abuse by the White House of various Executive branch agencies, Dean said—as though it had just come back into mind—"There was also maintained what was called an enemies list, which was rather extensive and continually being updated."

"I am not going to ask who was on it," Weicker said; "I am afraid you might answer."

The Ervin Committee, which had been almost a model of impartiality in its opening days, now broke into open combat over Dean. Senator Gurney and minority counsel Thompson tried to cast doubt on Dean's credibility, and Dean engaged in a particularly sharp give-and-take with Thompson.

"Mr. Dean," Thompson said on Tuesday, "let me ask you a few questions about your actions after the Watergate incident and by asking questions about your own personal involvement, I hope I am not appearing to be badgering you in any way, but I am sure you understand that your actions and motivations are very relevant?"

Dean responded icily: "In fact, if I were still at the White House, I would probably be feeding you the questions to ask the person who is sitting here."

The remark, a reminder that the man who faced up to the President of the United States would be no easy target for hostile elements of the committee, infuriated Thompson and set him to talking like Sam Ervin at a tired moment: "If I were here as I am, I would have responded as I have responded, that I do not need questions to be fed to me by anybody," Thompson said.

On the other side, Sam Dash and Ervin were protective of Dean. If Dean had felt a father-son relationship with John Mitchell, as he said he did, Ervin moved rapidly to fill the void and was almost fondling in his questioning. He and Dean turned the act of testimony into a minuet, bowing and pointing at a President who was not there.

On Wednesday, June 27, Dean entered for the record the notorious enemies list, with his own accompanying recommendations as to "how we can use the available federal machinery to screw our political enemies." Included were not only hundreds of names of prominent Americans, but memos from White House aides who had nominees for the list, or requests that certain people be removed from it.

From Nixon himself was a notation in the margin of one of the news summaries he was given every morning. Next to the name of Democratic national chairman Robert Strauss,

Nixon had written, interestingly enough, "Is he on our list?—Or should he be?"

As the nation began to ponder this new Watergate marvel, Ervin and Dean engaged in beautifully harmonious dialogue:

> *Ervin*: Didn't those in the White House interested in President Nixon's re-election and then the re-election committee classify among their enemies people who dissented from President Nixon's programs?
>
> *Dean*: As I say, those who were able to command an audience were singled out . . .
>
> *Ervin*: So we have here plans to violate the Fourth Amendment, which were approved by the President according to Mr. Haldeman; we have people being branded enemies whose mere offense is that they believed in enforcing the First Amendment as proclaimed by the Supreme Court of the United States just about a week ago.
>
> *Dean*: That is correct.
>
> *Ervin*: Yes. . . . And the President discussed again on St. Patrick's Day he was not willing for any of his aides past or present to appear before [this] committee and give testimony in person.
>
> *Dean*: Well, we had discussed that before he made that statement, Mr. Chairman, that he certainly did not want Mr. Haldeman and Mr. Ehrlichman coming up here before the committee nor did he want me appearing before this committee.
>
> *Ervin*: And this was on the 15th and the 17th day of March, about a month after Mr. Buzhardt says that the President was anxious for all the facts to be revealed. Do you know how facts can be revealed except by people who know something about those facts?
>
> (Laughter.)
>
> *Dean*: No sir, I do not. I think that the theory that was developing was that to take the very hard line initially and back down to written interrogatories. But that would be the bottom line. I believe that was as far as the President was willing to go because he felt that written statements could be handled and quite obviously it is much easier to prepare a written brief or a statement than it is to submit yourself to cross-examination.
>
> *Ervin*: I believe you discussed at that time the assertion that I made, I was not willing to accept written state-

ments because you cannot cross-examine a written statement.
Dean: Yes, and I had discussion with the President about that very statement.
Ervin: Just one other matter. Article II of the Constitution says, in defining the power of the President, Section 3 of Article II, "He"—that is, the President—"shall take care that the laws be faithfully executed." Do you know anything that the President did or said at any time between June 17 and the present moment to perform his duty to see that the laws are faithfully executed in respect to what is called the Watergate affair?

For Sam Ervin, the latter-day Dr. Johnson, the abuse by the King was clearly enormous, and Nature was, as Johnson had told Boswell, rising up and claiming her original rights.

Ervin, joined by Howard Baker, began to hint broadly and then demand outright that Nixon testify before the committee, possibly in a meeting at the White House. Instead, from the Executive mansion came an attack on Dean. Nixon's attorney, J. Fred Buzhardt, sent questions to be asked of the star witness, constructed in such a way as to put the onus for the Watergate coverup on him and referring to John Mitchell as Dean's "patron," a word frequently used in purges in Moscow but seldom applied to political relationships in this country. The questions were asked by Senator Inouye, who identified them as having come from the White House. They failed to make a dent in Dean, and before a day was out, the attack was disowned by another of Nixon's attorneys, Leonard Garment, who said the President had not been aware of Buzhardt's move.

Then, in a strange but not unforeseen way, when Dean's testimony was completed, things began to change. The next witness, John Mitchell, and the one following him, special counsel to the President Richard A. Moore, did the work of clean-up crews after a hurricane. Blame was aimed at Mitchell, who shouldered it while staunchly defending Nixon. Watergate had a tendency to be a story of what happened yesterday; Dean's testimony, as striking as it was, was getting stale.

By Friday, July 13, the day Moore took the stand, the Ervin hearings were almost a month old. They had opened at a time when there was unprecedented pressure on the President. Somehow, despite the abundant testimony by

Dean, Nixon seemed able to weather any attack. True, his popularity was down, but the worst, his defenders thought, was over. Ronald Ziegler reportedly told a White House speech writer that Dean had not "laid a glove" on Nixon.

Moore, older and kindlier appearing than most of those on the President's staff, was a specialist on public relations, especially with the communications media, and he was appearing at the special request of the White House in an obvious attempt to strike back at Dean. He was to pave the way for Ehrlichman and Haldeman, who were to appear later. But owing to a completely unforeseen event, the twisting and turning Watergate story began moving in another direction entirely.

2

Jo HORTON AND Charlotte Mary Maquire were students and good friends at the University of California at Los Angeles immediately after World War II, and they used to double-date. Their beaus were fellow students, Bob Haldeman and Alex Butterfield, and the young men became friendly through the girls.

"Even in college," Butterfield told me in June, 1974, "Haldeman was always efficient. He wasn't the kind of guy who would suffer fools easily. He was always suntanned, didn't drink, was a very nice guy. But little discrepancies would bother him."

Both men married their college sweethearts. The Haldemans stayed in California, where Haldeman began his climb with the J. Walter Thompson advertising agency and began to work in politics for Richard Nixon. The Butterfields traveled the world as Alex pursued a career in the Air Force. Over the years, the Butterfields and the Haldemans didn't see each other, but the wives exchanged Christmas cards, and, Butterfield told me, "We felt we knew them very well."

During the Lyndon Johnson Administration, Butterfield worked for a time in the Pentagon as one of Defense Secretary Robert MacNamara's military assistants. One of his associates was Alexander Haig, and both of them worked under Joseph Califano until Califano was called to the White House as special assistant to Johnson. Butterfield was a White House liaison officer, preparing press releases on astronauts and the like.

From there, Butterfield went to the National War College in Washington, a training ground for those who climb to the heights in the American military. In the summer of 1967 he was sent to Australia as a full colonel, the ranking American military official there. He had a title commensurate with high position—Commander in Chief Pacific Representative/Australia, or CINCPACREP—but a dull job.

His office was in charge of inspecting lamb that went to U.S. servicemen in the Pacific and of running the American dependents' school program and the R and R (rest and recreation) program for American fighting men in Southeast Asia who took their leave in Australia. He had a lawyer on his staff, four officers, eight enlisted men, a secretary, an airplane, and a car.

"It's the kind of place you'd want to go in your last year in service as you're getting ready to retire," Butterfield recalled.

After Richard Nixon won the 1968 election, Butterfield began to see Haldeman's name in the newspapers as the man who would be chief of staff and who was then helping the President choose his Cabinet. One Sunday early in January 1969, Haldeman telephoned Butterfield from Washington. "I complimented him on what he was doing," Butterfield said, "and he asked me, 'How would you like to be part of all this?'"

Butterfield's military file had been forwarded to Haldeman in the search for an aide for national security adviser Henry Kissinger. The man selected was Butterfield's former colleague, Alexander Haig. But Haldeman put Butterfield's file aside and thought of him for another job that he laid out in the telephone call from halfway across the world.

As Butterfield remembered it, Haldeman said, "You would be my immediate deputy. You'd be called deputy assistant to the President and work right with me and the President. We'd want you to get out of the military. I know you're a career officer, and I want you to think about it. You would have to come now, before the Inaugural."

Haldeman said he himself would be working with the President almost all the time, that Butterfield would serve as a backup man when Haldeman wasn't there. There was one possible problem, Butterfield recalled Haldeman saying—"The personal chemistry thing. The President is used to just a few men around him. It could be it won't work out. If that happens, we'll find something else for you."

Butterfield left for Washington the following Wednesday, his departure from the Air Force surprising some who saw him not only as a gung-ho career officer but one who was certain to advance higher up the ladder.

Since he was to work so closely with the President, Butterfield expected to be introduced to Nixon right away, but Haldeman kept putting that off. Finally, after about ten days, just before Haldeman was to go to California while the President stayed in Washington, Haldeman ushered Butterfield into the Oval Office. Butterfield's recollection of this meeting was similar to that described by Jeb Magruder, who said that in his own "great-to-have-you-aboard chat" with Nixon, he had been "struck by how ill at ease the President seemed."

Butterfield said the President stood up, shuffled his feet and dug them into the carpet, had his chin into his chest, looked down at the floor, and didn't seem to know what to do with his hands—making Butterfield so uncomfortable that he didn't know what to do with *his* hands. Haldeman was seated on a couch, and he shrugged as Butterfield looked at him, as if to explain that this was why the introduction had been so delayed.

In his first year, Butterfield had some political as well as administrative duties, most notably making contact with outside organizations—helping, as he put it, to get "the silent American majority to be identified and to stand up." Then, late in 1969, Charles Colson was brought to the White House on the recommendation of presidential adviser Bryce Harlow, and Colson took over contact with outside groups.

In January, 1970, Butterfield moved to Haldeman's office just outside the President's door as the chief of staff took over grand quarters known as the Vice-President's ceremonial office a few doors down. Butterfield assumed a great many of Haldeman's administrative duties, including the responsibility of seeing that the President's day ran smoothly. With a large staff to run White House operations, Butterfield personally would meet with Ronald Ziegler, the White House photographer, and anyone else necessary to set the schedule for the following day. He was trusted to read messages to the President from Henry Kissinger or others in high position, and sometimes he was asked to express his own views on matters.

By and large, however, Butterfield's role was not that of an adviser; his recommendations were made simply because he was in Haldeman's or Nixon's presence so much. He also served as secretary to the Cabinet, attending all its meetings when the President was sitting in on them, and often was a third person present on private meetings Nixon held with officials.

As time passed, Butterfield became fairly powerful in the White House in the ways that keepers of the keys are powerful in all institutions. When Ehrlichman asked that an important assistant be given use of a car, Butterfield could and did refuse; when Ehrlichman then went to Haldeman to protest, Butterfield politely asked Haldeman to stay out of it. He knew who was who on the staff as he saw them entering or not entering the Oval Office. He spent long periods of time with Nixon, especially on trips when Haldeman would stay behind.

On occasion the President went out of his way to show kind feelings to his aide. Butterfield, handsome in the way many Californians are—tanned, tall, and even-featured—had a daughter, "a beautiful girl," he told me, who suffered a broken leg and other injuries that required plastic surgery as the result of an automobile crash in which the driver of the other car died. Butterfield's daughter was hospitalized for a good while, and the day she was to return home, Nixon insisted that Butterfield take her to the White House to see him first.

"Her face was swollen and she was on crutches. The President talked to her about courage, and gave her a little gift. It was a nice gesture, something he wanted to do and obviously wasn't doing for publicity, because there was no press," Butterfield told me.

On one occasion, Nixon mentioned to Butterfield his own problem in making small talk and said he hoped that Cabinet members circulated some in the White House, that they introduced themselves to secretaries and staff members and chatted with them. "God knows," Butterfield quoted the President as saying, "I couldn't do that."

One day Haldeman's aide Lawrence Higby told Butterfield that Nixon wanted to keep an oral record of his conversations, and that Haldeman wanted Butterfield to have a taping system installed. Butterfield passed the message along to the Secret Service, whose technical division installed the system. The only ones who knew of its existence, according to Butterfield, were Nixon, Haldeman, Higby, Butterfield, Butterfield's secretary, and two or possibly three Secret Service men.

Butterfield monitored the tapes several times to ascertain that the system was adequate, and in his own judgment, the sound was clear. He started to show the President how the system had been installed, he said, but Nixon didn't seem interested. Butterfield felt Nixon was oblivious to the tapes.

Once Charles Colson came to Butterfield in alarm, saying

he was almost certain that Nixon's telephone was bugged. Butterfield told Colson that surely he was mistaken. Colson insisted, saying he had heard telltale clicking sounds, and he wanted Butterfield to run an electronic sweep. The possibility was then raised that perhaps it was Colson's telephone that had been bugged, and Colson asked if he could run a check on his own telephone.

As time passed, Butterfield, unaccustomed to staying in one place for very long, grew restless in his job and, although he doesn't like to talk about it, apparently unhappy with the Boy Scout atmosphere. As the first Nixon Administration drew to a close, all staff members were asked to submit pro forma resignations and to give Haldeman what Butterfield called "what I want to be when I grow up" letters. Butterfield put in for a job as undersecretary of transportation and several positions in the Department of Defense.

One Sunday, Butterfield told me, Nixon said, "Bob tells me you'd like to leave, although we'd been planning on you continuing here." They talked about a new assignment, and Nixon suggested that perhaps the aide would want to transfer to the State Department—a place where all Presidents are anxious to have high-level staff members who are totally loyal to them. The transportation job went to White House plumber Egil Krogh, and the question of where Butterfield would go was left open for a while.

Shortly after that, in December, 1972, the chief job at the Federal Aviation Administration became open and John Ehrlichman thought Butterfield would be perfect for it. Because of objections to Butterfield's military reserve status, his transfer was delayed until March 14, 1973, just as Watergate was heating up. At the end of February, as he was putting things in order, Butterfield told Haldeman that he felt he had to notify Steve Bull, an aide who was assuming some of his work, of the taping system. "Oh, sure, sure," Haldeman said. If Haldeman or Nixon had forgotten the existence of the tapes, Butterfield then gave Haldeman a reminder.

Late in April, 1973, Butterfield had his first experience as a witness before Watergate investigators. He was called to testify before Earl Silbert about his role in the placing of $350,000 of CRP money in a friend's bank account. Butterfield explained that he had been asked by Haldeman's aide Gordon Strachan if he knew someone who could be relied on to hold money, and he had no idea what the funds were for. Later, after the election, this money was returned to CRP and was used as hush money for the Watergate defendants, but Butterfield said he had no knowledge of that.

Butterfield described to me the eerie feeling of sitting down and counting all that money, and I asked him if he didn't feel there was something peculiar about the request to find a friend who would hold it. "When you work in the White House, for the President of the United States," he explained, "the last thing you think of is that you might be involved in some wrongdoing."

On July 13, 1973, as the Watergate Committee went through a second day of hearing public testimony from Richard A. Moore, Butterfield was called to testify in a closed session with committee staff aides. Most of the questioning was conducted by a young investigator, Scott Armstrong.

Armstrong asked Butterfield about how records were kept of conversations between Nixon and staff aides, and handed him a copy of notes taken from Nixon's Watergate attorney, J. Fred Buzhardt, on meetings between the President and John Dean. Butterfield studied the memorandum and realized immediately that it had to have come from the President's tapes. The notes described in brief detail what had been discussed in twenty-three conversations, and Butterfield told Armstrong that the President's memory was good, but not that good.

Butterfield knew that Haldeman and Higby had testified in closed session before he had, and he wondered whether either had mentioned the existence of the taping system. He felt the Senate committee should be told of the tapes, but he feared that public disclosure of the system would prove embarrassing to the President and to the United States as well, since all visits, including those by foreign dignitaries, were recorded. At the same time, Butterfield told me, he felt that if the existence of the tapes was to be made public, it was not exactly fitting for so peripheral a figure as he to tell the world of them. It would have been better, he thought, if a way could be found for the President to introduce them.

As Armstrong continued to ask questions, Butterfield sat toying with the Buzhardt memo and came to a decision: if asked a direct question, he would tell of the tapes. After about three hours, a Republican staff member, Donald Sanders, took over the interrogation. Sanders noted John Dean's suspicion that the President might have taped one of their conversations, and he asked whether there was reason for such a concern.

Here was the question. Butterfield said yes, there was. The Ervin Committee staff members showed no surprise as Butterfield described how the system had been installed in the Oval Office, the Executive Office Building of the President, the Cabinet meeting room, and on telephones used by Nixon at one other location in the White House and at Camp David.

"They were cool," Butterfield told me. "I had no idea whether what I was saying was new to them."

As the meeting came to a close, Butterfield asked, "Do these sessions serve as a prelude to public testimony?" The staff members said they often did, but not always. They all walked out, into a hallway. Armstrong left for a moment and then returned. Finally Butterfield said, "I realize as well as anyone the import, the fantastic significance of the information I have given you. If you had it before, fine. If you haven't had it before, I hope you handle it awfully carefully."

Butterfield mentioned that he was to leave for Moscow Tuesday, July 17, on FAA business. While the meeting was important, he could, if need be, send an aide. Should he change his plans? he asked. Armstrong indicated that he felt not. On Saturday, Butterfield flew to Nashua County, New Hampshire, for the dedication of a new air traffic control center. When he returned home, around 6 P.M., his wife said, "My gosh, what an active day. Phone calls from the office and a young man came out to the house from the Senate committee. He said they forgot to ask you the name of your secretary."

The request convinced Butterfield that he had been the first to testify about the tapes. He called Armstrong, who confirmed that and said he was recommending that Butterfield be called to testify publicly on Monday. The news of the taping system was dynamite, Armstrong said.

"Scott, I think that's wrong," Butterfield said. "Are you sure you've considered it enough?"

Either that night or Sunday morning, Butterfield told me, he telephoned Senator Howard Baker and asked if he could call on him. "I didn't know Ervin, and I knew Baker slightly as a member of the President's political party," Butterfield said in way of explanation. "I went to his house at 2 P.M. Sunday. He didn't act as though he knew anything about my testimony. I told him my concern that there would be embarrassment, that in seeing him I wanted to make sure there were some mature, senior people considering the ramifications of the release of that information.

"Baker said, 'Alex, first of all, I've got to tell you I do know about this situation. I've got the whole file upstairs. With regard to going public, I hate to admit it, but we can't keep anything under wraps. Everything leaks. I understand your concern, but I'll be surprised if it keeps for the weekend.'"

Butterfield said he tried to impress upon Baker how bad it would look for such a peripheral figure to explode so great a time bomb on the public. Baker told Butterfield there was a good chance he might not have to testify right away, and that he would let him know on Monday.

As Butterfield left, Baker asked whether he had informed anyone in the White House of his testimony. No, he hadn't, Butterfield said, but he intended to, just as he had informed White House attorney Leonard Garment of his testimony before Earl Silbert a few days after giving it.

"From Baker's house, I went to the Windsor Park Hotel, had my driver stop there, and I telephoned the White House and asked for Garment. He was out of town, due back that night. He called me at home, and I think he must have been at work, because I believed Buzhardt was with him." Butterfield told Garment what he had testified to, and Garment was shocked. "He said something like, 'Jesus Christ,' or some other expression of alarm and concern," Butterfield said in answer to my questioning.

On Monday morning between 11:10 and 11:20, Butterfield was at the barber shop in the Sheraton Carlton Hotel on 16th Street, near the White House, where the barber who cuts Nixon's hair runs his own shop. Butterfield's secretary called and said that James Hamilton, an assistant chief counsel on the Ervin Committee, was trying to get him, and shortly after that, Hamilton called. He told Butterfield that he was to be interrogated publicly right away, as soon as Richard Moore's testimony was completed and before the next scheduled witness, Herbert Kalmbach.

Butterfield told me that his first reaction was one of anger; everything he feared might happen was happening. He hadn't heard from Baker and he didn't know exactly what to do. He gave me this account of the conversation:

"I won't appear," Butterfield said.

"What?" asked Hamilton.

"I'm not coming."

Hamilton explained that Senator Ervin had demanded that he appear. Butterfield said, the hell with Ervin, or words to that effect; he was not going. Hamilton said it was only fair to warn Butterfield that he would pass the message on to Ervin as Butterfield had given it.

Twenty minutes later Hamilton called back, just as Butterfield was leaving the barbershop. He said, "I whispered your message in Ervin's ear, and Ervin raised his eyebrows and said, 'If he's not in my office at 12:30, I will have law enforcement officers come and get him.'"

At 12:40, Butterfield, somewhat contrite, apologized to Ervin, saying that he was upset because things were running so fast. Once more, he explained his feeling that the revelation of the tapes would be very embarrassing to the President and the nation, and said he wasn't sure that he should be the one to tell the world about them.

But shortly after 2 P.M., Monday, July 16, 1973, Alexander P. Butterfield, one of the few surprise witnesses before the Ervin Committee, was asked by minority counsel Fred Thompson, "Mr. Butterfield, are you aware of the installation of any listening devices in the Oval Office of the President?"

"I was aware of listening devices; yes, sir."

If John Dean had identified President Nixon as the culprit in the Watergate coverup, Butterfield told the world where the evidence could be found. The Watergate saga was never the same after the existence of the tapes was revealed. The Senate Watergate Committee and Special Prosecutor Archibald V. Cox immediately moved to obtain a small number of the taped conversations, selecting ones that seemed most important on the basis of Dean's testimony. The President fought to block their release.

Once the Watergate Committee had uncovered the existence of the tapes, its real usefulness, at least in the pursuit of Richard Nixon, had largely come to an end. Although the committee did make other findings that were damaging to the President and his close associates—in particular the revelations regarding Nixon's friend, Bebe Rebozo, and the $100,000 funneled from billionaire Howard Hughes to Rebozo—all other testimony about Nixon and about his top aides became of secondary importance.

The committee's stated function was to investigate 1972 presidential campaign activities with an eye toward creating legislation that might keep such scandals as Watergate from recurring. Legislation, however, was not what most people concerned about the scandal were looking for; what was sought was a means of dealing with perpetrators of crimes now that the scandals had been exposed.

So despite the fact that the Watergate Committee continued to remain active, interest in it waned after the summer of 1973. Its signal contribution will be remembered as the discovery of the existence of a taping system in the White House. But in a broader sense, in terms of the future of politics and governing in this country, the Ervin hearings will serve as a model of how well the "system" of democracy may work in the United States.

The committee was, however, not without its imperfections. Its members had been selected by the Democratic and Republican parties, people who may have wanted to teach Nixon a lesson but never gave any indication that they wanted to punish him severely. Sam Dash told me that as he introduced himself to the members of the committee after his appointment by Ervin, each senator claimed to have been drafted for the job. Not one, Dash said, told him that he had asked to be on the committee. Only one senator, Lowell Weicker, through his own probing and constant attacks on the White House, became a leader in the fight to expose the moral barrenness of the Nixon Administration. While other senators showed occasional signs of fury at what they heard, Weicker alone acted as a prosecutor might in chasing down the crime of the century.

Ervin's questioning of Maurice Stans was bold and incisive. Senator Talmadge's assault on John Mitchell was electrifying. But questioning of reluctant witnesses by the senators was often flaccid. They, and the staff members too, were incredibly soft with Richard Helms and Vernon Walters of the CIA, men who for a time had loaned themselves to the Watergate coverup. Former Attorney General Kleindienst and his assistant, Henry Petersen, were praised by senators instead of hounded.

Even so, the hearings represented a triumph of great dimensions for openness in government. Because they were televised, people in great numbers could form their own judgments as to where guilt or innocence lay. When the chief of staff of the President of the United States, a man not chosen for that role because he has no memory, comes into millions of homes and says 150 times over the space of three days "I can't remember," or, "I have no recollection," something begins to register.

If, as Nixon suggested about Baker, any senators on the committee intended to hold sensational hearings for a brief time and then allow them to subside, the massive scrutiny of the TV cameras and the press helped prevent that. The fact that the hearings were on television, then, contributed to an unprecedented assault on the politics of cooperation and rescue. Scrutiny kept politicians honest; the risk of public humiliation runs high on TV.

A year earlier, before the 1972 election, judges, prosecution and defense lawyers, Nixon campaign officials, and members of Congress had espoused a theme that publicity about Watergate would interfere with the processes of justice. With that rationale, they effectively hid the crimes of the Nixon re-election campaign until after the President emerged triumphant—and thereby thwarted justice. The lesson of the televised hearings was that the glare of publicity could serve the cause of proper governance. In this regard, the Ervin Committee hearings resulted in a great public exploration and kept the citizenry better informed than any forum in the criminal justice system could have.

But the triumph of openness and disclosure seemed more inflicted on the Watergate senators and other members of Congress than it was welcomed by them. As the burden of inquiry shifted to Special Prosecutor Archibald Cox, the elected leadership on Capitol Hill shrank from drawing conclusions, from assessing their findings and apportioning guilt or innocence. Senator Baker piously asserted that he would withhold judgment until the last piece of evidence was in hand. Three of the Democrats on the committee, Inouye, Talmadge, and Montoya, while occasionally being severe with individual witnesses, generally refrained from making any overall judgments except to point to and deplore the general rot. Once, after the testimony of John Ehrlichman, Inouye mumbled, "What a liar," into an open microphone. Beyond that, almost all members of the committee were scrupulous in their refusal to interpret for the American people the importance of their findings at a time when the nation was looking for solutions to corruption and not simply further evidence of scandal.

Ervin and Weicker, who made no secret of their disgust with Nixon, failed to take the obvious next step: to assert, in line with their newfound positions as moral as well as political leaders, that on the basis of their findings, the President was either fit or not fit to hold office. Instead, almost all members of the committee said at one time or another that it was not their function to judge, but only to make inquiry and recommend legislation.

Even in July, 1974, when the Senate Watergate Committee issued its final report, it refrained from making judgments about the role of Nixon in the Watergate coverup. Samuel Dash told me, as the report was being finished, that the committee's findings would be very clear, that "we're saying here's two plus two, and people can add that up." Senator Ervin, in his homey way, said at about the same time, "There are two ways to draw a picture of a horse. One is to draw a horse, and the other is to draw a picture of a horse and write under it, 'Horse.' "

Ordinarily, such a conclusion might have been unassailable. But the failure of the elected leadership to express judgments after hearing so much evidence resulted in extreme frustration for large numbers of the citizenry who had followed the hearings closely and were now waiting to hear, from their leaders, the wise expression of informed opinion. What was lacking, after almost three months of unrelieved, harsh disclosure, was any endeavor to place the crimes of the Nixon Administration in a perspective. The public could see that crimes had been committed. But politics is foreign to most people. Were Nixon's activities common in Washington, or were they aberrant? It was the function of leadership to analyze, explain, and interpret Watergate, yet not only the members of the Watergate Committee, but the leaders of both political parties failed to make an attempt.

As the summer of Watergate hearings came to a close, one man—Nixon himself—moved to fill that void. On August 15, 1973, a week after the hearings recessed, the President, in a nationally televised address, with a perfect understanding of the problem, said that he would "provide a perspective on the issue for the American people," exactly what all others had failed to do. He then denied any personal involvement in wrongdoing and blamed Watergate on the attitude of a few overzealous people who assumed that "their cause placed them beyond the reach of those rules that apply to other persons and that hold a free society together."

It was the same attitude, he said, as that of individuals and groups who, in the 1960's, "asserted the right to take the law into their own hands, insisting that their purposes represented a higher morality," and whose attitude "was praised in the press and from some of our pulpits as evidence of a new idealism."

"One excess begets another," Nixon said. "The extremes of violence and discord in the 1960's contributed to the extremes of Watergate." He said that "after twelve weeks and two million words of televised testimony, we have reached a point at which a continued, backward-looking obsession with Watergate is causing this nation to neglect matters of far greater importance to all the American people."

As he had in the past, and as he was to continue to do, Nixon said it was his "constitutional responsibility to defend the integrity of this great office against false charges," attempting to make an attack on him appear to be an assault on the democratic process.

Thus began the final round in the Watergate battle as it played itself out before the public. On the one side was the amassing of mounds of incriminating information leading to the belief that the President of the United States was deeply involved in and responsible for the worst corruption imaginable, but with almost no elected official saying, "Look, the Emperor has no clothes on." On the other side was the President, with a diminishing but staunch number of defenders, either maintaining that he was innocent or saying that his conduct was not any different from that of his predecessors.

Nixon, as tough as the metal he likened himself to, could withstand the most punishing disclosures. In the courts, as the Ervin Committee and the Special Prosecutor fought to get hold of the tapes of his conversations, attorneys for the President maintained that in order to protect all future presidents and to insure the fundamental constitutional provisions of the separation of powers, the President was dutybound not to relinquish the tapes. The President's principal attorney at the time, Charles Wright, continually issued the ultimate dare—Congress could impeach the President, but it could not force the tapes out of him.

In September, 1973, as Congress returned from its midyear recess, the first thing the leadership made clear was that it had no intention of impeaching Nixon. Senate Majority Leader Mike Mansfield spoke about the need to bring the Watergate hearings to a speedy conclusion, and several of his Republican counterparts insisted that the public was bored with Watergate and, as Nixon had said, anxious to get on with the nation's more important business, such as the battle to stop inflation.

Senator Baker, who on the basis of the Watergate hearings had arranged perhaps the most extensive and lucrative lecture tour ever undertaken by a member of Congress, had the audacity to say that Watergate was taking so much of his time that his other work was suffering.

It was not the behavior of a leadership that was intent on rooting out the worst corruption in the nation's history; it seemed more the old politics of rescue at play.

Watergate by then was clearly the ultimate in political crimes. There had been abundant testimony that under Nixon the CIA had been dragged into domestic affairs; the investigation and findings of the FBI had been subverted; the Justice Department had engaged in malicious prosecutions of some people and failed to act in instances where it should have; the Internal Revenue Service had been used to punish the President's alleged enemies while ignoring transgressions by his friends and by the President himself; the purity of the court system had been violated; congressmen had been seduced to prevent an inquiry into campaign activities before the election; extortion on a massive scale had been practiced in the soliciting of illegal contributions from the nation's great corporations; the President had secretly engaged in acts of war against a foreign country despite the wording of the Constitution that gives Congress the sole power to declare war; and agents of the President were known to have engaged in continued illegal activities for base political ends.

PART VII

"Saturday Night Massacre": The Road to Impeachment

1

ON FRIDAY NIGHT, October 19, 1973, President Nixon began what many people have since come to regard as the most reckless step of his political career. Plagued by the Watergate and related scandals, and ordered by the courts to relinquish the tapes of nine of his private conversations, Nixon announced that he had effected a "compromise" that would both allow him to maintain the confidentiality his office required and give Special Prosecutor Archibald V. Cox the material he needed to conduct his investigation at the same time.

Under the plan, Nixon would submit summaries of the relevant portions of the tapes to Judge John J. Sirica, and an independent verifier, Senator John Stennis of Mississippi, would be allowed to listen to the tapes to authenticate the version given the judge. It would be Nixon's last bow to Cox—the Special Prosecutor would have to agree not to use the judicial process to seek further tapes or other records of Nixon's conversations in the future.

Because of this shortcoming and others in the plan, Nixon's aides knew that Cox would not accept it. On Saturday, as he refused, White House chief of staff Alexander Haig ordered Attorney General Richardson to fire Cox. Richardson resigned instead. Haig then ordered Deputy Attorney General William Ruckelshaus to fire him, and Ruckelshaus also resigned. Finally, the number-three man in the Justice Department, Solicitor General Robert Bork, was named acting attorney general, and he fired Cox. White House press secretary Ronald Ziegler announced that the Office of Special Prosecutor had been abolished, and FBI agents were dispatched to prevent Cox's staff members, whose status was in limbo, from taking their files out of their offices.

What came to be known as the "Saturday Night Massacre" then unleashed the torrent of public anger at Nixon that had been building across the nation. In a period of ten days, more than a million letters and telegrams descended on members of Congress, almost all of them demanding Nixon's impeachment. Before long, according to some, there were three million letters and telegrams, and an impeachment inquiry was begun.

All this was a result of what seemed at first to have been an impetuous action by the President. But Nixon's firing of Cox was by no means a rash, sudden action. The President, who knew how dangerous a special prosecutor could be, agreed to the appointment of one in the spring of 1973 only after severe pressure had been placed on him. By the middle of June, 1973, Nixon's aides were complaining about Cox. Nixon himself voiced extreme displeasure in the first days of July, and by early October—at least twelve days before the Saturday Night Massacre—he announced privately that Cox would be fired.

Occasionally, and early on, the President broke through his own veil of insulation and revealed his thinking to his third attorney general, Elliot Richardson. Through subsequent testimony before the Senate Judiciary Committee, and the House Judiciary Committee, and in statements to intimates, Richardson dispassionately put into the record strong evidence that Nixon's behavior during this period continued to be that of a man bent on using any and all means to block the pursuit of justice.

When Archibald Cox settled in as special prosecutor in May, 1973, he told friends he expected to be in Washington for three to possibly seven years. His assignment was monumental. He was given carte blanche to investigate as he saw fit in a public pledge by Elliot Richardson at the Attorney General's Senate confirmation hearings. Only the Attorney General could fire Cox, and then only for what Richardson said would be "extraordinary improprieties."

President Nixon, in his May 22, 1973, statement, had promised that "Executive privilege will not be invoked as to any testimony concerning possible criminal conduct, in the matters presently under investigation, including the Watergate affair and the alleged coverup." Cox had the authority and the blessing to seek and get any and all information, or so it appeared.

But on May 25, the day Richardson was sworn in, the President told the new Attorney General in a conversation in the Oval Office that he had used the word "testimony" *advisedly*, that he had meant it to apply only to oral testimony and not to documents.

Earlier, on April 30, when Nixon spoke to Richardson about the appointment of a special prosecutor, the President mentioned only Watergate and not related scandals. The statement was vague; Nixon didn't specifically rule out investigations of incidents other than the break-in and bugging. But it served to alert Richardson that there might be trouble on down the road, possible problems he should note and come back to at another time. Richardson didn't have to wait long before the problem came back to him. Almost immediately afterward, John Ehrlichman, although he resigned the morning of April 30, called to say that the Special Prosecutor had to be kept away from "national security" matters.

Nevertheless, as Cox began to settle in, there was an air of optimism at his office and at that of the Attorney General's as well. Richard Darman, who had followed Richardson as a close aide from the Office of Health, Education and Welfare to the Defense Department and then to the Justice Department, explained it to me in this manner: "Those first days at Justice were euphoric for anyone who could remember how hard it was to get anything from the White House while at HEW. Now there was cooperation."

It was a moment when the President was at his weakest—under pressure from every quarter in March and April, he had let go of Haldeman and Ehrlichman only to be smashed by the Ellsberg revelations and the CIA testimony and the opening of Senate Watergate hearings in May. For a period of about a month, Nixon and his new chief of staff, Alexander Haig, under constant battering, submitted to requests for materials by both the Senate Watergate Committee and the Special Prosecutor.

Cox also had the fruits of the work done by the original Watergate prosecutors, Silbert, Glanzer, and Campbell, who had broken the case by the time of his appointment. He was getting cooperation from at least four of the men who were conspirators in the bugging or the coverup and in other related scandals: John Dean, Jeb Magruder, Herbert Kalmbach, and Frederick C. LaRue.

With such a fast start, and a $2.8 million annual budget that allowed him ninety employees, Cox immediately extended the Watergate inquiry so broadly that the term "Watergate" had little to do with much of his investigation; it was only a convenient label to attach to the many probes of the Executive branch under Nixon.

Cox was looking into the work of the White House plumbers, the early White House wiretaps, and illegal campaign contributions to Nixon, including those that had allegedly been a payoff to Nixon by the dairy industry for the promise to raise milk price supports. He was investigating the role of the White House in the ITT merger plans, and dirty tricks aside from Watergate in the 1972 campaign. Much of his inquiry paralleled that of the Senate Watergate Committee, with one crucial difference: Cox worked through the criminal justice system and had the power, therefore, to follow his investigation through with criminal prosecutions. So while the Ervin Committee gave public airing to the most sensational charges of corruption ever made about a presidential staff, Cox quietly began putting together material for indictments.

In the middle of June, Haig called Richardson to express displeasure at the scope of Cox's investigations. Then, on July 3, three and a half months before the Saturday Night Massacre, came the first warning that the President was considering firing Cox.

That morning, the *Los Angeles Times* reported that Cox's staff had begun a preliminary inquiry into the President's acquisition of his estate at San Clemente and improvements made on it. The report, according to Cox, who was forced to issue a denial later in the day, was incorrect. What had happened, he said, was that he had been asked so frequently about San Clemente at press conferences that he requested an aide to get him newspaper articles on it to increase his understanding of the subject. The aide called the *Los Angeles Times* and asked for all their clips on San Clemente, which led to the writing of the July 3 article.

Nixon was in Key Biscayne when the story appeared. Haig, who was with him, telephoned Richardson, who was in the midst of a meeting with Baltimore U.S. attorney George Beall and three of his assistants. Richardson excused himself to take the call in another office. Haig said that Cox was overstepping his bounds enormously if he was looking into San Clemente, and that Cox would be fired if he didn't shape up.

As though the Haig warning were not serious enough business in itself, when Richardson returned to his visitors, Beall and his assistants began to spell out to the Attorney

General, for the first time, the incriminating testimony they had been gathering against Vice-President Spiro T. Agnew in the course of an investigation of kickbacks and corruption in Maryland. As this new, terrifying scandal was being thrust in his lap, Richardson had to leave the room several more times to talk to Cox or Haig. Finally he was able to tell Haig that Cox was only asking for newspaper clippings to read, that he was not investigating San Clemente.

Nixon broke into the call himself, angrily demanding that the Attorney General have Cox issue an immediate denial of the *Los Angeles Times* story. Cox did, explaining, however, that he had ordered a review of "relevant public knowledge" of the purchase of and improvements on the property.

From then on, Nixon's aides—Haig and attorneys Leonard Garment and J. Fred Buzhardt—repeatedly complained to Richardson about Cox and his staff. Richardson was warned that Nixon would not tolerate a prosecution of Ehrlichman, Charles Colson, or plumber Egil Krogh because national security projects would be brought to light at a trial, and that was impermissible. The President had begun to rebound from his losses of the spring; the White House returned to its earlier hard-line stance, and cooperation with investigators came to a virtual halt.

By July 16, when Alexander Butterfield revealed the existence of the White House taping system, the early euphoria that Richardson's aide Darman had spoken of was gone. On July 18, Cox wrote Buzhardt asking for the tapes of nine conversations. Five were of talks between Nixon and Dean, the others between Nixon and Haldeman, Ehrlichman, or Mitchell in the thirteen days following the Watergate arrests of June 17, 1972. On July 20, having received no reply, Cox wrote again. This time he got an answer from Charles Alan Wright, the University of Texas law professor who was to serve as Nixon's principal attorney in the battle over the tapes.

Wright told Cox that Nixon would not surrender the tapes either to the Ervin Committee, which had requested five of them, or to the Special Prosecutor. Since Cox planned to use the tapes in the courts, a separate branch of government, Wright wrote, the principle of Executive privilege would be violated were Nixon to give Cox the tapes. "The successful prosecution of those who have broken the laws is a very important national interest, but it has long been recognized that there are other national interests that, in specific cases, may override this," he said. Nixon felt he had to maintain the confidentiality "that is imperative to the effective functioning of the presidency," Wright said; the President would stand by this decision even at the risk of having prosecutions arising from Watergate thrown out of court.

On July 23, realizing he was at an impasse, Cox served a subpoena on Nixon's attorneys. The President refused to obey it, throwing the battle of the tapes into the courts, before Judge John Sirica, for the first time. On August 29, Sirica, saying Nixon's arguments on the separation of powers were unpersuasive but that he wanted to "walk the middle ground," ruled that the tapes should be given to him, and he would decide what to forward to the Special Prosecutor and what would be kept secret on the basis of presidential confidentiality. Nixon was in San Clemente that day; the White House issued a statement saying the President "will not comply with this order."

Wright appealed to the U.S. Circuit Court of Appeals, whose judges urged that Cox and Wright seek a compromise and avoid the constitutional confrontation that would arise through pushing the argument to a conclusion in the courts. On September 20, both sides notified the Appeals Court that they could reach no agreement, and on Friday, October 12, the Appeals Court ruled that Nixon would have to turn the tapes over to Sirica.

Out of that ruling, Nixon forced the confrontation with Cox that led to the Saturday Night Massacre. The fact is, however, that in late September or early October—before the court ruling, some time prior to the forced resignation of Vice-President Agnew on October 10—Nixon told Richardson that he was going to fire Cox.

Agnew at the time was struggling to avoid a criminal prosecution, claiming that as Vice-President he could not be indicted. Richardson went to Nixon to seek approval for the final steps to be taken against Agnew. The President concurred, but he said, "After this, we're going to get rid of Cox."

On the weekend following the Appeals Court ruling on the tapes, Nixon's resolve hardened. He could have taken the tapes case to the Supreme Court, but he decided not to. He was insistent on firing Cox. On Sunday night, October 14, Haig called Richardson on the telephone and asked him to come to the White House the following morning. It was the beginning of seven days of negotiations, during which, at times, Haig warned Richardson that the United States was on the edge of a possible confrontation with Russia in the Middle East and that Richardson should weigh the possible international effect of any decision he made that went against the President's wishes.

From 9 to 11:30 A.M. on Monday, October 15, Richardson met at the White House with Haig and Buzhardt. He was told that despite the ruling that Nixon had to submit the tapes to Sirica, the President had his own plan: he would prepare an "authenticated version" of them, and he would fire Cox. Once Cox was gone, Nixon would not be in violation of a court order since the agent requesting the order— the Special Prosecutor—was no longer in existence.

Under the terms of Cox's appointment, however, only the Attorney General could fire him. Richardson reminded Haig and Buzhardt that he had pledged not to dismiss Cox except for "extraordinary improprieties" and said that if Nixon went ahead with his plan, he would resign.

During the day, Haig backed off on the necessity to fire Cox, and between Monday afternoon and Thursday evening, Richardson served as a middle man between the White House and Cox, trying to effect a compromise. Cox seemed receptive, but he objected to various aspects of the proposal given him. On Thursday evening, October 18, Richardson transmitted Cox's written response to Haig, Buzhardt, Garment, and Wright. The Nixon aides seized on Cox's objections, said he had rejected the plan, and that he should be fired. They suggested that Richardson and Assistant Attorney General Henry Petersen take charge of the investigation. Richardson was incredulous. He said the public would not have faith in such an investigation.

"I wondered whether I was the only sane man in the room or whether I was the one who was crazy," Richardson said later. He urged Wright to speak with Cox before any action was taken. Wright agreed—but Richardson was warned that if Cox could not be persuaded to accept the offer, he would be dismissed.

Richardson went home fully expecting the worst. He sat down and wrote out a letter titled "Why I Must Resign." He discussed the conversation at the White House with intimates, saying, "You won't believe what those guys think they're going to get away with." The question arose as to whether the President's assistants were serious in their hard-line position— Cox, after all, had the court ruling on *his* side—or whether they adopted such an extreme position in hopes of having Richardson help get Cox to capitulate.

Meanwhile, Wright called Cox and they failed to reach an agreement. After the conversation, Wright sent Cox a note, saying that "if you think there is any purpose in our talking further, my associates and I stand ready to do so. If not, we will have to follow the course of action that we think in the best interest of the country." The letter spelled out a requirement that Cox not pursue further requests for additional tapes or documents, where the earlier proposal had not.

Friday morning Cox wrote Wright to tell him exactly why it was wrong to call the Stennis plan a "very reasonable" proposal, as Wright had. After repeating objections he had given to Richardson earlier, Cox noted, in addition, that he simply could not promise there would be no "further legal challenges to claims of Executive privilege. I categorically assured the Senate Judiciary Committee that I would challenge such claims so far as the law permitted. The Attorney General was confirmed on the strength of that assurance. I cannot break my promise now."

Notified of the impasse, Richardson asked Haig if he could meet with the President to submit his resignation. Haig said Nixon could see him immediately. The Attorney General told his aides as he left that it looked like it was all over. Resignation in hand, he went to the White House, going directly to Haig, who occupied the grand Vice-Presidential ceremonial office that had been Haldeman's before him. But Haig took Richardson by surprise. He said the firing of Cox might not be necessary after all, and Richardson didn't go to the Oval Office.

Buzhardt, Garment, and Wright joined the conversation. Richardson was shown Cox's letter to Wright, and the reference Cox had made to further legal challenges confused him—he was not aware, he said later, of Wright's stipulation to Cox. But Richardson saw a glimmer of hope. Several new proposals were discussed, including one Richardson thought might have promise, calling for Judge Sirica to rule on the merits of the Stennis plan. The so-called "linked proposal"—combining the Stennis verification plan and agreement by Cox that he not seek access to other tapes or documents—was also aired. Richardson said he felt Cox would resign before accepting it.

When Richardson returned to the Justice Department, it was his understanding that no decision on a final course had

The Road to Impeachment

been made, and that he would be consulted before any was. He and his three closest aides went to his private dining room for lunch. They were joined by Deputy Attorney General Ruckelshaus, and they remained there for hours, trying to come up with an acceptable solution.

Three times during the afternoon, Richardson spoke on the telephone with Haig or Buzhardt. The Appeals Court had given Nixon until Friday to move the case before the Supreme Court; it was now late Friday afternoon and time was running out. Nixon could always ask for an extension and no doubt get it—but he had to do something.

During the day, Senator Ervin and Senator Baker were called to the White House separately and asked if they would consent to a plan in which Senator Stennis would authenticate a version of the tapes prepared by Nixon for use by their committee. The courts earlier had ruled that the Ervin Committee was not entitled to the five tapes it had sought, and both senators—who stood to gain no access to material from the tapes otherwise—agreed to the Stennis plan.

At 7 o'clock Friday, Haig called Richardson and read a letter to him from the President instructing the Attorney General to order Cox not to go to court to seek any further records of presidential conversations. Richardson, taken by surprise, realized he could not comply with such an order.

Expecting Nixon to make public the letter to him, Richardson prepared a press release in which he termed the Stennis authentication plan a reasonable compromise but objected to tying it to a promise by Cox not to seek further material through the courts. "I plan to seek an early opportunity to discuss this plan with the President," Richardson's statement said.

Richardson had no need to release his statement, however. At 8 o'clock, bypassing Richardson, the President announced that he was implementing the "linked proposal," calling it a compromise. It was Nixon's last, failing attempt to shake loose from Watergate.

Noting the strain that the scandal had imposed on the American people, Nixon said the possibility of a constitutional confrontation was especially damaging. At home, he said, Watergate "has taken on overtones of a partisan political contest," and such divisiveness could "tempt those in the international community . . . to misread America's unity and resolve in meeting the challenges we confront abroad."

For these reasons, the President said, "I have concluded

that it is necessary to take decisive actions that will avoid any possibility of a constitutional crisis and that will lay the groundwork upon which we can assure unity of purpose at home and end the temptation abroad to test our resolve."

The President said he was confident that the Supreme Court would have reversed the Appeals Court ruling on the tapes, but "that it is not in the national interest to leave this matter unresolved for the period that might be required for a review by the highest court."

The President then announced the details of the Stennis plan, saying that Senator Ervin and Senator Baker had accepted it as a means of forwarding information from the tapes to the Senate Watergate Committee, but that the Special Prosecutor rejected the proposal. Nixon said he would go ahead with the plan anyway, that his aim was

> ... to bring the issue of Watergate tapes to an end and assure our full attention to more pressing business affecting the very security of the nation.
>
> Accordingly, though I have not wished to intrude upon the independence of the Special Prosecutor, I have felt it necessary to direct him, as an employee of the Executive branch, to make no further attempts by judicial process to obtain tapes, notes, or memoranda of presidential conversations.

Every shibboleth that has come to be equated with Nixonism was contained in this statement. The President said he was seeking to assuage damages to the nation, making no mention of damages to himself. He invoked the threat of danger from foreign powers should an investigation of his own honesty be pursued. He charged that those seeking to find the truth about Watergate, or those disturbed by the crimes that had become so apparent, were motivated by partisan interest and not by a desire to clean up corruption. Throughout, he attempted to give the appearance of being above the fray, and he concluded with a statement that he was cooperating with the Watergate inquiry when, in fact, he was defying a court order.

Cox immediately issued a statement charging that the President had refused to abide by the court decrees and stating he would bring that to the attention of the court. "For me to comply with these instructions," he said, as he had written Wright earlier in the day, "would violate my solemn pledge to the Senate and the country to invoke judicial process to challenge exaggerated claims of Executive privilege. I shall not violate my promise. Acceptance of these directions would also defeat the fair administration of justice."

True to form, the first reaction from leadership on Capitol Hill was one of siding with Nixon. Senate Majority Leader Mansfield, while saying he thought Cox had been given independent powers, termed the President's Stennis plan "a move to avoid a constitutional confrontation." Minority Leader Hugh Scott said he felt "a very wise solution had been reached and a constitutional question avoided." Senator Baker, who reportedly was unaware that Cox had objected to the proposal, said through his press aide that it seemed "very good, totally in the best interests in the country."

On Saturday morning, Richardson still thought it possible that the firing of Cox could be avoided. In response to the directive Nixon had sent him the previous night, he sent word to the President that he hoped Nixon would allow the courts to decide on whether the Stennis plan was in compliance with court rulings.

By early afternoon he had not heard back. Any possibility that Nixon might reconsider vanished, as Special Prosecutor Cox called a press conference and spelled out, for the first time, the story of the months of resistance he had received from the White House. He complained that long before the tapes conflict arose, the White House had established a pattern of failing to turn over information necessary for his inquiry, that papers "of many White House aides—Haldeman, Ehrlichman, Krogh, Young, Dean, and others—were taken into custody and they're in a special room, and many of their papers were taken out of the usual files and put in something special called presidential files." He said the White House had refused his request for an inventory of those papers, and he suggested that the President's refusal to relinquish the tapes be seen in that light—the tapes were not the only information the President was withholding; this was only the most recent and sensational example of Nixon's failure to cooperate in the inquiry.

In answer to questions, Cox said he might seek an order to have the President placed in contempt of court.

"Mr. Cox, I think you believe that Attorney General Richardson will not fire you," one reporter said. Cox said that whether or not Richardson would dismiss him, the President could always find a way of forcing him out, citing a precedent in which Andrew Jackson fired a Secretary of the Treasury, named a new one, and had to fire him as well before a third appointee could be found who would follow a presidential order. "Eventually a President can always work his will," Cox said. Nixon was to work his sooner rather than later.

At 2:20 P.M., Haig called Richardson and told him to fire Cox. Richardson said he couldn't do that, that he would come to the White House at Nixon's convenience and resign. An hour later, Haig invited the Attorney General to see Nixon and, on his arrival, ushered him into the Oval Office. Richardson said he would have to resign. Nixon brought up the problems in the Middle East, Richardson said later, suggesting that resignation right then might have a bad effect. The President asked Richardson to think less of his pledge to the Senate—his personal commitment—and more in terms of the national interest. Richardson said that, in his view, he was thinking of the national interest.

"It is fair to say," Richardson said later, "that I have never had a harder moment than when the President put it on me in terms of the potential repercussion of my resignation on the Middle East situation. I remember a long moment when the President looked me in the eye and I said:

" 'Mr. President, I feel that I have no choice but to go forward with this.' I had the feeling, God, maybe the bombs are going to drop."

Haig then called William Ruckelshaus and asked him to fire Cox, again issuing a warning that a decision not to could have bearing on the Middle East situation. Ruckelshaus, who had already told Richardson he would also resign rather than fire Cox, has been quoted as telling Haig that if the situation in the Middle East were that ticklish, "Why don't you put off firing Cox?"

Haig responded, "Your commander-in-chief has given you an order." Ruckelshaus then resigned.

Both Richardson and Ruckelshaus had spoken to the third in command at the Justice Department, Solicitor General Bork, who had told them that someone would certainly eventually be found to fire Cox, so he would do it and then resign. Richardson suggested that Bork fire Cox and stay on, as someone was needed to run the shop.

At 8:25 P.M., Ronald Ziegler announced the developments of the afternoon to the press, saying that the office of the special prosecutor had been abolished. "Its function to investigate and prosecute those involved in the Watergate matter will be transferred back into the institutional framework of the Department of Justice, where it will be carried out with thoroughness and vigor." From Ziegler's statement it was unclear whether Cox's staff would continue to exist at all. The possibility arose that Nixon had, in one daring maneuver, put an end to the entire investigation, placing responsibility in the Justice Department, which had been so maligned for submitting to White House control the first time around.

At least six FBI agents were sent by the White House to the office of the special prosecutor, where some twenty or more attorneys who worked under Cox were gathering in their moment of crisis. The agents refused to allow staff members to remove any files—"They won't even let me take a pencil out," one lawyer complained. FBI agents sealed off Richardson's and Ruckelshaus's offices at the Justice Department as well.

In a brief statement, Cox said, "Whether ours shall continue to be a government of laws and not of men is now for the Congress and ultimately the American people to decide."

Nixon had made a terrible miscalculation.

Contacted by reporters, members of both parties attacked the President. Democrat Jerome Waldie of California said he would immediately introduce an impeachment resolution, charging that Nixon "in one wild move, has removed the few remaining men of demonstrable integrity in the Administration." The action, he said, left no doubt that release of the tapes would prove the President's guilt in obstructing justice.

A leading Republican congressman, John B. Anderson of Illinois, stated Nixon had "precipitated a constitutional crisis" and said he was certain impeachment resolutions would be immediately introduced.

Senator Edward Kennedy, in his most outspoken moment during the Watergate scandal, said the firing of Cox was "a reckless act of desperation by a President who is afraid of the Supreme Court, who has no respect for law and no regard for men of conscience." He said it was "obvious that Mr. Nixon is bent on maintaining the Watergate coverup at any cost. The burden is now on Congress and the courts to nullify this historic insult to the rule of law and to the nation's system of justice."

Republican Edward Brooke, Kennedy's colleague from Massachusetts, who had long been critical of Nixon, said the act was "sufficient evidence which the House of Representatives should consider to begin impeachment proceedings."

At least half a dozen other members of the House and Senate of both parties made similar remarks. Gerald Ford, Nixon's nominee as successor to Agnew, hollowly defended the President, saying Nixon "had no other choice after Cox, who was, after all, a subordinate, refused to accept the compromise solution to the tapes issue." But hardly any other voices were raised in support of Nixon.

The next day, Sunday, in the middle of the long Veterans Day holiday weekend, thousands of telegrams began to descend on empty offices on Capitol Hill, and motorists on Pennsylvania Avenue in front of the White House were exhorted by demonstrators holding signs to honk if they favored impeachment. The noise disturbed Nixon and his attorneys inside as they prepared to defend the President's action in court during the week.

His opinion solicited by a reporter, Senate Majority Whip Robert C. Byrd charged that the President had "defied the courts, defied Congress." Byrd said "this sounds like a brown shirt operation thirty years ago—gestapo tactics." Byrd said the President had left Congress no choice but to impeach him.

Others in the Senate saw a need to reestablish the special prosecutor's office, this time assuring through legislation that the prosecutor was not responsible to the President. The members of Cox's staff—their positions in limbo since Nixon had abolished their office—decided they would continue to investigate under the direction of the Justice Department if they were allowed to do so.

A press aide for the Cox staff, James Doyle, told a reporter, "It's really a very extraordinary situation for Washington D.C. The White House said we were abolished, but if they say the sky is green and you look out and see it's blue, well . . ."

On Monday a few members of the House Democratic Party leadership met with Speaker Carl Albert and launched plans to begin a preliminary study on possible impeachment—a means of *preventing* the institution of immediate formal impeachment proceedings. Reaction from Republicans to Nixon's firing of Cox continued to be unfavorable. "I've carried Nixon's flag faithfully for five years," said Congressman William Whitehurst of Virginia, "and it's getting awfully heavy." California Republican Jerry Pettis said, "I'm bending

The Road to Impeachment

over backwards to believe him. I'm bending over so far backwards my fifth vertebra is about to break."

Across the country, sentiment poured in from quarters that had been previously silent. Raoul Berger, a Harvard Law professor who had written what was considered the definitive work on impeachment, said, "I have hesitated to say it before, but after the events of the past few days, he must be impeached." Berger said Nixon was in violation of a court order by offering to produce a summary of the tapes when he had been ordered to release the tapes themselves. "Disobedience of the law is a subversion of the Constitution, which is an impeachable offense," he said.

Berger said that "obviously more serious than the Middle East War is the attempt of the President to set himself above the law. We just cannot permit that. It's the road to tyranny, dictatorship, and Hitlerism. Democracy cannot survive if a President is allowed to take the law into his own hands."

Other noted constitutional lawyers agreed, and the deans of fifteen major law schools, acting as a body, urged that Congress create a special committee "to consider the necessity of presidential impeachment."

Equally ominous for Nixon was the word on Monday that Judge Sirica, who had been out of town Saturday and Sunday, had been in touch with his own staff and was known to be considering holding the President in contempt of court for failure to comply with the court order. No President had ever been held in contempt of court. The force of such an order was undetermined—no one expected the President to pay fines or go to jail. But such an order would be one more item to add to an impeachment bill of particulars, and anger from Sirica would undoubtedly fan the enormous flames of public discontent.

On Tuesday morning, with Western Union officials saying their wires to Washington were running at triple their normal rate, Republican leaders warned the President through emissaries he sent to Capitol Hill that they could not defend him against an impeachment move unless he surrendered the tapes. Some demanded that he also appoint another special prosecutor, or run the risk of seeing the Senate appoint one.

Elliot Richardson, who was to become immensely popular for having resigned rather than fire Cox, held a televised press conference in a large hall at the Justice Department and was greeted by a sustained ovation that lasted more than two minutes as about five hundred Justice employees expressed their appreciation for the man who had restored a semblance of honor to their agency. Richardson deplored the President's actions but stopped short of impugning his motives. He said, in answer to a question, that he would have done what Cox had done. He recommended that the President appoint another special prosecutor, and said that impeachment was a question not for him, but for the American people.

"Although I strongly believe in the general purposes and priorities of his Administration, I have been compelled to conclude that I could better serve my country by resigning from public office than by continuing in it," Richardson said.

No one asked, and Richardson had no reason to mention that he had seen the President once since his resignation Saturday. He had been called to the White House Monday after Nixon heard that he was to hold the press conference. The President urged Richardson to cast things in a favorable light for him.

Nixon had accomplished one of his goals, the firing of Cox. But it was only at his own peril, for the public saw his insistence on confidentiality in the light that H. R. Haldeman had anticipated on March 22, 1973.

"On legal grounds, precedence, tradition, constitutional grounds, and all that stuff you are just fine," the Nixon transcripts show Haldeman saying. "But to the guy who is sitting at home who watches John Chancellor say that the President is covering this up by this historic review blanket of the widest exercise of Executive privilege in American history and all that—he says, 'What the hell's he covering up, if he's got no problem why doesn't he let them go talk?'"

Nixon had been subject to extreme pressures on Watergate for seven months, from the end of March, 1973. He had seen a great tide against him swell with the Ellsberg-CIA disclosures in May, and he had been trying to weather it. Transcripts of his private conversations show that he was always the first to explain to others one of the constant, immutable laws in the science of public opinion: no matter how angry citizenry may get, it will quiet down. A politician must learn to withstand clamor, to wait, and not to take rash actions in the heat of the moment.

The President believed in and practiced bold, decisive maneuvers—but only when the timing was right, as a means of surprising others, and only after careful thought. For him, the months since March had represented a gradual, sometimes precipitous capitulation, but even in his surrenders, he refused to act in haste. The decision to have Haldeman and Ehrlichman resign preceded by two weeks their actual resignation. He considered firing Cox for months and made his final decision at least twelve days before dismissing him.

Nixon may have been given to defending himself from charges the moment they were made, but when it came to taking action he almost invariably waited and watched before moving. It was one of his great strengths as a politician.

But on October 23, 1973, Nixon collapsed under pressure. As his emissaries came back from Capitol Hill with the message that Republicans there felt helpless, the President sent his attorney Wright to Sirica's court to say that Nixon had relented. "This President does not defy the law," Wright told Sirica; he would now submit the nine tapes in accordance with the ruling by Sirica and the Appeals Court.

Still the clamor did not subside. In the midst of it, and exacerbating the tension, Henry Kissinger went on television Thursday, October 25, to announce in a press conference that American armed forces had temporarily been put on alert as a result of suspected movement of Russian troops and equipment, and the fear that the Soviets would take unilateral military action in the Middle East. The threat that Haig and Nixon had made privately to Richardson and Ruckelshaus the previous week, the warning that Nixon had given in his Friday night announcement of the Stennis plan, was now being played out before the American people in a terrifying manner.

Kissinger, the practitioner of secret diplomacy, described how a serious confrontation had been avoided, but refused to spell out exactly what actions by the Russians had created the situation. To more conspiratorial-minded Americans, Kissinger's statements, while possibly true, smacked of a plot to rescue Nixon. The great bugaboo of threats from foreign powers had been used forever as a means of pressuring a populace to rally to its leaders. For some of the reporters assembled before the highly respected Secretary of State, the request that his statements be taken at face value was unacceptable. They questioned whether Nixon had manufactured an international situation.

Kissinger was furious. "It is a symptom of what is happening to our country that it could even be suggested that the United States would alert its forces for domestic reasons."

When the record is published, he said, it will be seen that "the President had no other choice."

A reporter asked the Secretary of State whether he felt Nixon's decision was "totally rational." Another, refusing to let go of the theme that Watergate and Nixon's self-preservation possibly had dictated the alert, said, "It seems to me that you are asking the American people . . . who are already badly shaken by the events of the last week, to accept a very traumatic military alert involving nuclear forces on the basis of a kind of handful of smoke without telling them exactly why. . . . I wonder if you can give us any more information that will help convince people that there's some solid basis for the action that has been taken?"

Kissinger replied, "We are attempting to preserve the peace in very difficult circumstances. It is up to you ladies and gentlemen to determine whether this is the moment you try to create a crisis of confidence in the field of foreign policy as well. . . . There has to be a minimum of confidence that the senior officials of the American government are not playing with the lives of the American people."

The arguments put forward by Kissinger that day were to form the basis for a major element of Nixon's future strategy when the problem of impeachment became much more serious. Fundamentally, Kissinger's press conference represented an appeal for the nation to rally behind its President. These were difficult times in the conduct of government. There was recurrent war in the Middle East; an embargo on the sale of oil by Arab nations had contributed to an energy crisis at home. Those who questioned the motives of the President were jeopardizing the security of all. The blame for any international disasters would fall heavily on those individuals and groups who, under such circumstances, were reckless or malicious enough to continue to question or attack Nixon. Skeptics in the press—not Nixon—were creating the "crisis of confidence."

The long-range effect of such an argument was to throw a new consideration into the question of impeachment. It was this: the Congress and the nation were being asked ever so subtly not to judge the President on his guilt or innocence in the Watergate coverup and related scandals alone, but on other questions based on *what was good for the country*. Nixon had established détente with Russia and China; under him, Kissinger had negotiated withdrawal of American troops from South Vietnam and was later to play a major role in what many thought might lead to ultimate peace in the Middle East. Did not these accomplishments offset any role the President may have played in the Watergate scandal? Wasn't Nixon *needed* as President?

This argument against impeachment was made in a more obvious manner in the summer of 1974 when Nixon flew to the Middle East and then to Moscow for summit meetings. But it had its roots in the stance taken by Kissinger in the press conference of October 25, 1973, as he warned that "one cannot have crises of authority in a society for a period of months without paying a price somewhere down the line," and urged the press and the nation to follow a politics of faith instead of skepticism.

The immediate result of Kissinger's appeal was to heighten inquiries as to whether Nixon had drummed up a war scare rather than to quiet them. The following night, Friday, October 26, the President himself held a news conference, in what was possibly the most jarring public clash ever between a Chief Executive and any group. Nixon began by saying that tension between the United States and Russia had eased as a result of diplomatic maneuvers coinciding with the troop alert. From a discussion of the Middle East, he turned to "the subject of our attempts to get a cease-fire on the home front," which, he said, was "a bit more difficult."

Nixon said that arrangements were being made to work out a delivery of the tapes to Judge Sirica, and that some time in the following week, Acting Attorney General Bork would appoint a new special prosecutor. "The special prosecutor will have independence. He will have total cooperation from the Executive branch, and he will have as a primary responsibility to bring this matter which has so long concerned the American people, bring it to an expeditious close. . . . It is time for those who are guilty to be prosecuted, and for those who are innocent to be cleared."

In answer to the first question from a member of the press, however, Nixon indicated that in a crucial way he would be no more cooperative with the new prosecutor than he had been with Cox. The question was whether the President would be receptive if the prosecutor went to court to obtain evidence from Nixon's files—the issue Cox was fired over. "I would anticipate that that would not be necessary," the President responded. "I believe that as we look at the events which led to the dismissal of Mr. Cox, we find that these are matters that can be worked out and should be worked out in cooperation and not by having a suit filed by a special prosecutor within the Executive branch against the President of the United States."

The President then went on to say that everyone had approved the Stennis plan except Cox. "Attorney General Richardson approved of this proposition. Senator Baker, Senator Ervin approved of the proposition. Mr. Cox was the only one that rejected it. . . . I had no choice but to fire him." In setting forth this view, Nixon was lying outright to the public in some aspects of his statement and misleading them in others.

Richardson had no complaints with Nixon's method of making the tapes public, but he sided with Cox in his refusal to accept the plan as a whole. Furthermore, in accepting the Stennis plan, neither Senator Baker nor Ervin agreed with Nixon's understanding of how it would work. Both said they thought they were to be given actual transcripts of tapes.

The President was then asked whether he would agree to submit documents beyond the nine tapes to the special prosecutor on his request. He said, "We will not provide presidential documents to a special prosecutor. We will provide, as we have in great numbers, all kinds of documents from the White House, but if it is a document involving a conversation with the President, I would have to stand on the principle of confidentiality. However, information that is needed from such documents would be provided." The obvious implication was that the President would be the one to decide what was needed.

As the news conference continued, questions that most reporters never would have dared put to a President in quieter times began to be aired. Dan Rather of CBS-TV asked what went through Nixon's mind when he heard people friendly to the President call for impeachment. Peter Lisagor, a Chicago newspaper writer and nationally known TV commentator, asked if the President had evidence that Cox was out to get him. Finally, in response to a question on whether the nation had suffered so many shocks that it was drained of energy and ready to rebel against change and progress, Nixon erupted in anger, blaming any public lack of confidence on the media, and especially television.

> I have never heard or seen such outrageous, vicious, distorted reporting in twenty-seven years of public life. I am not blaming anybody for that. Perhaps what hap-

pened is that what we did brought it about, and therefore, the media decided that they would have to take that particular line.

But when people are pounded night after night with that kind of frantic, hysterical reporting, it naturally shakes their confidence. And yet, I should point out that even in this week, when many thought that the President was shell-shocked, unable to act, the President acted decisively in the interests of peace, in the interests of the country.

Later, when a reporter said, "A lot of people have been wondering how you are bearing up emotionally under the stress," Nixon said, "The tougher it gets, the cooler I get. Of course, it isn't pleasant to get criticism. Some of it is justified, of course. It isn't pleasant to find your honesty questioned."

Nixon was asked exactly what it was about television coverage that angered him so. "Don't get the impression that you arouse my anger," he said. "You see, one can only be angry with those he respects."

2

IN EARLY NOVEMBER, 1973, Richard Nixon's attorneys said that two of the nine tapes Nixon had finally promised to relinquish never existed in the first place. Then it was revealed that the tape of a conversation with H. R. Haldeman only three days after the bugging arrests had a gap in it—a hum—of 18½ minutes duration.

If there were reasonable people who still felt the President wanted to bring out the facts of Watergate, surely many of them were convinced otherwise by that hum. No one could satisfactorily explain it, and a group of experts jointly chosen by the Court and the White House later concluded that it was the result of a segment of conversation being manually erased between five and nine times.

The erased part came near the start of the conversation on Nixon's and Haldeman's first day back at the White House after the Watergate arrests. Nixon had just spoken to John Ehrlichman, who was gathering information about the bugging and the inquiry into it, and Haldeman had spoken to Ehrlichman, John Mitchell, John Dean, and reportedly to Attorney General Richard Kleindienst as well. It would have been a perfect occasion for the President and his chief of staff, his most trusted aide, to make plans that they would never want to have surface.

The hum was particularly damaging to Nixon in that it was difficult for people to understand why he would have allowed the tape to be erased if he were truly innocent in the coverup. With the vast resources of the White House at his disposal, it would have been the easiest thing in the world for Nixon to insure that the tape he turned over to a court of law would not be erased before it got there. One simple procedure would have been to have a copy made of each tape.

Nixon's secretary, Rose Mary Woods, could transcribe from the copy, thus preventing each tape from being damaged.

The fact that any tape of such importance should be marred in any way, let alone be erased between five and nine times, seemed reason enough to conclude that the President wanted some of the conversation to be lost forever. There was another alarming aspect to the mysterious erasure as well. Could a President who couldn't protect a spool of tape really be trusted to safeguard the interest and security of two hundred million people?

The 18½-minute gap subjected Nixon to scorn and humiliation as well as suspicion; the President of the United States became the nightly butt of late-hour TV entertainment shows, and in Washington a prevailing joke was that a secretary could get a job at the White House if she could erase a hundred words a minute. The ridicule never ceased, and after April 30, 1974, when Nixon made public his own incomplete, embarrassing, and misleading version of the transcripts of the tapes of forty-three meetings and telephone conversations between himself and his associates, it got worse.

Long before then the President was simply a man trying to hold onto his office, capable of any effrontery but essentially powerless. He could compare himself to Lincoln, tell newspaper editors in Disney World that he is not a crook, travel the world over in hopes of persuading Americans that they needed him as President. But his fate was to be controlled by a forum outside his control, the Congress of the United States.

As impeachment resolutions were introduced in the House of Representatives in October and November, 1973, the House Speaker, Carl Albert, referred each of them to the Judiciary Committee for consideration. Impeachment was seen as a remedy that could work for the President as well as against him. According to the thinking of many people at the time, there was little sentiment in Congress for removing Nixon from office, and a verdict in his favor could help clear the air. The first serious public discussions of impeachment had, in fact, come from the Nixon side—from Richard Kleindienst in April, 1973, and then from the President's attorneys as they argued in court over the tapes that summer.

But many in Congress viewed impeachment as a cure that was worse than the disease. A devastating impeachment battle would further the divisiveness among an already unsettled populace, some said. It could be viewed as a partisan endeavor by the majority party, the Democrats, to revoke the enormous mandate Nixon had received from the electorate in 1972. Others said, echoing Nixon, that evidence against him in the Watergate coverup was based largely on the word of one man, John Dean, a turncoat—hardly enough to convince many members of Congress to start down a road from which there was no turning back. Aside from the Watergate coverup, some of the accusations laid at Nixon's door had to do with his accepting illegal or questionable campaign contributions, and many members of Congress were not exactly pure themselves in that area.

Impeachment was fraught with problems for elected officials, whose careers depended on winning elections. It was difficult for even the most dedicated, serious, and honest members of Congress to view impeachment simply as a search for the truth, a trial in which Nixon's actions alone would be considered. It was only natural that other concerns entered the thinking process, such as, would impeachment help or hinder a congressman's re-election drive?

Ordinarily, a Republican who voted to impeach a Republican President might expect to lose a hard core of constituent support; a Democrat who voted to impeach had little to gain. A Republican who took a stand against impeachment might be threatened by insurgent candidates of his own party and, at the least, stood to lose support from Democratic switchover voters that was necessary to win a seat in many areas. Democrats who voted against impeachment, it was thought, would be doing so at their peril.

But, since public opinion was volatile and the time was early, there was no certain way of predicting how a stand on impeachment would affect the future of any individual member of Congress. The one thing that was clear was that impeachment was, more than anything else, a headache. So as the impeachment drive began, along with it came cries for Nixon to resign, a solution that would take Congress off the spot. The overwhelming number of congressmen had consistently turned their backs on Watergate until it surrounded them. They were still reluctant to deal with it, hoping Nixon would solve what was becoming their dilemma. The President, however, undertook a counteroffensive, scheduling public appearances before carefully selected audiences in a campaign called "Operation Candor." He began meeting in the White House with groups from Congress, mostly Republicans, and told them the move against him was a partisan one. He said he would not resign under any circumstances.

On November 7, 1973, a highly respected Republican senator, eighty-one-year-old George D. Aiken of Vermont, a former governor of his state and a U.S. senator since 1940, called on members of Congress to realize that pleas for Nixon to resign were dishonorable, and urged them to "either impeach him or get off his back."

In his first major public statement on Watergate, Aiken said:

> ... the White House has handled its domestic trouble with such relentless incompetence that those of us who would like to help have been like swimmers searching for a way out of the water only to run into one smooth and slippery rock after another.
>
> I am speaking out now because the developing hue and cry for the President's resignation suggests to me a veritable epidemic of emotionalism. It suggests that many prominent Americans, who ought to know better, find the task of holding the President accountable as just too difficult ...
>
> To ask the President now to resign and thus relieve the Congress of its clear congressional duty amounts to a declaration of incompetence on the part of the Congress.

Aiken said he was particularly disturbed by "those who now would have us believe that President Nixon and his associates alone are the ones who corrupted America. If the politics of righteous indignation succeeds in persuading the President to resign and relieving the Congress of its clear duty, how long will it be before our politics is corrupted by competitive self-righteousness?"

Eight days later, on November 15, the House of Representatives voted 367 to 51 to assign one million dollars to the Judiciary Committee to enable it to hire staff to conduct its inquiry. The committee was not yet authorized to make impeachment findings; its function was to recommend whether a true impeachment proceeding should be begun. But it seemed clear that if the committee decided to drop its inquiry, sooner or later an impeachment resolution would be brought to the House floor anyway. Ultimately members of Congress would have to deal with the problem.

The inevitable difficulties in having elected officials decide the question of impeachment had been anticipated long ago, when the Founding Fathers decided to put the fate of a suspect President in their hands. In the Federalist Papers No. 65, Alexander Hamilton spelled out the reasoning—and the dangers—in having the legislative body conduct such proceedings. Hamilton said the offenses considered in an impeachment stemmed from the "misconduct of public men, or, in other words, from the abuse or violation of some public trust. They are of a nature which may with peculiar propriety be denominated POLITICAL as they relate chiefly to injuries done immediately to the society itself."

Hamilton saw that regardless of the nature of the charges against the person being impeached, passions would be inflamed and the "whole community" would divide "into parties more or less friendly or inimical to the accused. In many cases it will connect itself with pre-existing factions, and will enlist all their animosities, partialities, influence, and interest on one side or on the other; and in such cases there will always be the greatest danger that the decision will be regulated more by the comparative strength of parties than by the real demonstrations of innocence or guilt."

With the recognition then, that impeachment would be "a national inquest into the conduct of public men," that the difficulties of divorcing justice from politics were enormous, Hamilton asked, "Who can so properly be the inquisitors for the nation as the representatives of the nation themselves?"—the House of Representatives. Impeachment was a "bridle in the hands of the legislative body upon the executive servants of the government."

Hamilton went on to state why the U.S. Senate, not a court, should constitute the jury: "Where else than in the Senate could have been found a tribunal sufficiently dignified, or sufficiently independent? What other body would be likely to feel confidence enough in its own situation to preserve, unawed and uninfluenced, the necessary impartiality between an individual accused and the representatives of the people, his accusers?"

The problems of factionalization as envisioned by Hamilton came to the fore in the early exploration of whether impeachment proceedings should be instituted against Nixon. Unlikely as it seems, given the nature of the evidence against the President, the Judiciary Committee immediately divided itself along strict party lines.

In its first vote, the committee's twenty-one Democrats all

The Road to Impeachment

chose to allow Chairman Peter W. Rodino, Jr., of New Jersey to decide what information and which witnesses would be subpoenaed, overriding the vote of all seventeen Republicans who wanted the power to veto any of Rodino's subpoenas. Then, in a second rigidly party line vote immediately following, the Democrats refused to allow the Republicans on the committee the right to issue subpoenas of their own.

Anyone who felt the aim of the Rodino Committee was to seek out the truth about Richard Nixon had to view these votes with great alarm. For while divisions among reasonable people may always occur, it is almost inconceivable that thirty-eight men and women, all of them attorneys, could divide strictly according to party in settling on the proper approach for ferreting out the truth. Defenders of the President, and Nixon himself, seized every opportunity thereafter to claim that the impeachment committee had embarked on a partisan witchhunt.

The question that had to arise from the deliberations of the Rodino Committee was whether the committee, the House of Representatives, and, perhaps, ultimately the Senate, could be counted on to put politics aside and vote up or down on impeachment on the merits of the case.

But certain members of the committee viewed partisanship as a false issue, one that would evaporate as findings for or against Nixon began to come in, and as members of the committee got further soundings from constituents about the depth of feeling toward impeachment.

On January 24, 1974, as one means of dispelling charges of partisanship, Rodino relented on the matter of subpoena power, agreeing to share it with the senior Republican on the committee, Edward Hutchinson of Michigan. At that point the committee was still simply conducting an inquiry to determine whether impeachment proceedings should begin. Rodino and Hutchinson agreed to ask the full House to pass a resolution recognizing the Judiciary Committee as the body that would make a formal impeachment inquiry.

Five days later, the President, at the conclusion of his State of the Union address, extended a challenge to both the new special prosecutor, Leon Jaworski, and the Rodino Committee. Saying that "one year of Watergate is enough," Nixon asserted that he had provided Jaworski "all the material that he needs to conclude his investigations and to proceed to prosecute the guilty and to clear the innocent. I believe the time has come to bring that investigation and the other investigations of this matter to an end."

Nixon said he recognized that "the House Judiciary Committee has a special responsibility in this area, and I want to indicate on this occasion that I will cooperate with the Judiciary Committee in its investigation. I will cooperate so that it can conclude its investigation, make its decision, and I will cooperate in any way that I consider consistent with my responsibilities to the Office of the Presidency of the United States."

He said he would not do anything that "impairs the ability of the Presidents of the future to make the great decisions that are so essential to this nation and to the world."

It was the old Nixon position on the need for confidentiality, now being extended to apply to an impeachment proceeding. Nixon, the prospective defendant, was telling the Judiciary Committee, which was in many ways equivalent to a grand jury, that he, not the committee, would decide what evidence was germane.

About three weeks earlier, I had asked a member of the Judiciary Committee, Democrat Paul Sarbanes of Maryland, what would happen if the President refused to submit material requested by the committee. "I think this constitutional argument to keep from turning over documents is 98 percent hokum," Sarbanes said. "Our role is to exercise ultimate discretion. If the President refuses material, he would be failing to obey a mandate of the Constitution. Secondly, when materials or knowledge are not handed over, by established legal principle you can judge the worst. Failure to turn over material may provoke a constitutional issue strong enough to go to the Senate with all by itself."

On hearing Nixon's State of the Union address, several members of Congress said the President's offer to cooperate was no offer at all and took the same stance that Sarbanes had with me: that refusal to submit material could be an impeachable offense in itself.

On February 6, 1974, the full House voted 410 to 4 to have the Judiciary Committee "investigate fully and completely whether sufficient grounds exist for the House of Representatives to exercise its constitutional power to impeach Richard Nixon, President of the United States of America." The House gave the committee authorization to subpoena any witness and any information "it deems necessary to such investigation."

In the following days, the Nixon position hardened as the President's attorney, James St. Clair, refused to submit material to either the Special Prosecutor or the Judiciary Committee. On February 14, Jaworski complained that some quests for material from the White House had gone unmet since the previous August. He said that during a brief period of cooperation after the firing of Cox, the White House had submitted eleven tapes on Watergate, three that had bearing on the Nixon decision to raise milk price supports, three on possible Nixon interference in the ITT merger, and one on the White House plumbers. But then cooperation had stopped, and requests for twenty-seven additional tapes had been turned down. Jaworski said he had spelled out the need for each of the tapes, that he was not on any fishing expedition.

That same day Judiciary Committee counsel Doar met with St. Clair in hopes that he could establish procedures to acquire White House data. The meeting was said to be a friendly one, but no procedures emanated from it. At that stage in its inquiry, the Rodino Committee was receiving information and data from the Senate Watergate Committee and from other committees on the Hill that had looked into aspects of the Nixon scandals. But the committee could not count on receiving material from the special prosecutor's office, especially anything that had been the subject of grand jury deliberations, as Jaworski said he did not have the authority to release confidential grand jury records. So the Rodino Committee, now a true impeachment panel, while charged with a more solemn responsibility than any congressional committee in the hundred years since an earlier President was impeached, was being denied material to conduct its inquiry properly. Doar asked St. Clair to submit to him at least the same documents, including tapes, that had been given to the Special Prosecutor, and he set a deadline in early March for the answer, threatening a congressional subpoena for failure to comply.

On March 1, the Watergate grand jury issued its major Watergate indictment, charging H. R. Haldeman, John Ehrlichman, Charles Colson, John Mitchell, Gordon Strachan, Robert Mardian, and re-election committee attorney Kenneth Parkinson with crimes in the coverup. Secretly naming Nixon as an unindicted co-conspirator, the grand jury requested that all the information it had gathered on the President be submitted to the Judiciary Committee, including tapes of conversations. In court, two bulging satchels were given to Judge Sirica as he was asked to decide on the grand jury's request.

On March 5, before Sirica had issued any ruling, the Rodino Committee, having failed to get any response from the White House to its demands, announced that it would subpoena the documents and tapes it sought. Failure to comply could result in a contempt of Congress citation against Nixon. The following day, St. Clair said the President would give the committee the same material that had been offered the Special Prosecutor.

At a press conference that evening, March 6, Nixon was asked whether he would relinquish other material sought by the Rodino Committee. The President said "those matters will continue to be under discussion between White House counsel and Mr. Doar." He said the material turned over to Jaworski included nineteen tapes and over seven hundred documents, and that he felt he had made a "very forthcoming offer" to the Rodino Committee in pledging to respond under oath to written interrogatories and offering to "meet with members of the committee, perhaps the chairman and the ranking minority member of the committee, at the White House to answer any further questions under oath that they may have."

Nixon was still maintaining his right to determine what evidence would be produced against him; a position that neither Doar nor Jaworski could accept. As Doar got some of the material that had been submitted to the Special Prosecutor, he continued to press a demand on the White House for forty-two additional tapes, all of them having to do with the latter stages of the Watergate coverup in February, March, and April, 1973. Jaworski went to court, seeking enforcement of a subpoena for sixty-four tapes, including those of conversations in the first days after the June 17, 1972, arrests. He won a favorable ruling from Judge Sirica but the White House said it would not abide by it, and Jaworski then appealed directly to the Supreme Court. On April 11, the Rodino Committee subpoenaed the forty-two tapes which it had originally requested on February 25.

On the 29th of April, as time for a response to the Rodino Committee subpoena was running out, the President went on television to announce one of his striking capitulations, another act in which he cooperated yet did not cooperate at the same time. But this event was more dramatic than any in the past, even his firing of Archibald Cox.

The President told the American people:

> In these folders that you see over here on my left, are more than 1,200 pages of transcript of private conversations I participated in between September 15, 1972 and April 27th of 1973, with my principal aides and associates with regard to Watergate . . . I have been well aware that my effort to protect the confidentiality of presidential conversations has heightened the sense of mystery about Watergate and, in fact, has caused increased suspicions of the President. Many people assume that the tapes must incriminate the President, or that otherwise, he would not insist on their privacy.

Nixon said he was making a major exception to the principle of confidentiality, that he was turning over the transcripts of conversations—but not the tapes themselves—to the Rodino Committee. The transcripts, he said, "include all the relevant portions of the subpoenaed conversations that were recorded." He said he would invite Rodino and the senior Republican on the committee, Hutchinson, to the White House to listen to the full tapes to determine for themselves that the transcripts are accurate and all the relevant information presented.

> Because this is an issue that profoundly affects all the American people, in addition to turning over these transcripts to the House Judiciary Committee, I have directed that they should all be made public—all of these that you see here.

Nixon said he realized that the transcripts would lead to many sensational news stories, that parts would seem contradictory, that they would embarrass him and others. He said that those who read the raw transcripts would see why the principle of confidentiality is essential and must be maintained in the future. He made it as clear as he could that this was his final contribution to those who were investigating him.

The President had given edited transcripts instead of tapes. There were no transcripts at all for eleven of the forty-two tapes that had been subpoenaed. Nixon said that portions of the tapes were unrelated to Watergate and were therefore omitted, so that neither the public nor anyone on the committee but its two chief members could determine the reliability of the tapes. Rodino and Hutchinson were not thought to be expert enough to tell if the tapes had been falsified in some way, and, in all probability, neither of them was expected to be as alert as committee staff members to important material that had been deleted. (Rodino and Hutchinson did listen to the tapes, however, and found some glaring differences from what Nixon had made public.)

On May 1, the Judiciary Committee, in a 20 to 18 vote split almost along party lines, directed Rodino to send this note to Nixon:

> Dear Mr. President:
> The Committee on the Judiciary has directed me to advise you that it finds as of 10 A.M. April 30, you have failed to comply with the committee's subpoena of April 11, 1974.

3

IN THE FEW days following the release of the edited transcripts, the shortcomings in the version of the tapes released by Nixon became readily apparent. It was discovered that two dictationists had transcribed an overlapping segment of a conversation between Nixon and Assistant Attorney General Henry Petersen. The typed versions of what they heard were so different that both accounts were inadvertently put, one after the other, in the final edited transcripts—as apt a demonstration as any that the entire package of more than 1,200 pages was worthless insofar as it purported to be an accurate rendition of what was on the tapes.

The transcripts, though incomplete, were seized on by publishers and became overnight best-sellers, with the *Washington Post* and *The New York Times* making immediate arrangements with paperback firms for rapid printing and distribution. A rush, hardcover edition was also circulated. The phrase "expletive deleted" became the latest popular addition to the lexicon of Watergate; "a limited hang out" (a story half told) and "stonewalling" (remaining silent) took their place next to the slang of 1973, the year of "stroking calls," "talking papers," and "that point in time."

Everyone had favorite portions of the transcripts or phrases that stuck in their heads, such as Ehrlichman's reference to John Mitchell as "the big enchilada."

There were bizarre parts, as when Nixon and Haldeman spoke to Ehrlichman about getting his office geared up to tape a conversation. Ehrlichman, who did not know of Nixon's taping system, questioned the legality of such a procedure although he himself had taped telephone calls before. Haldeman readily explained the law in detail as he understood it. In the first transcript, that of a conversation on September

15, 1972, Nixon closed a telephone call with Mitchell by saying, "Get a good night's sleep. And don't bug anybody without asking me? OK?" Later on, Nixon lamented his Watergate predicament, saying he was, after all, a law-and-order man.

There was also boastfulness and occasional sadness as well, with the President expressing concern over family problems that Haldeman was having and talking about how difficult it was for him to turn against Mitchell.

But what struck many people more than anything else was the apparent moral barrenness in the White House, the absolute failure to approach problems through any principled course of action, the hour upon hour of scheming privately while publicly claiming to be above the scandal, and the clear indications that despite his protestations, the President was deeply involved in the coverup.

The question arose that if this was the best face Nixon could put forward through his own edited version of the transcripts, then how much more incriminating might the real tapes be? Gradually an answer came.

Because Nixon had made public his version of some tapes that had been given to the Special Prosecutor, the Rodino Committee staff was able to compare Nixon's editing with the actual tapes that had been turned over to them. They found immediately that in key areas, the President, whether purportedly to remove expletives or to excise material that allegedly did not pertain to Watergate, had, in fact, distorted meaning and left out damaging sections entirely. The best example was a crucial segment of Nixon's March 21, 1973, conversation with Dean and Haldeman. Attorneys for Nixon maintained, even after the release of the tapes, that the President had never approved of the payment of hush money to Howard Hunt, that he had only explored options in discussing blackmail with Dean and Haldeman, and that in the end, he ruled out such payments. The edited Nixon transcript showed this dialogue over whether or not to get money for Hunt:

Nixon: Would you agree that that's the prime thing that you damn well better get that done?
Dean: Obviously, he ought to be given some signal anyway.
Nixon: (Expletive deleted), get it. In a way that—who is going to talk to him? Colson? He is the one who is supposed to know him?

These lines were possibly damaging to Nixon, but one could see where the President might only be sounding out his aide. The Judiciary Committee listened to the tape, however, and heard the expletive that had been deleted. The President's actual words, amounting to a clear order, were, *"For Christ's sakes, get it, in a way that, uh—who's going to talk to him, Colson? He's the one who's supposed to know him."*

Several committee members were so infuriated over this distortion that they released the corrected account to the press, as well as segments of other conversations in which Nixon's version was at variance in crucial areas with the actual tapes. As they did, presidential aides such as Kenneth Clawson, who had been promoted to the position of White House communications director, charged that the corrections were "leaks" that demonstrated the partisan nature of the Rodino Committee. A new wave of obfuscation began as presidential speech writer Patrick Buchanan challenged the press to address itself to the problem of leaks as a worthwhile subject for news stories.

The audacity of such criticism was unparalleled—the President had put out statements to the nation that were deliberately misleading, doing much of the editing himself. What these congressmen had done was to correct those statements. Yet a claim was made that the congressmen had violated principles of confidentiality.

Later, the Judiciary Committee made public even larger sections of the tapes in which Nixon's version was at variance with what actually had been said. More than ever, the President's own words were incriminating to him.

In the edited version released by Nixon, for example, the March 21, 1973, conversation showed the President saying to H. R. Haldeman and John Dean, in regard to blackmail demands by Howard Hunt: ". . . his price is pretty high, but at least we *can* buy the time on that."

In the Judiciary Committee version, Nixon was heard to say: ". . . his price is pretty high, but at least, uh, we *should*, we *should* buy the time on that, uh, *as I pointed out to John.*"

In the tape of a conversation on March 22, 1973, between Nixon, John Mitchell, John Ehrlichman, Haldeman, and Dean, the Nixon transcript omitted an entire section in which the President said, at one point, "I don't give a shit what happens. I want you all to stonewall it, let them plead the Fifth

Amendment, coverup, or anything else, if it'll save it—save the whole plan. That's the whole point."

At the White House, Ronald Ziegler criticized the committee for its release of a 131-page comparison of conflicting passages in the transcripts, saying the committee was conducting a "hypoed PR campaign" against Nixon, that "they have chosen the public relations route which will focus the news media only on one section of the tapes." Ziegler said the committee "should release the full body of evidence all together, all at once and not in piecemeal fashion."

Of course, had Nixon not edited the way he did, there would have been no need for the committee to release any comparison of the transcripts. If Ziegler's complaint sounded lame, the fact was that by then, the middle of July, 1974, there were virtually no trump cards left in the Nixon hand. The tapes, even in the form presented by the President, were ruinous to him, and any defense from the White House rang hollow, the mutterings of an emperor trying to convince a citizenry that his clothing was just a little soiled, when they could see that he had none at all.

As time passed, the House Judiciary Committee, which had begun its work in October, 1973, fell far behind its planned schedule. Hoping at first that its work would be completed by April, Chairman Rodino kept pushing the date back, aiming at the last to have its recommendations ready by the end of July. The committee spent weeks listening to the Nixon tapes and hearing witnesses in secret sessions. As they would emerge each day, certain committee members expressed the conviction that the testimony was damaging to Nixon; others would say that it wasn't.

The President's attorney, James. St. Clair, developed a strategy aimed at focusing the impeachment debate as narrowly as possible. Maintaining that a President could be impeached only for actions that were criminal offenses, he discarded almost all the vast accumulation of charges against Nixon except for those dealing with the Watergate coverup. Then he singled out the one accusation that had become most prominent in recent months—that Nixon had ordered the payment of hush money to Howard Hunt on March 21, 1973. St. Clair said he could demonstrate that regardless of those words, payment made to Hunt had been arranged before Nixon spoke to Dean, without the President's knowledge. Therefore, he said, Nixon had not been instrumental in seeing that Hunt was bribed to keep silent. Had Nixon been in

China, St. Clair said, the March 21, 1973, payment to Hunt would have been made anyway. No other charge against Nixon was as serious as that one, St. Clair maintained. Ergo, the President should not be impeached.

By July, 1974, many of the events dealt with in this book—and many others not gone into here—were largely out of the minds of large numbers of citizens; Watergate, as ever, had a tendency to be yesterday's newspaper story. What was remembered was the most recent shock. Reporters covering Capitol Hill returned to their offices saying that if St. Clair could demonstrate what he said he could demonstrate, well then . . .

The question, then, was whether Congress would cooperate in St. Clair's strategy or not. It was they, not he, who were to decide Nixon's fate. For many weeks there was no way of predicting what would happen. At just that point, the committee began to release the voluminous testimony it had gathered during its months of work, tracing the pattern of Nixon's behavior from the earliest days of his presidency. As the material became public, the vast majority of members of the House and Senate continued to state that they stood to be *judges* and therefore should not venture an opinion on the likelihood of a successful impeachment. A few members of Congress attacked the President, at the risk of being labeled partisans. There was a vocal group who, despite the existence of a record two years in the making, said that they saw no evidence of wrongdoing on Nixon's part.

Public opinion and government policy feed on each other. As people clamor, elected officials act. As officials act, people's understanding of events is shaped. In mid-July, 1974, a public that had grown tired of clamoring became somewhat quiet. The Rodino Committee released millions of words of information it had gathered, but not a single sentence explaining the signficance of its findings.

Then, on the 19th of July, the committee acted in a striking fashion. The senior counsel to both the Democrats and the Republicans, John Doar and Albert E. Jenner, Jr., urged the committee to endorse sending impeachment of Nixon to the Senate on one or more of several broad impeachment charges:

- Obstruction of justice in the Watergate coverup and related scandals.
- Abuse of government agencies by the President.

- Contempt of Congress and the courts by Nixon in his defiance of subpoenas.
- Failure to observe his constitutional duty "to see that the laws be faithfully executed."
- Denigration of the presidency through Nixon's underpayment of income taxes and the use of federal funds to improve personal property.

The charges were backed up by twenty-nine potential articles of impeachment and a thick summary of the committee staff's findings, containing harsh judgments as to Nixon's conduct in office—both before and after Watergate.

Doar's first proposed article of impeachment read:

> Beginning almost immediately after the burglary and continuing up to the present time, Richard M. Nixon, using the powers of his office, acting directly and personally and through his personal agents at the seat of Government and their immediate subordinates, has made it his policy to cover up and conceal responsibility for the burglary, the identity of other participants, and the existence and scope of related unlawful covert activities.
>
> The means of implementing this policy have included the subornation of perjury, the purchase of silence of those directly participating in the burglary, the obstruction of justice, the destruction of evidence, improper and unlawful interference with the conduct of lawful investigation by the Department of Justice, including the Federal Bureau of Investigation and the Office of the Special Prosecutor, improper and unlawful misuse of other agencies of the Executive branch, including the CIA, and the release of deliberately false and misleading statements from the White House and by the President.

"For all this, Richard M. Nixon is personally and directly responsible," Doar's report said.

As the House Judiciary Committee moved to bring its findings to Congress, the Supreme Court entered Watergate for the first time when asked by Special Prosecutor Jaworski to decide whether the President could keep from him sixty-four additional tapes that he had requested. The Court was thereby given an uncertain role in impeachment proceedings, as the President's attorneys argued that any material given Jaworski would find its way to the Judiciary Committee despite Nixon's claim that the committee had all the evidence it needed, and his insistence on the need for confidentiality. "In effect court process is being used as a discovery tool for the impeachment proceedings—proceedings which the Constitution clearly assigns to the Congress, not the courts," Nixon's attorneys maintained in a brief in advance of oral arguments in the case.

The brief urged the High Court not to be swayed by the "passing needs of the moment" at the expense "of those enduring constitutional doctrines that have preserved our system of ordered liberty through the ages.

"Of those doctrines, none is more fundamental to our governmental structure itself than the separation of powers—with all of its inherent tensions, with all of its necessary inability to satisfy all the people or all institutions all of the time, and yet with the relentless and saving force that it generates toward essential compromise and accommodation over the longer term if not always in the shorter term."

By attempting to invoke the principle of confidentiality to keep from submitting tapes to the Special Prosecutor and the Rodino Committee, Nixon's Watergate defense became absurdly empty, for while the President chose to rest his public posture on a high constitutional issue, he had, in the Watergate transcripts, shown time and again that he had not the slightest concern with separation of powers or Executive privilege as historic, constitutional matters. The private Nixon was known by anyone who could read the English language as a President who saw confidentiality exclusively as a means of preventing harmful disclosure. In the transcripts he made public, he ridiculed the historic aspects of Executive privilege.

Beginning with his February 28, 1973, conversation with Dean—in which Nixon referred to Executive privilege as the "kind of a line" he wanted to take—there were more than five dozen references to Executive privilege, some of them running for many pages. In every instance the so-called principle of confidentiality was discussed as a tool to save Nixon or his closest associates, and not the "presidency" or future Presidents.

In their February 28, 1973, conversation, for example, Nixon and Dean agreed on a plan to invoke Executive privilege to keep presidential aides from appearing before the Ervin Committee. The aides instead would respond under oath to written interrogatories, and if more information was desired, the aides would answer questions put to them, in the

White House, by the chairman and ranking minority member of the Ervin Committee. The idea was that written questions were easier to answer.

In their March 13, 1973, conversation, the transcripts show, Dean and Nixon left no doubt why they preferred interrogatories. Speaking about the possibility that Dean might be called to testify at the Senate confirmation hearings for L. Patrick Gray as permanent FBI director, the young counsel said, "You can handle written interrogatories, where cross-examination is another ball game."

"That's right!" Nixon responded.

In the early part of that day's conversation, while Haldeman was present, Nixon, Dean, and Haldeman talked specifically about using Executive privilege fraudulently. Charles Colson had left the White House to enter private law practice three days earlier, and the discussion opened on whether Colson's severance papers should be amended to state that he remained an unpaid consultant to Nixon. Such a change, Haldeman noted, should be "backdated" so that the Executive privilege claim could be continuous.

If that were done for Colson, the President asked, could it also be done for Dwight Chapin, who had left the White House earlier? Dean said the former appointments secretary didn't have quite the same problem that Colson did, but Haldeman disagreed.

Nixon then said, "Well, can't—that would [be] such an obvious fraud to have both of them as consultants, that that won't work. I think he is right. You would have to leave Chapin." Evidently it was not fraud that disturbed Nixon, only obvious fraud.

On the 20th of March, in a telephone conversation with Dean, Nixon expressed concern that people outside the White House would see Executive privilege for what it was, an attempt to "stonewall" Congress. He asked Dean to circumvent that problem by preparing a statement for the President's use—but not too revealing a statement. The transcripts show the President saying:

> You've got to have something where it doesn't appear that I am doing this in, you know, just in a—saying to hell with the Congress and to hell with the people, we are not going to tell you anything because of Executive privilege. That, they don't understand. But if you say, 'No, we are willing to cooperate,' and you've made a

complete statement, but make it very incomplete. See, that is what I mean.

Nixon explained that he wanted such a statement for its effect on Cabinet members and other leaders. "It might just be very salutary. You see, our own people have got to have confidence or they are not going to step up and defend us. You see the problem there, don't you?"

Dean suggested that at the same time, these Nixon supporters be given a statement explaining Executive privilege, saying, "It is tremendous to have a piece of paper that they know they can talk from."

"Pointing out," said Nixon, "that you are defending the Constitution; responsibility of the separation of powers; and we have to do it." It was no jump at all for the President to go from a request for an incomplete complete statement to a constitutional principle—they were both part of the same defense.

When the Constitution did arise, or any reference to history and principle at all, it was discussed in terms of a "scenario," exclusively as a means through which Nixon, Mitchell, and Dean envisioned hoodwinking Sam Ervin.

Nixon: It is a record for the future. Maybe you can tell Ervin on the mountaintop that this is a good way to set up a procedure for the future. You know what I mean, where future cases of this sort are involved. We are making a lot of history here, Senator.
Mitchell: And the Senator can be a great part of it.
Nixon: A lot of history. We are setting a stirring precedent. The President, after all, let's find out what the President did know, talk about the Hiss case.
Dean: Ervin away from his staff is not very much and I think he might just give up the store himself right there and lock himself in. You know, I have dealt with him for a number of years and have seen that happen.

And finally, when Nixon decided to capitulate on Executive privilege before the Senate Watergate Committee after Ervin remained adamant, he showed no remorse for future Presidents. In a late night phone call to Ehrlichman on April 14, 1973, Nixon said, "I think, frankly, let's get off of the damned Executive privilege." He told his aide that to surrender the principle would put the President in the position of appearing forthcoming, suggesting that he wanted the facts out, "and that's that."

Nixon said to Ehrlichman, "We have won lots of things with the Congress. We lost one. But you, in interpreting it, would say we have reached a compromise with the committee, that we limited it to this, to charges of wrongdoing."

At that point, the President waived his power to decide on what was privileged and agreed to Ervin Committee ground rules which said that while aides to the President could assert Executive privilege, the committee itself would make the final decision. Two days later, though, when Nixon became alarmed that Dean might testify against him, the President once more returned to his hardline position, urging Dean not to report the substance of their conversations, much of which dealt with, as Nixon phrased it, "that damn Executive privilege and all that."

On July 24, 1974, the Supreme Court rendered a unanimous 8-0 verdict that the President had to turn over the sixty-four tapes requested by Special Prosecutor Jaworski.

At one point citing the eloquent language of a 1935 High Court case that "guilt shall not escape or innocence suffer," the Court, in a thirty-one page opinion delivered by Chief Justice Warren Burger, decided:

> We conclude that the ground for asserting privilege as to subpoenaed materials sought for use in a criminal trial is based only on the generalized interest in confidentiality, it cannot prevail over the fundamental demands of due process of law in the fair administration of criminal justice. The generalized assertion of privilege must yield to the demonstrated, specific need for evidence in a pending criminal trial.

That same day, with its final decision considered by many a foregone conclusion, the House Judiciary Committee began its debates—which were televised—to work out the exact language of its impeachment recommendation to Congress.

With the record of his conduct exposed through Nixon's own words, and with the Judiciary Committee's strong findings, it seemed highly unlikely that a large enough number of the members of Congress could combine to rescue Nixon from impeachment. Nixon knew that. He seemed half resigned to the worst, alternately charging that impeachment was partisan-motivated, deploring his "enemies," saying his aides could not get a fair trial in Washington, D.C.

At the same time, he tried to extricate himself from the ever-pulling undertow by rallying public opinion behind him, as though impeachment were an election campaign. As the summer began, Nixon, once more attempting to appear above the fray, flew to the Middle East and then to Russia for summit talks. One might recall how his trip to Moscow in 1972 had helped enormously in public opinion polls. This time when the President went overseas, it was reported that he was the victim of phlebitis, a blood clot—an ailment that sometimes requires people to undergo extensive periods of rest or run the risk of losing their lives.

When Nixon returned from Russia, then, and after the Supreme Court ruled, the seeds for any possible turn of events had been planted. The evidence against him was being gathered and disseminated. He had a small, staunch corps of defenders who predicted that he would not be impeached. And, with a Congress likely to be importuning him once again, he could resign and attempt to call it "a compromise."

4

ALMOST UNTIL THE end, Nixon fought to dodge impeachment or resignation. His last tactic was to have members of Congress judge him not on evidence of his complicity in one or more aspects of scandal, but on the question of whether the nation could afford to lose him as president. Nixon, the theme went, was *needed*. The position was formally articulated on July 22, 1974, when the assistant minority counsel to the House Judiciary Committee told committee members, "The question is, did the President do it, and if so, what are the implications of that for the nation *in light of all competing interests*."

In the last week in July, 1974, as the Judiciary Committee held its final deliberations in lengthy and spellbinding televised sessions, it was apparent that this strategy had failed to move all but a few members of the committee. Nixon had given little in the way of assistance to the Judiciary Committee, generally defying their counsel's requests and subpoenas for evidence. Nevertheless, the committee, working largely from material gathered in earlier investigations by other bodies, presented an overwhelming case against him in the form of three articles of impeachment.

Each article stated that Nixon had violated "his constitutional oath faithfully to execute the office of the President of the United States" and "his constitutional duty to take care that the laws be faithfully executed."

Article One charged that Nixon, "using the powers of his high office, engaged personally and through his subordinates and agents in a course of conduct or plan designed to delay, impede, and obstruct the investigation of such unlawful entry (the Watergate break-in); to cover up, conceal and protect those responsible; and to conceal the existence and scope of other unlawful covert activities."

The article charged that one or more of nine means had been used to implement such conduct, including the making or causing false or misleading statements to investigators; withholding evidence; "approving, condoning, acquiescing in, and counseling witnesses" to make false or misleading statements; interfering or attempting to interfere with investigations of the Justice Department, the FBI, the office of the Watergate Special Prosecutor and congressional committees; approving payment of "substantial sums" of money to buy silence or influence the testimony of witnesses or others involved in illegal entry or other illegal activities; attempting to misuse the Central Intelligence Agency; disseminating Justice Department information to subjects of investigations to help them avoid criminal liability; making false and misleading statements to deceive the American people into believing that a thorough and complete investigation had been held, and endeavoring to cause prospective defendants and convicted individuals to expect favored treatment in return for their silence or false testimony.

Article Two charged that Nixon "has repeatedly engaged in conduct violating the constitutional right of citizens, impairing due and proper administration of justice in the conduct of lawful inquiries, of contravening the law of governing agencies to the executive branch and the purposes of these agencies."

The second article dealt with Watergate and also with Nixon's role in other matters that had been uncovered as the Watergate coverup collapsed. Included were charges dealing with abuse of the Internal Revenue Service, the FBI, the Secret Service and "other executive personnel"; the practice of unlawful electronic wiretapping; the creation and continuance of the White House special investigative unit (the "plumbers"); the failure to act when he knew that aides had behaved illegally, and the misuse of executive power by interfering with agencies of the executive branch.

Article Three held that the President should be impeached for his refusal to comply with Judiciary Committee subpoenas. "In refusing to produce these papers and things," the article stated, "Richard M. Nixon, substituting his judgment as to what materials were necessary for the inquiry, interposed the powers of the Presidency against the lawful subpoenas of the House of Representatives, thereby assuming for himself functions and judgments necessary to the exercise of the sole power of impeachment vested by the Constitution in the House of Representatives."

During the months of closed deliberations of the Judiciary Committee, most members refrained publicly from drawing any conclusions on the evidence the committee staff had assembled. That changed dramatically in the televised sessions as the proposed bill of particulars was drawn, and at the end of each impeachment article, this language appeared:

"In all of this, Richard M. Nixon has acted in a manner contrary to his trust as President and subversive of constitutional government, to the great prejudice of the cause of law and justice, and to the manifest injury of the people of the United States.

"Wherefore, Richard M. Nixon, by such conduct, warrants impeachment and trial and removal from office."

The last article was approved July 30. Subsequently, the committee debated but refused to recommend impeachment on two other charges: Nixon's secret bombing of Cambodia in violation of the constitutional requirement that Congress approve such action, and possible fraud in his payment of personal income taxes.

As the Judiciary Committee completed its televised sessions, it was clear that its thorough and largely bipartisan efforts had made it difficult for most other members of Congress to vote against impeachment without discrediting themselves. The evidence against Nixon was too strong. Still, the vote on impeachment was thought to be treacherous for individual Representatives and Senators in that segments of their constituencies might be angered regardless of how warily they moved. For that reason, and because some leaders felt a Senate trial would be jarring to the nation, a cry emanated from Capitol Hill for Nixon to resign. It was not the first time such a plea had been made, and, at the outset, Nixon responded the way he had in the past; with a firm refusal. It appeared that impeachment would go down to the wire.

It was in such a setting that Nixon was felled by the blow from which there was to be no recovery, the release of new tapes that showed his involvement in dragging the Central Intelligence Agency into the Watergate coverup. "The smoking gun," these tapes were called. Fittingly, as had happened so frequently in the course of the scandal, it was Nixon himself who forced the issue.

The role of the CIA in the coverup has been dealt with at length in this book. Long before the contents of these last tapes became known, from data on the public record, the evidence was overwhelming that within a week of the arrests of five men at Democratic National Committee headquarters, Nixon plotted to have the CIA block crucial aspects of the FBI's Watergate inquiry.

The "smoking gun" phrase referred to three of the sixty-four tapes that were ordered made public by the Supreme Court. They were records of meetings between Nixon and Haldeman on June 23, 1972. The tapes demonstrated once and for all that Nixon knew all about the Watergate coverup at its outset.

They showed that only six days after the initial Watergate arrests, Nixon and Haldeman discussed strategy to keep the FBI from moving into what Haldeman called "productive areas." As Haldeman spelled out the plan in its details, Nixon issued his approval, saying, "All right, fine." The President then instructed Haldeman on how to elicit cooperation from Richard Helms, the director of the CIA at the time, and from Vernon Walters, Helms's deputy.

The tapes also revealed for the first time that the President knew by June 23, 1972, of the involvement of one of the White House plumbers, G. Gordon Liddy, in the break-in and bugging. Yet five more days were to pass before Liddy was questioned by FBI agents—and then, as is described in this book, it was only through accident that Liddy was uncovered, not because Nixon or any other high officials who knew of his involvement reported him to investigators.

On the first weekend in August, 1974, Nixon met with several of his remaining close advisers and notified them of what was recorded in the June 23 conversations before relinquishing them to investigators. Two of the advisers reportedly said that the material was so damaging that Nixon had no choice but to resign. On Monday, August 5, with the knowledge that the tapes could not be kept from Congress for long, the President made their contents public.

He noted that "this additional material I am now furnishing may further damage my case," and pointed out that portions of the tapes "are at variance with certain of my previous statements." But he was still not ready to give up the fight.

Nixon made a last, futile appeal to Congress and to the public, saying he was convinced that the record, "in its entirety, does not justify the extreme step of impeachment and removal of a President. I trust that as the constitutional process goes forward, this perspective will prevail."

Members of Congress felt otherwise. For more than two years, the President had lied to the people about his role in the Watergate coverup. As he relinquished the last three tapes, he admitted that he had kept them from the House Judiciary Committee with the awareness that they "presented potential problems . . . that those passing judgment on the case did so with information that was incomplete and in some respects erroneous."

To a one, Nixon's strongest defenders on the Judiciary Committee stated publicly that they could no longer support the President. Several of them were near tears in televised interviews in which they expressed the view that they had been betrayed by Nixon. Most of them, and other leaders on Capitol Hill, once more pleaded that the President resign.

By Wednesday, August 7, as the weight of the new evidence sunk in, impeachment no longer seemed a difficult matter for any member of Congress. A vote against impeachment might be costly, but not a vote for it. The President's complicity in the great coverup was so amply demonstrated by these tapes that Capitol Hill head counters predicted Nixon could expect no more than fifteen votes from the Senate to keep him in office. He needed thirty-four. The end had come.

5

ON THURSDAY, AUGUST 8, 1974, a drizzly and gloomy day in Washington, D.C., Richard Milhous Nixon, the thirty-seventh President of the United States, announced his resignation from office. The man who for five and a half years had held the highest position in the world's mightiest nation had been driven out of power.

That evening, in his last televised address as President to the American people, Nixon referred only briefly to the scandal that had destroyed his career. "I regret deeply any injuries that may have been done in the course of events that led to this decision," he said. "I would say only that if some of my judgments were wrong—and some were wrong—they were made in the best interests of the nation."

Four times in his sixteen-minute talk Nixon referred to "the good of the nation" as his sole motivation in twenty-eight years of making decisions in public life. With an estimated one hundred thirty million citizens watching—the greatest number ever to see a single televised event—Nixon said he hoped his legacy would be that he had made the world "a safer place today, not only for the people of America, but for the people of all nations . . . that all of our children have a better chance than before of living in peace, rather than dying in war."

With the knowledge of the President's private thoughts rubbed in their consciousness through transcripts of the most revealing conversations, there could be but few Americans who accepted those words at face value. They had come to learn that the public and private Nixon were two very different men.

Outside the White House, as Nixon spoke, two thousand or more people gathered. Some were solemn and sad but others, the majority, cheered the news of his departure. One placard waved in front of the television cameras was inscribed "Jail to the Chief." It was a strange, perhaps inevitable climax to the Watergate saga, to more than two years of what many may have come to regard as the most bizarre and tragic scandal of modern times.

The following morning, August 9, Nixon assembled his White House staff and members of the Cabinet for an emotional parting in which the President, at times in tears, said, in effect, that life must go on despite the greatest of setbacks. Shortly after that he left Washington on Air Force One, "The Spirit of '76," for his estate at San Clemente.

While he was in flight, somewhere over the great heartland of the United States, Gerald Ford was sworn in as his successor. The immediate transition, after such wrenching years, was painless. In Alexandria, Virginia, the suburb of the nation's capital where Ford kept his home, crowds watched for the first days as the new President came and went. In California there were crowds to see the Nixons arrive, and truckloads of flowers were sent to the Nixon family there. A sign at the outskirts of San Clemente that proclaimed the city as "the home of the Western White House" was taken down.

Epilogue

At first, Gerald Ford had indicated that he would not pardon Richard Nixon. The question had come up indirectly in November 1973, at Senate hearings on Ford's nomination to succeed Spiro T. Agnew as vice-president. At the time, impeachment or resignation of Nixon was a concept that had just begun moving from the realm of the ridiculous to that of the remotely possible. Therefore, when the chairman of the Senate Rules Committee asked whether a new president could "terminate any criminal investigation or prosecution involving the President," Ford did not have to answer in detail. He said, "I do not think the public would stand for it," and let it go at that. Although he did not say so in as many words, the suggestion was, of course, that Ford was against a pardon.

It was fitting that Ford put himself on record at that early stage as looking to public opinion in the consideration of a pardon. It made it that much clearer later on, when he issued one, that Ford knew he was thwarting the desires of most Americans, for whom justice in Watergate meant putting Nixon on trial like any other citizen.

Ford held his initial news conference as president on August 28, 1974, twenty days after Nixon resigned. The first question put to him was this: "Do you agree with the bar association that the law applies equally to all men, or do you agree with Governor Rockefeller that former President Nixon should have immunity from prosecution. And, specifically, would you use your pardon authority, if necessary?"

Nelson Rockefeller, then vice-president designate, had commented that Nixon had been "hung" and should not now "be drawn and quartered." Ford responded to the question by saying, "The expression made by Governor Rockefeller, I think, coincides with the general view and the point of view of the American people. I subscribe to that point of view."

Ford had got the progression of public opinion exactly backward. The previous November, when he said Americans would not tolerate a pardon, the question was not really a part of the public debate. But by late August, 1974, it obviously was. The fate of the "unindicted co-conspirator," as Nixon had come to be called, was for many the number-one matter before the nation. And in an odd coincidence, on September 2, only five days after Ford's news conference, the "point of view of the American people" became known through the findings of a new Gallup poll. In it, a majority of citizens interviewed, 56 percent, said they felt Nixon should "be tried for possible criminal charges arising from Watergate." Little more than one-third, 37 percent, were opposed, and 7 percent expressed no opinion.

Nevertheless, on Sunday, September 8, Ford eliminated the chances of prosecution by proclaiming "a full, free, and absolute pardon unto Richard Nixon for all offenses against the United States which he, Richard Nixon, has committed or taken part in during the period from July 20, 1969, through August 9, 1974." (The first date on the original pardon was wrong, being six months after Nixon had taken office. To be on the safe side, Ford had the document changed to start from January 20, 1969.)

As he issued the proclamation, Ford said, "I cannot rely on public opinion polls to tell me what is right." He said his aim was to restore tranquility.

The public had greeted Ford warmly as Nixon's replacement, but many citizens rejected him after the pardon. He immediatey plummeted more than twenty points in the Gallup presidential approval ratings, and he never recovered. When he lost the 1976 presidential election to Jimmy Carter, a political outsider who ran with no real support from his own party leaders, the major polls cited the pardon as among the keys to the election. Ford himself has said it would have to be considered a contributing factor to his defeat, since the election was so close.

As I have tried to demonstrate in this book, there was much that went wrong with our system during the course of the 784 days. Most of the press was derelict, there was some taint in the courts and continued collusion in Congress. But much also went well, especially in the latter stages. The processes of justice were balky, but they began to work, moved by the powerful force of public opinion. Some who were once involved in the coverup underwent great personal trauma and what dramatists would have called change in character, emerging erect and loyal to a better cause than the service of a corrupt president.

In these regards, Watergate had the elements of a classic Greek tragedy, with people and events moving toward a fitting denouement—the trial of Nixon, and a subsequent national cleansing. The pardon, of course, blocked that. Many people maintain that Nixon's forced resignation was sufficient punishment for him, and that to have put him on trial would have further divided the nation. In this view, the uncovering of the Watergate scandal and Nixon's resignation are proof of the strength and resilience of the democratic system as practiced in the United States. Others, however, hold that the pardon had the appearance and effect of being one last move in the politics of cooperation, a demonstration that for some there are special standards, that equal justice does not apply.

In the years since Watergate we have come to know more about sordid activities by earlier presidents. We are aware of plots to assassinate foreign leaders, of presidents who used their political careers for personal financial gain, of presidents who regularly cheated on their wives. We know that Franklin Roosevelt, Dwight Eisenhower, John Kennedy and Lyndon Johnson secretly taped conversations in the White House.

Each time a revelation is made, there are those who state that what Richard Nixon did wasn't so different after all, except for the fact that Nixon got caught. In one sense, what Nixon did certainly does not appear to be very different. Most recent presidents, it seems clear, have decided somewhere along the line that moral and ethical demands made on society do not apply to them. As we say in my business, however, that's not news. Eleven years before the Watergate break-in, Saul Bellow, in his novel *Herzog*, had his main character write these words in a fictitious letter to the *New York Times*:

"In every community there is a class of people profoundly dangerous to the rest. I don't mean the criminals. For them we have punitive sanctions. I mean the leaders. Invariably the most dangerous people seek the power."

The fact is, shabby behavior by other presidents rings hollow as a defense for Nixon. As dangerous as others may have been, we still know of none with a record quite like his. And more importantly, as Sam Ervin put it, the existence of crimes in past generations "hasn't made murder meritorious or larceny legal."

Index

ABC (American Broadcasting Company), 105
Abplanalp, Robert, 3, 128
Address books of burglars, 10
Advertising Age, 33
Agnew, Spiro T., 118, 159, 167, 215, 216, 261
Aiken, George D., 235
Albert, Carl, 70, 71, 224, 233
Alch, Gerald, 119
Alsop, Stewart, 155
Americans for Democratic Action, 178
An American Life (Magruder), 17
Anderson, Jack, 133
Anderson, John B., 223
Andreas, Dwayne, 39, 68, 76
Anti-war veterans, arrest of, 168
Armstrong, Scott, 200–201
Athens (Ga.) Housing Authority, 78
Associated Press, 14

Bagdikian, Ben H., 105
Baker, Bobby, 115
Baker, Howard, 123–24, 130, 184, 185, 193, 205, 208
   Butterfield and, 195–203
   Stennis plan and, 218–221, 230
Baldwin, Alfred C., III, 5–10, 76, 113
Banco Internacional of Mexico City, 39, 61
Barker, Bernard L., 7, 9, 27, 38, 63, 143
   bank account of, 38–40, 61–63, 117
   Nixon and, 187–188
   sentencing of, 143, 146, 149–150
   trial of, 111–119
Barrett, John, 8–9

Bates, Charles W., 45
Beall, George, 214
Beard, Dita, 35, 136
Bellow, Saul, 263
Berger, Marilyn, 90–91
Berger, Raul, 225
"Berlin Wall," 34
Bernstein, Carl, 59–60, 61, 62, 106, 156, 159, 163
   investigative and reporting strategies, 82, 97–99
   Miami investigation and, 60–61
   Mitchell interview, 85
   Whitehouse Correspondents' award, 163
Bittman, William O., 115, 148
Boggs, Patrick, 13
Bork, Robert, 211, 222, 229
Boyd, Marjorie, 77–79
Bradlee, Benjamin C., 98–99, 105
   Colson attack on, 103–104
Brasco, Frank, 77
Bremer, Arthur, 26
Brezhnev, Leonid, 188
Broder, David S., 25, 90
Brooke, Edward W., 166, 223–224
Brown, Garry, 73, 76
Buchanan, Patrick, 95, 245
Bull, Steve, 199
Burger, Warren, 112
Butterfield, Alexander P., 14, 160
   background on, 197–199
   on Nixon, 70n
   as Senate witness, 200–203
   White House role, 196–200
Buzhardt, J. Fred, 193, 200, 202, 215, 218
Byrd, Robert C., 134–135, 141, 142, 224
Byrne, W. Matthew, 159, 168, 172, 175, 176

Caddy, Douglas, 11, 113
Califano, Joseph, 22, 121
California Democratic primary, 27
Campaign financing, illegal, 39–40, 51–52, 214
Campbell, Donald E., 49, 52, 55, 158, 169–170, 213
Canuck letter, 25–26, 90
Carter, Jimmy, 28, 262
Caulfield, John J., 13, 20, 76, 185
Center, People and Power in Political Washington, The (Alsop), 155
Central Intelligence Agency, see CIA
CBS (Columbia Broadcasting System), 105, 230
Chambers, Whittaker, 129
Chancellor, John, 226
Chapin, Dwight L., 51, 92–95
  Nixon and, 120
  Post stories on, 94–95, 97
  Segretti and, 139
Chappell, Bill, Jr., 78–79
Chicago Eight, 113
China, Nixon détente with, 228
Chisholm, Shirley, 24
CIA (Central Intelligence Agency), 5, 204, 208, 213, 226
  Ellsberg's psychiatrist break-in, role in, 169, 173–177
  FBI, obstruction of, 37, 40–43, 46–47
Clawson, Kenneth W., 90–92, 245
  Canuck letter written by, 25, 90, 92
Colson, Charles W., 18, 129, 130, 136, 197, 199, 250
  on Bradlee, 103–104
  FBI investigation and, 38
  Hunt and, 13–14, 125
  indictments of, 239
  McCord on, 155, 156
  Nixon and, 21, 36, 121, 129, 166, 167
  Shapiro and, 121
Columbia Journalism Review, 105
Committee for the Re-election of The President, see CRP
Common Cause, 40n
Connally, John, 73
Cook, Dick, 72
Corrupt Practices Act, 51
Cox, Archibald V., 178, 203, 205
  San Clemente estate inquiry, 214
  as special prosecutor, 212–223, 239
Cronkite, Walter, 105
CRP (Committee for the Re-election of The President), 4
  Democratic damage suit against, 22–23, 35, 125, 165
  dirty tricks of, 24–26, 167
  employees interviewed, 82–85
  FBI investigations of, 13–14, 37–38, 44–47, 50–56
  public polls rigged by, 167
  records destroyed at, 37, 136
  secret campaign funds, 39–40, 199
Cuban exiles, 7, 10, 59, 114, 115

Dade County, Fla., 60–61
Dahlberg, Kenneth H., cashier's check of, 38–40, 61, 62, 63, 68, 76, 177
Dairy industry payoff, 214
Daley, Richard, 28
Dardis, Martin, 60–61
Darman, Richard, 213, 215

Index

Dash, Samuel, 45, 123, 126, 143, 150, 187, 188, 191, 204
  FBI, interference with, 121
Dean, John Wesley, III, 40, 51, 76, 81, 95
  background of, 18–20
  charges made by, 162, 163, 166, 185–194
  Gray and, 37–38, 44–46, 134, 135
  Hunt and, 45–46
  immunity fight, 164, 165, 185–187
  implicated in coverup, 134–138, 141
  Liddy and, 158
  Nixon and, 81–82, 121–123, 171, 172, 186, 234
  papers withheld, 221
  Patman Committee and, 71–73, 79
  Washington Post and, 95
Dean, Maureen, 95, 241
"Deep Throat" (*Washington Post* news source), 87–88, 90, 157
Democratic campaign, Republican disruptions of, 24–26
Democratic National Committee, 38
  burglary of office, 5–11
  civil damage suit, 22–23, 125, 165
  Mitchell role with, 166
Democratic National Convention, 28
Des Moines Register and Tribune, 96
Diem, Ngo Dinh, assassination of, 35, 168
Dirty tricks, 92–93
  Canuck letter, 25–26, 90
  disruptive calls, 24–25
District of Columbia police, 8

Doar, John, 53, 239, 240, 247–248
Dole, Robert, 96, 101
Doyle, James, 224

Eagleton, Thomas F., 28, 64
Eastland, James, 132, 143
Ehrlichman, Jean Fisher, 33
Ehrlichman, John D., 13, 18, 19, 55, 121, 130, 163, 213, 251–252
  background of, 33–34
  Dean and, 18–20
  Gray and, 45–46, 135, 137–138
  indictments of, 239
  Nixon and, 34–37, 160–163, 215
  papers confiscated, 221
  resignation of, 175
  Senate Watergate Committee and, 123
  wiretapping and, 177, 178
Eisenhower, Dwight D., 263
Ellsberg, Daniel,
  burglary of psychiatrist of, 35, 47, 169–173, 226
  trial of, 159, 168, 175–176
  White House campaign against, 164, 169
Enemies list, 73–74, 191, 192
Energy crisis, 228
Ervin Committee, *see* Senate Watergate Committee
Ervin, Sam, 155, 164, 183–84, 205, 206, 264
  Dean and, 191–193
  Nixon and, 122–123, 251
  Stennis Plan and, 218–221, 230
Executive clemency, 128, 185
Executive privilege, 79, 138, 164, 165
  Cox and, 217–218
  Nixon on, 212, 226, 249–252

FBI (Federal Bureau of Inves-

tigation) 133
  Bernstein-Woodward interviews with, 97
  CIA interference with, 40–43, 46–47
  Cox files guarded by, 211, 223
  CRP investigations by, 13–14, 37–38, 40, 44–47, 50–55, 83
  Haldeman and, 97–99
  Justice Department and, 52, 134, 223
  Liddy and, 7
  McCord and, 5, 145
  White House use of, 133–141
  see also Gray, L. Patrick, III
Federal Aviation Administration, 160, 199
Federal Communications Commission, 107
Federalist Papers No. 65, 236
Federal Reserve Board, 68
Felt, W. Mark, 45
Fielding, Fred, 20, 189
Fielding, Dr. Lewis, 169–173
  see also Ellsberg, Daniel: burglary of psychiatrist
Fiorini, Frank, *see* Sturgis, Frank
Flug, James, 126
Ford, Gerald, 263
  Liddy and, 7
  Nixon and, 72, 224, 264

GAO (General Accounting Office)
  CRP investigated by, 64, 66–69, 81, 101
Garment, Leonard, 193, 202, 215, 217, 218
Gemstone operation, 7, 14, 27
Gerstein, Richard, 60
Gettys, Tom S., 78
Glanzer, Seymour, 49, 51, 52, 55, 158, 213

Goldwater, Barry, 82, 159
Goldwater, Barry, Jr., 18
Gonzalez, Virgilio R., 10
  trial of, 114–117
Graham, Katharine, 85, 101, 104
Gray, L. Patrick, III, 15, 20–21, 44
  Dean, working with, 37–38, 44–46
  Ehrlichman and, 45–46, 135, 137, 138
  Hunt's files, disposition by, 45–46, 136
  Nixon and, 44–45, 127, 137, 138, 140, 141
  Senate confirmation hearing revelations, 127, 131–142, 155
Gregory, Thomas, 115, 116
Griffin, Charles H., 78
Gulf Resources and Chemical Co., 39, 40
Gurney, Edward J., 128

Haig, Alexander, 36, 178, 211
Haiphong (Vietnam), phony support for mining of, 167, 168
Haldeman, H.R. (Bob), 5, 21, 130, 226
  background of, 33–34, 195–200
  coverup involvement, 36–37, 70–71, 96–97, 129
  FBI, interference with, 42
  indictment of, 142, 239
  Nixon and, 17, 18, 33–37, 158–163
  papers confiscated, 221
  resignation of, 175
Hall, Joan, 54
Hamilton, Alexander, on impeachment, 236
Hamilton, James, 202–203
Hanna, Richard, 79
Harlow, Bryce, 197

Index

Harmony, Sally, 76, 85
Harris, Louis, presidential candidate polls, 23–24
Hart, Philip, 134
Helms, Richard, 42, 45–47, 170, 176, 177, 204
Hennings, Thomas, 18
Hersh, Seymour, 116
Higby, Laurence, 198
Hiss, Alger, 129
Hoffa, James, 115
Hoffman, Julius, 113
Hoover, J. Edgar, 20, 131
Horner, Garnett, 103
Horton, J., 195
House Banking and Currency Committee, 66
House Judiciary Committee, impeachment considerations by, 235–242
House Un-American Activities Committee, 129
Hughes, Howard, 203
Hughes, Philip S. (Sam), investigation made by, 66–70, 178
Humphrey, Hubert, 23, 24, 26, 27, 39
Hunt, E. Howard, Jr., 47, 59, 121
  in address books of burglars, 14
  background of, 7, 149
  blackmail by, 142, 171, 244–245
  Colson and, 14
  documents in safe, 45–46
  Ellsberg's psychiatrist burglarized by, 47, 168
  executive clemency for, 128
  FBI investigation of, 14, 50
  Gray's disposition of documents, 45–46, 137, 168
  immunity given to, 157
  indictment of, 82
  Kennedy investigation by, 24
  McGovern spy and, 115, 116
  sentencing of, 143, 148–150
  trial of, 111–119
  White House telephone of, 106
Hush-money payments, 116, 121–22, 142, 159, 164, 167, 177, 244–245
Hutchinson, Edward, 237, 241

Impeachment resolutions, 233–253
  charges, 247–248
Indictments
  of Colson, 239
  of Ehrlichman, 239
  of Haldeman, 142, 239
  of Hunt, 82
  of Liddy, 82
  of Mardian, 239
  of Mitchell, 239
  of Parkinson, 239
  of Strachan, 239
Internal Revenue Service, 208
International Telephone and Telegraph, White House and, 35, 136, 208, 214, 239
Issues and Answers (television program), 188

J. Walter Thompson, advertising agency, 33
Jackson, Henry, 24
Jaworski, Leon, 237, 239, 240, 248
Jenner, Alfred E., Jr., 247
Johnson, Lyndon B., 263
Justice Department, 49–50
  burglary of Ellsberg's psychiatrist office and, 169–176
  FBI and, 52, 134
  McCord on, 144–145, 151
  Silbert prosecution, interference with, 50
  see also Kleindienst, Richard

Kalmbach, Herbert, 95, 121, 164
  burglars, payments to, 47
  Cox and, 213
  Gray on, 136, 138–139
  Nixon and, 128
  secret fund of, 167
  Segretti, payments to, 51
  Senate Watergate Committee and, 164
Kehrli, Bruce, 14
Kennedy, Edward, 27, 223
  CRP on, 24
  Gray questioned by, 136, 138–139
  Hunt's investigation of, 35, 168
  investigation made by subcommittee of, 64, 119, 126–127
  Senate Watergate Committee and, 119, 126–127
Kennedy, John F., 105, 265
  Hunt sabotage and, 35, 168
  wiretapping and, 127, 263
Kennedy, Robert, 127
Key Biscayne estate of the President, 128
Keyes, Paul, 17
King Timahoe, 18
Kissinger, Henry, 127, 166, 196, 197
  troop alerts and, 227–228
Kleindienst, Richard, 204
  Bernstein-Woodward, advice to, 163
  Gray and, 134
  on impeachment, 233
  on Magruder problem, 55
  on McCord, 151
  on McGovern, 56
  resignation of, 175
  Senate Watergate Committee and, 122–24, 129
  White House and, 56, 129, 163, 165, 174
Knap, Ted, 163

Krogh, Egil (Bud), in Plumbers, 54, 121, 170, 199, 215, 221

LaRue, Frederick C., 4, 12, 37, 48, 76, 84, 159, 213
Laundered money, 69
Lawrence, John, 113
Leary, Dr. Timothy, 7
Leeper, Paul, 8–10
Liddy, George Gordon, 4, 37, 52, 76
  background of, 7, 146–147
  burglary of Ellsberg's psychiatrist office, 168, 170
  burglary of Watergate, 5–7, 12–13
  immunity given to, 158
  indictment of, 82
  McCord on, 155
  money received by, 53
  sentencing of, 143, 146–148, 150
  trial of, 111–119
Life Magazine, 7
Lindsey, John, 24
Lisagor, Peter, 230
Loeb, William, 25
Los Angeles Times, 105, 113, 164, 214, 215
  Baldwin interview in, 8*n*

McCardle, Dorothy, 106
McClellan, John L., 176
McCord, James W., Jr.
  background of, 5, 145
  burglary of Watergate by, 5–7, 9–10
  executive clemency offered to, 177, 185
  letter to Sirica, 144–45, 147, 150–151
  trial of, 111–119
  Watergate committee testimony by, 155–158
McGovern, George, 23, 79, 95, 112

campaign infiltrator, 115, 116
Kliendienst on, 56
as presidential candidate, 23, 27–29
MacGregor, Clark, 36, 79, 96, 101
Mafia, 77
Magruder, Jeb Stuart, 4–5, 76, 118
An American Life, 17
in Commerce Department, 120
Cox, cooperation with, 213
Gemstone files and, 14
knowledge of Watergate by, 155–197
money received by, 53, 84
phony testimony of, 52
White House implicated by, 162, 166
Maguire, Charlotte Mary, 195
Manchester, New Hampshire, *Union Leader*, 25
Mankiewicz, Frank, 64
Mansfield, Mike, 119, 188, 207, 221
Mardian, Robert C., 4, 12, 37, 76, 84, 239
Maroulis, Peter, 146, 147, 150, 158
Marriott, Willard, 118
Martinez, Eugenio R., 114
burglary of Watergate, 10
trial of, 114–117
Mathias, Charles McC., Jr., 157
May Day protests of 1971, 19
Meany, George, 28
Mein Kampf (Hitler), 147
Mexico City, Mexico, Barker's money from, 39, 61, 62, 69
Meyer, Lawrence, 106, 112
Meyers, Robert, 92
Miami (Fla.), prosecuter's office in, *see* Dardis; Martin

Miami men, *see* Watergate burglars
Middle East Crisis, used by Nixon, 227–229
Mitchell, John N., 4–5, 23, 76, 79, 84, 193
Bernstein's telephone conversation with, 85
Dean and, 19, 193
Democrats' civil suit and, 23, 125, 165, 166
grand-jury testimony of, 168
indictment of, 239
knowledge of Watergate by, 34–37, 84, 97, 136–137, 159, 162
McCord on, 156
O'Brien on, 67–68
Nixon and, 18, 36–37, 125, 129–130
resignation of, 16, 47–48
on Watergate burglary after it happened, 14–15, 23, 193, 194
Mitchell, Martha, 4, 5, 16, 47, 136–137, 157, 178
Mitchell, Marty, 4
Mollenhoff, Clark, 96
Moore, Richard, 95, 189, 190, 193, 200
Muskie, Edmund, 23, 27, 158
Republicans disrupt campaign of, 24–26, 115
Muskie, Jane, 25

NBC (National Broadcasting Company), 105
National Commission on the Reform of Criminal Laws, 19
Nedzi, Lucien, 176, 177
New Hampshire Democratic primary, 24–26
Newporter Inn, Newport Beach, Calif., 15–16
Newsweek Magazine, 25, 156

New York Times, The, 60–62, 105, 116, 157, 166, 176
  Pentagon Papers in, 212–213
Nixon, Patricia, 4
Nixon, Richard M.,
  campaign always run by, 70*n*
  Colson and, 21, 36, 121, 129, 215
  vs. Cox, 211–223
  dairy industry payoff and, 214
  Dean and, 81–82, 121–123, 142, 161, 163, 165, 166
  Ehrlichman and, 34–37, 160–163, 215
  on Ellsberg case, 171, 172
  Ervin and, 123–124
  executive clemency and, 128, 177, 185
  executive privilege and, 79, 138, 164, 165, 212, 226, 249–252
  Ford and, 263
  and Gray, 44–45, 127, 137, 138
  Haldeman and, 17, 18, 33–37, 160–163
  on Hunt payments, 142, 171, 244–245
  impeachment threat to, 223–253
  inauguration, 118
  I.R.S., use of, 189
  ITT merger and, 208, 214, 239
  knowledge of Watergate by, 35–38, 41–42, 44–45, 67–75, 94, 163–166, 244–246
  O'Brien on, 67–68
  Operation Candor, 234–235
  pardon of, 261–263
  Patman Committee and, 66–67, 69–70
  personal traits of, 17–18, 35–36, 196–198
  politics of cooperation of, 71–74, 123–125
  on the press, 125–126, 230–231
  San Clemente estate of, 128, 214
  on second-term goals, 107
  Stennis plan of, 217–221, 227
  support for Democratic candidates, 74
  tax dereliction of, 128
  transcripts (edited), 233, 240–246
  trust funds and, 128
  as unindicted co-conspirator, 142, 239
  on *Washington Post,* 81
  on wiretapping, 82, 128–129

O'Brien, Lawrence F., 22–23, 27
  civil suit against CRP, 22–23, 35, 125, 165
  as CRP target, 6
  on Watergate coverup, 67–68
Odle, Robert C., Jr., 12, 85
Office of Federal Elections, 67, 178
Ogarrio, D'Aguerre Manuel, 38–40, 45–46, 61
Oliver, Spencer, 6
Omnibus Crime Control Act of 1970, 19
"Operation Candor," 234–235
Osnos, Peter, 102

Packwood, Robert, 157
Parkinson, Kenneth Wells, 68–69
  indictment of, 239
Patman, Wright, 66
  Patman Committee, investigation, 64, 66, 68–69, 71–72, 76–80, 81, 124, 142, 166

on Hughes report, 68
Nixon and, 69, 71–73
Pentagon Papers, *see* Ellsberg, Daniel
People's Party, 27
Petersen, Henry E., 13, 158–159, 170–174, 187, 204, 243
  Gray repressed by, 51–52
  Nixon pressure on, 51, 55, 163–166, 170–171
  Patman Committee, letter to, 76–77, 166
  proposed as Cox replacement, 217
  Silbert repressed by, 53–55, 170–171
Pettis, Jerry, 224
Piper, Virginia, 63
Porter, Herbert, 52, 118
  money received by, 53, 84
Presidential abuses of power, 265–266
Primary elections, *see* Democratic campaign; Dirty tricks
Public opinion, White House attempts to manipulate, 167–168

Rafferty, Joseph, Jr., 11
Rather, Dan, 230
Rebozo, C.G. (Bebe), 128, 203
Republican National Committee, 168
Republicans, opposition to Nixon, 223, 224, 225, 235
Reuss, Henry S., 166
Ribicoff, Abraham, 131
Richardson, Elliott, 18, 77n, 178
  Agnew scandal and, 215
  Cox-Nixon confrontation and, 211–222, 225–226, 230
  resignation of, 211, 222, 225–226

Richardson, Michael, 38
Rietz, Kenneth, 167
Rockefeller, Nelson, 33, 263
Rodino Committee, *see* House Judiciary Committee
Rodino, Peter W., Jr., 237
Roosevelt, Franklin D., 263
Rosenfeld, Harry M., 59, 87, 98
Rothblatt, Henry, 115–116, 149
Ruckelshaus, William D., 222–223
Russia, 227–229, 253
Rugaber, Walter, 61
Russo, Anthony, 176

Sadat, Anwar, 266
San Clemente estate of the President, 215, 260
Sanders, Donald, 200–201
Sans Souci, 91
Sarbanes, Paul, 238
"Saturday Night Massacre," 212, 214
Schultz, Daniel, 149
Scott, Hugh, 188, 221
Scripps-Howard syndicate, 163
Secret fund, 39, 40, 53, 84, 103, 199–200
Secret Service, 13–14
Segretti, Donald H., 50
  access to FBI files, 132–33
  Bernstein-Woodward investigation of, 88–94
  Chapin and, 51, 92–95, 120
  FBI investigation of, 50–51, 133, 139–40
  grand jury appearance of, 54n
  money received by, 51, 92
  as political saboteur, 26
  Post stories on, 94–95, 97
Senate Watergate Committee (Ervin Committee), 64, 65, 74, 120, 123–124, 144, 170, 183–194, 251–252

Gray, questioned by, 131–142
Kennedy influence, 126–27
McCord and, 155–156
Nixon and, 164–165
Nixon, relationship to, 122–129
Ziegler discredits, 157
Shapiro, David, 121*n*
Shipley, Alex, 88–89
Shoffler, Carl, 8–9
Shumway, Devan L., 4
Silbert, Earl, 49–55, 106, 158, 164, 186, 187, 199, 213
   conduct of investigation, 49–55
   conduct of prosecution, 112, 113–115
   Ellsberg case, 170–175
   Hughes and, 67
   Peterson interference with, 51, 53–55
   Sirica and, 112–115
Simons, Howard, 60, 87, 98–99, 102
Sinatra, Frank, 61
Sirica, John J., 106, 111–112, 143, 145–146, 264–265
   on Ervin Senate Committee, 119
   interrogation of burglars, 116–117
   McCord's letter to, 144–45, 147, 150–151
   sentencing of Watergate burglars, 143–150
   trial procedures, 111–113, 115–117
   White House tapes and, 211, 216, 217, 218, 225, 240
Six Crises (Nixon), 49
Sloan, Hugh Walter, Jr., 12, 20, 40, 84, 185
   briefcase full of money of, 39–40, 53
   Hughes and, 68
   Post as source on Watergate, 84, 96–97, 100
Spock, Benjamin, 27
St. Clair, James, 239, 240, 246, 247
Stans, Maurice, 39, 40*n*, 54, 68–69, 79, 184, 185, 204
   Hughes and, 67, 68
   and Patman investigation, 68–69
   subpoened for grand jury appearance, 49
Stennis, John, 211
Stennis Plan, tape authentication, 211, 217–221, 227
Stephens, Robert G., 78
Stephenson, Dennis P., 8
Strachan, Gordon, 20, 95, 120–21, 199
   indictment of, 239
   on support of Democrats, 74
Strauss, Robert, 125, 165, 191–192
Strickler, Frank, 166
Sturgis, Frank, 10
   trial of, 114–117
Sullivan, William, 127

Tapes of Nixon White House, 35
   battle over, 211–225
   gaps in, 232–233
   Stennis plan on, 211, 217–221, 227
   transcripts (edited) published, 233, 240–246
Taping as Presidential practice, 265
Talmadge, Herman E. (Senator), 204
Teamsters Union, 121
Thomas, Helen, 16
Thompson, Fred, 123, 187, 191, 203
Time magazine, 95, 129, 156
Titus, Harold, 163
Tunney, John V., 135–136

Ulasewicz, Anthony, 34, 47, 185
United Air Lines, Chapin employed by, 120
United Press International, 16
U.S. Attorney's office, investigation of Watergate burglary, 49–55
United States Information Agency, 120–21

Vance, Robert, 28
Vietnam War
opposition to, 23, 167–68
White House-staged support for, 167–168

Waldie, Jerome, 223
Wallace, George, 24, 26, 87
Wall Street Journal, The, 159
Walters, Gen. Vernon A., 45–47, 169, 176, 177, 204
on CIA funding for burglars, 46–47
Warren, Gerald, 151
Washington Monthly, 77–78
Washington Post, 25, 59–108
attacked by White House, 103–104, 106–107, 139–140
CRP interest in, 4
early Watergate coverage, 59–64, 156
Haldeman story in, 96–100
Inaugural section on Nixon, 118
Nixon on, 81
Pulitzer Prize awarded to, 160
television stations of, 107
Washington Star, 103, 105, 167
Watergate burglars
address books of, 10, 59
attorneys for, 115
CIA and, 46–47
money received by, 46–47, 116–117
sentencing of, 143–150
trial of, 111–119
Watergate Committee, *see* Senate Watergate Committee

Watergate complex
description of, 5
residents of, 5
Watergate jurors, 111, 118
Weicker, Lowell, 74, 124, 127, 131, 158, 168, 188, 190, 204, 206
"White House horror stories," 35, 47
White House Tapes, *see* Tapes
Whitehurst, William, 224
Whitten, Leslie, 133
Widnall, William R., 72, 77–78
Wills, Frank, 6, 8, 59
Wilson, Jerry V., Nixon and, 13
Wilson, John J., 166
Wiretapping, 6–7, 35, 82, 214
WJXT in Jacksonville, Fla., 107
Women's Wear Daily, 25
Wong, Alfred (Secret Service) investigation, 14
Woods, Rose Mary, 5, 160, 233
Woodward, Bob, 59–60, 62, 63, 87, 106, 138, 156
"Deep Throat" and, 87–88, 90
investigative techniques, 82, 87, 97–99
Whitehouse Correspondents' award, 163
WPLG in Miami, Fla., 107
Wright, Charles (D.C. police), 10
Wright, Charles Alan, 207, 215–218, 227

Yorty, Sam, 24
Young, David, 54
Young, Lawrence, 92–93

Ziegler, Ronald, 41, 92, 95, 100–101, 165, 197
 on Gray hearings, 140
 on Office of Special Prosecutor, 211
 on Rodino Committee, 246
 on *Washington Post* errors, 100–101
 on Watergate Committee, 157